Helping Students to Learn

Helping Students to Learn

Teaching, Counselling, Research

Kjell Raaheim
Janek Wankowski
John Radford

The Society for Research into Higher Education
& Open University Press

Published by SRHE and
Open University Press
Celtic Court
22 Ballmoor
Buckingham
MK18 1XW

and
1900 Frost Road, Suite 101
Bristol, PA 19007, USA

This Revised Second Edition First Published 1991

British Library Cataloguing in Publication Data

Raaheim, Kjell
 Helping students to learn: teaching, counselling, research. – 2nd. ed.
 1. Learning by students in higher education institutions
 I. Title   II. Wankowski, Janek   III. Radford, John *1931*–378.1981

 ISBN 0-335-09320-5
 ISBN 0-335-09319-1 pbk

Library of Congress Cataloging-in-Publication Data

Raaheim, Kjell.
 Helping students to learn:teaching, counseling, research/Kjell
Raaheim, Janek Wankowski, John Radford.
  p. cm.
 Rev. ed. of: Helping students to learn at university.
 Includes bibliographical references (p. 159) and index.
 ISBN 0-335-09320-5 (hard). – ISBN 0-335-09319-1 (pbk.)
 1. College student orientation. 2. College teaching. 3. Study,
Method of. 4. Personnel service in higher education.
I. Wankowski, Janek. II. Radford, John. III. Raaheim, Kjell.
Helping students to learn at university. IV. Title.
 LB2343.3.R33 1991
 378.1'98–dc20   90–7987
                                         CIP

Typeset by Rowland Phototypesetting Limited
Bury St Edmunds, Suffolk
Printed in Great Britain by St Edmundsbury Press Limited
Bury St Edmunds, Suffolk

Contents

List of Figures and Tables

Introduction

This book is a considerably revised second edition of *Helping Students to Learn at University* by Kjell Raaheim and Janek Wankowski (Bergen: Sigma Forlag, 1981). The revisions are of three kinds: updating of the original text where that has been retained; the addition of new material from further research; and a contribution from a new, third, author, John Radford.

There is also a revision of the title, which is minor but nevertheless indicates something about the nature of the book as it now is. We have dropped the word 'university' because no one any longer equates universities and Higher Education, which is what we are concerned with. And we have added the subtitle *Teaching, counselling, research* because we have, we think, something to say about all these; and because we all three have some experience of all of them, although in different proportions. It is in the interaction and co-operation of these three processes, we suggest, that the best hope lies of helping students to learn.

We offer views of teaching, counselling and research which are consistent and complementary; but we have not tried to write as if we were one person. Rather we give three personal perspectives; each chapter is the work of one author, though we have all discussed the contents. The contributions of the three authors need not necessarily be read in the order in which we present them. The plan of the book, however, is that John Radford first offers a selective review of published research as a background; Kjell Raaheim and Janek Wankowski then present their own research, experiences and conclusions; finally John Radford compares these with his own teaching experience and with other publications.

All three of us agree that, whatever may be the philosophical or political aims of Higher Education, there is a pressing need for it to become more self-consciously effective; professional, one may say. This is so both from the point of view of the investment of national resources and from that of individual satisfaction. This view is gaining ground due to many authors besides ourselves, and undoubtedly far more is understood about the learning and teaching process at higher levels than even a decade ago, when the first version of this book appeared.

At the same time this is not a teaching handbook. We refer to several excellent examples of such books in the final chapter. What we hope to do is to stimulate teachers and others involved with Higher Education to think about what is done, and what might be done, in the light of evidence and considered experience. If our book adds to debate and awareness, and supplies some helpful suggestions, we shall be amply repaid.

Kjell Raaheim
Janek Wankowski
John Radford

1

Teaching and Learning: A Selective Review

John Radford

The problem

When I was a (mature) undergraduate I heard a lecturer argue that lecturers should not be too efficient at their job as it would make things too easy for students, thus confusing the natural distinction between the good and the less good. Certainly I came across not a few who acted as though they believed this, though no others stated it explicitly.

It need hardly be said that this view (which perhaps, one may hope, was not seriously held) is diametrically opposite to the standpoint of the present authors. Without going into arguments about the purposes of higher education, it is clear as a minimum that it is something for which the bulk of the costs are paid by society, which is entitled to expect an efficient return; and it is something in which many thousands of young, and some older, individuals invest much effort and many hopes, which it is wasteful and destructive to disappoint.

Yet the outcome of higher education is far from clearly established. The most obvious measure is examination results. Perhaps the one thing that is un-equivocal about these is that they vary widely between different institutions, and indeed subdivisions within institutions, and between different categories of student. Johnes and Taylor (1987) examine variations in degree quality between United Kingdom universities in the period 1976 to 1984. Similarly, Johnes and Taylor (1989) analyse variations in noncompletion rates for the years 1979 and 1980. These range from about 3.5 per cent to as high as 28 per cent. In general, Cambridge has the best rate, and the Scottish universities the worst, although Brunel also records one of the highest. As Johnes and Taylor point out, such comparisons by themselves tell us little, partly due to the non-equivalence of institutions. For example Scottish universities normally offer four year courses as compared to three in England and Wales. An interesting fact to emerge from these analyses is that the single most important source of the variance is the GCE 'A' level scores, which have generally been considered a rather weak predictor of future academic success – despite the fact that most institutions have relied heavily on them for selection. As far as degree quality goes, the other major factors are library spending as a proportion of total spending, and percentage of students living at home during term. In the case of noncompletion rates, the factors, after 'A' levels, are the proportion of students reading for a business studies or social sciences degree (or languages in the case of females), and the proportion of students accommodated in a hall of residence. There is little suggestion of an important role for either teaching quality or study methods. But these may work at too fine a level to show up; they vary widely within institutions.

While completion rates and degree quality are obvious measures, one would wish equally, if not more, to know of more lasting effects. After all if Higher Education has any purpose, part of it must be to have some result beyond successful completion. But research seems to be scanty. Powell (1985) obtained autobiographical accounts from 22 Australian graduates, who attached most importance to learning high level intellectual skills and to developing attitudes and values of personal and professional significance. Powell and Cracknell (1987) interviewed 27 professional biologists about their degree experiences. The most significant outcomes identified by the group were: the understanding of basic principles, mastery of techniques, development of higher intellectual skills, engendering a deep interest in science, and the acquisition of attitudes towards the manner in which scientific work should be conducted. Little mention was made of the gaining of factual knowledge, though this may have been taken for granted. Opinions about teachers were both positive and negative but, perhaps surprisingly, did not feature prominently.

Brennan and McGeevor (1988), in a survey of 4,000 recent CNAA (Council for National Academic Awards, i.e. non-university) graduates from 122 courses, found that graduates from virtually all academic disciplines considered that their education had led to improvements across a wide range of cognitive skills, most especially in critical thinking, independence, writing ability and applying knowledge. But there was considerable dissatisfaction in some subject areas with the provision of general transferable skills such as communication and numeracy. These studies examined what graduates themselves considered important; there were no independent measures of whether it had in fact been achieved.

Dahlgren (1984) reviews research on the cognitive effects of higher education, at three levels: specific factual knowledge, both within and outside the subjects formally studied; understanding of basic concepts in a certain area; and awareness of the nature of scientific knowledge. The most positive effect is found at the first level, but the permanence of this is doubted. There is also a positive effect at the third level, and least at the second. McMillan (1987) reviews 27 studies that investigated the effect of instructional methods, course, pro- grammes and general college experience on changes in college students' critical thinking. He concludes that critical thinking does improve while students are at college, but that it is unclear what factors bring this about: instructors and content areas may be significant. McMillan points out that only two of these studies used true experimental designs, and that most research relies on single measures whereas multiple measures are needed. From another extensive review Pascarella (1985) concludes that, put simply: 'As compared to freshmen, seniors not only tend to know more, but also to possess more highly developed reasoning and thinking skills'. But he points out that design flaws make it impossible to conclude that the relationship is causal.

It is perhaps hard to distinguish cognitive effects very clearly from the non-cognitive: such qualities as independence and critical thinking have aspects of both. Brennan and McGeevor found that graduates irrespective of subject placed almost equal weight on employment, personal development and subject interest as the main areas of benefit from Higher Education. Nucci and Pascarella (1987) discuss the influence of college on moral development; and Rest (1988), reviewing the evidence, concludes that college attendance (in the USA) is indeed associated with the development of moral judgement. He offers six possible interpretations of how this comes about: simple age/maturation; learning specific knowledge or skills; generalized understanding; intellectual stimulation; and self-selection. Findings from longitudinal, correlational, educational and life-experience studies suggest that the last three factors have priority over the first three. Clearly there is some way to go before precise causes can be specified, if indeed that is possible.

Brennan and McGeevor were concerned also with the employment prospects of graduates. They showed that employment rates for graduates in different disciplines narrow considerably in the first three years after graduation, and that there is much job-changing in those years. This of course might conceal differences within disciplines reflecting advantages of better or worse teaching.

One might expect that employers would have both strong and clear views on what they want from the new graduates they take on, but in general this seems not to be so. 'Employers do not speak with a single voice, nor a small number of aggregated voices,' (Roizen and Jepson, 1985). Cannon (1986) for example points out, as many have done, that the dangers of the low proportion of Higher Education in the United Kingdom, and the mismatch of its programmes with the needs of industry, have been argued for well over a hundred years, for example by the Royal Commission on the 'Great Depression' of the 1880s and by at least three other Royal Commissions in the later 19th century. But Cannon found, in discussions with middle and senior executives from a number of industries, that what industry says it wants in graduates tends to be inconsistent, and not to match what it actually selects. There is 'a worrying level of indifference and apathy among managers to the universities and colleges.' This he contrasts with the much closer relationship in the USA. On the other hand Boys and Kirkland (1988) found from a survey of 6,000 final year undergraduates, of whom some 1500 were followed up three years later, that there was a general conviction that their period in Higher Education would lead to advantages in the labour market, although in terms of salary these might be deferred.

Formally, the burden of seeing that the public is getting value for money from education falls, in the United Kingdom, on Her Majesty's Inspectorate. One of this body, Gibson (1986), suggests, with due caution, that many HMIs 'might come close to asking the following questions': Does the course provide experiences which will: (a) develop the students' intellectual and imaginative powers; (b) be useful to the students themselves and to society . . . whether the study programmes are perceived as academic, vocational, or a mixture; (c) offer at least some learning which is of short-term, survival utility, and some of longer-term value, offering a basis for continued learning growth and development; (d) inculcate a capacity to see their subject/specialism in relation both to other fields of knowledge and to social and economic changes; and (e) enhance students' ability to contribute as 'thinking graduates' in industry, commerce, the professions or elsewhere. However, just how all this is to be assessed, other than intuitively, is perhaps not very clear.

The process of Higher Education

Whatever the hoped-for outcome, it would seem sensible to maximize students' success; at its simplest, improve completion rates. However, education as a whole does not lend itself easily to research of an orderly experimental kind, and even when good evidence is available this is often not given much weight by those who determine policy, as Eysenck (1988) for example points out. (Of course the same might be said of many aspects of behaviour, e.g. criminality – Hollin, 1989.) Foster (1985) among others has remarked that even psychologists appear to pay little attention to research findings in their own teaching practices. More generally Apps (1988) says:

> There is great irony involved in examining the faculty at most colleges and universities. On the one hand, most faculty members pride themselves on being liberal and open-minded and constantly searching for new ideas and new approaches, particularly when they are related to their disciplinary interests. But on the other hand, when it comes to their own teaching, their own departmental structure, and their view of educational aims, they are extremely conservative. They generally see no need to change and resist change at every turn.

While informed change is undoubtedly hard to achieve, there is little doubt that, despite the difficulties, much more is reliably understood about the process of education, including Higher Education, than even, say, twenty years ago. One aspect of this, as Entwistle (1990) says, is a change from attempts to apply general psychological theories, particularly theories of learning, to education, towards the analysis of the educational process itself. Again this can be paralleled in other fields. But the power of the analysis derives from the methodological sophistication of psychology, so that it is possible to advance beyond tradition, intuition and prejudice. One aspect of such sophistication consists in making the most of a number of techniques of objective investigation, not just that of experiment.

Entwistle himself has been at the forefront of this movement, and among his major contributions have been, first, an analysis of the different modes of learning that students adopt and, second, an awareness of the complexity of the whole environment within which learning takes place. Entwistle and Tait (1989) offer a 'heuristic model' of the teaching–learning process in Higher Education. (see Fig. 1.1)

This model is heuristic in that, as Entwistle points out, the precise relationship between the variables has in many cases still to be established.

Fraser, Walberg, Welch and Hattie (1987) summarize the findings of a large number of studies of educational productivity in numerous countries, and conclude that learning is dependent upon the following variables:

Student aptitudinal variables: 1. ability
                                            2. development or age
                                            3. motivation
Instructional variables: 4. quantity of instruction
                                            5. quality of instruction
Environmental variables: 6. home environment
                                            7. classroom environment
                                            8. peer group environment
                                            9. mass media environment.

Although this applies to school education it is, *mutatis mutandis*, by no means inconsistent with Entwistle's model. Fraser *et al.* found that other social and political factors, such as class size and financial expenditure per student, also influence learning but less directly.

> The nine factors in the model appear to compensate, substitute, or trade off for one another at diminishing rates of return ... Also, all factors seem important in that, without at least a small amount of each, students are likely to learn little. Furthermore, the results reported here appear to be surprisingly robust. Most of the meta-analyses which included consideration of student characteristics (e.g. gender, grade level) and design characteristics of the studies (e.g. method of sample selection) suggested that the more powerful factors appear to benefit all students in all conditions ... Changing the more alterable factors in the model seems to hold out the best hope for improving educational productivity.

Among the more alterable variables, of course, would be motivation, and the quantity and quality of instruction.

This argument is not necessarily invalidated by recognition of the importance of individual differences in student learning. Indeed Snow (1986) for example argues that such recognition may be among the most useful contributions of psychology to education. Snow (in his Editors' words): 'views education as an adaptive development program, in which adaptations that are responsive to individual differences will help provide both equality and optimal diversity of educational opportunity'.

Individual differences are almost by definition infinite, and psychology has generally tried to bring order into diversity by some kind of classification. Two

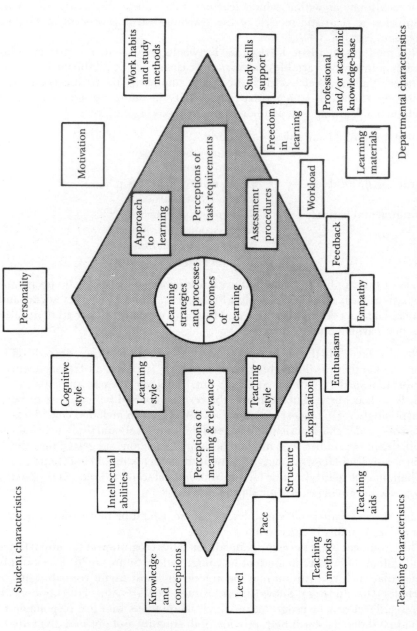

Student characteristics

Teaching characteristics

Departmental characteristics

Work habits and study methods

Study skills support

Professional and/or academic knowledge-base

Motivation

Freedom in learning

Learning materials

Perceptions of task requirements

Approach to learning

Assessment procedures

Workload

Feedback

Personality

Learning strategies and processes

Outcomes of learning

Empathy

Cognitive style

Learning style

Enthusiasm

Teaching style

Explanation

Perceptions of meaning & relevance

Structure

Intellectual abilities

Teaching aids

Pace

Knowledge and conceptions

Level

Teaching methods

Figure 1.1 A heuristic model of the teaching–learning process in higher education
From Entwistle and Tait (1989). For a more complex version of this model see Entwistle (in press).

approaches that are particularly relevant to education are the analysis of different modes of learning, and the examination of different categories of student.

As mentioned above, Entwistle has worked extensively on the first of these, though as Richardson (1989) points out there have been several sources of the ideas now current. One impetus from experimental psychology was the analysis by Craik and Lockhart (1972) of learning and memory in terms of 'levels of processing', which postulated a direct relationship between the durability of a memory trace and the level at which information was encoded within a hierarchical system of representations. Another was the work of Gordon Pask (e.g. Pask and Scott, 1971) on 'serialist' and 'holist' strategies of learning; and another that of Walter Perry (1970) on the developmental stages through which, he believed, a student ideally moves in the course of Higher Education. But perhaps the most important source has been the work of Ference Marton and colleagues. From this derives the now well known analysis of students' study styles and strategies, an analysis which is still undergoing modification, and appears in slightly different versions. A recent one (Entwistle, 1990) is shown as Table 1.1.

While there is now considerable evidence for these syndromes, they are of course abstractions, so that any individual student may well manifest characteristics of two or all three approaches. In particular perhaps the strategic approach may overlap with the deep approach. It is likely that the higher up the

Table 1.1   Categories of approaches to learning

Deep approach	Intention to understand Vigorous interaction with content
	Relating new ideas to previous knowledge Relating concepts to everyday experience
	Relating evidence to conclusions Examining the logic of the argument
Surface approach	Intention to complete task requirements
	Treating task as an external imposition Unreflectiveness about purpose or strategies
	Focus on discrete elements without integration Failure to distinguish principles from examples Memorizing information needed for assessments
Strategic approach	Intention to obtain highest possible grades
	Gear work to perceived preferences of teacher Awareness of marking schemes and criteria Systematic use of previous papers in revision
	Organizing time and effort to greatest effect Ensuring right conditions and materials for study

educational ladder one goes, the greater will be the preference, as least ostensibly, of teachers for the deep approach. Many teachers at secondary level make no bones about seeking to inculcate the strategic approach. This, of course, may be a major factor in the difficulties of transition from school to Higher Education which are discussed later. It is also possible, though apparently untested as yet, that the approaches would relate systematically to the shorter term and longer term aims and effects of education (as mentioned by Gibson, for example).

Then too, while the deep approach intuitively has some kind of higher status than the others, it is not necessarily the best for all individuals in all circumstances. Entwistle (1987) remarks that a deliberate attempt to use it, when there is insufficient time to do so properly, may result in what he calls improvidence, the accumulation of facts without overview, or globetrotting, personal conclusions without evidence. (The preferred method, one observes, of public figures who pontificate about education.)

Individual teachers may seek to foster one or other of the approaches to studying, but there is also evidence for more subtle effects of the academic environment. Terenzini and Wright (1987), among others, point to the complexity of the college-related growth process; see also Mumford *et al.* (1988). Entwistle and Tait (1989) report for example that those departments where there is consensus among the students that little freedom is allowed in learning, or there is a particularly heavy work load, are likely to contain a higher proportion of students relying on rote learning. But it is also true that what seems to be important is the students' perception of the situation, rather than that situation alone. One recalls John Stuart Mill, who regarded his prodigious childhood achievements as quite ordinary, since his father had ensured that he had no contemporaries with whom to compare his strangely demanding regime (Mill, 1873).

Different approaches to study clearly interact with the characteristics of students. Entwistle (1987) remarks that stable introverts are more likely to have better organized study methods, work longer and get better results. But extraverts who do, in fact, adopt efficient methods achieve just as good results.

There is considerable concern about the educational achievements of certain groups of students, especially those who may be regarded as disadvantaged. There is noticeably less concern, at least in the UK, about opportunities for the gifted. The most obvious concomitants, not to say causes, of disadvantage are race, socio-economic class and gender. Thus Clarke (1988), analysing UK degree results 1976–79, found large differences in the overall performance of men and women, with men generally doing better but also having a tendency to get the weakest degrees. But the matter is not simple: the underachievement of women, at any rate at First Class level, is more marked in certain subjects than others; and the differences do not exist in mature students. (On such students in general see, for example, Boud, 1987; Brookfield, 1986; Rogers, 1989.) Clarke attributes the underachievement to differences in 'A' level grades on entry (which of course only pushes the question back one stage) and to social pressures and sex stereotyping including bias in examining. However Kornbrot

(1987), examining the population of English and Welsh graduates 1980–82 (UK-based, under 24), found that the two social groups, women and lower class origin students, who are substantially under-represented in the undergraduate population, are actually more successful than upper class origin and male students at getting respectable degrees of Lower Second Class or better. Women are highly successful in many disciplines which are stereotypically male and where they are currently under-represented. Kornbrot remarks:

> Girls who are doing well at both arts and science at school should be advised that they are likely to do at least as well at science at university as they would at arts, maybe even better. This is important since there is evidence that one reason bright girls avoid science is that they believe there is nothing between Curie-level genius and school teaching!

As Eccles (1985) puts it in respect of the gifted, the important question is not why women are not more like men, but why both sexes make the sequence of choices they do; and perhaps the same could be said of every category of student.

Cognitive aspects

Chipman and Segal (1985) remark: 'the development of higher cognitive skills that enable students to be independent learners and independent, creative problem-solving users of their knowledge has always been a very important goal for educators. There is evidence, however, that explicit instruction in these skills is rare and that students' mastery of them is frequently inadequate'. It is also the case, as Richardson (1989) points out, that much of the research on inculcating such skills has been done at primary or secondary, rather than tertiary level. Possibly, it is easier to achieve results in a more controllable situation. For example, Savell, Twohig and Rachford (1986), reviewing studies of what is perhaps one of the most successful programmes, Reuven Feuerstein's 'Instrumental Enrichment', found the majority of positive effects in the 12–18 age range. They also found that most studies were difficult to interpret, usually due to inadequacies of design or implementation, or to lack of information in the report; and these problems also are widespread.

On the other hand Derry and Murphy (1986) are more confident: 'Research and cognitive theory amply support our contention that improvement of learning ability is an important and viable training goal for school districts, military services and industrial organizations'. Adams (1989) reviews the varying approaches to 'thinking skills' curricula. She points out that all share a fundamental assumption, namely that there exists a certain set of skills or processes that are common to thinking in general, regardless of person, domain or purpose. They subdivide, however, into two groups, according to whether they are organized around 'ecologically valid', real-life problems and materials, and aim to encourage 'macrological skills' such as creativity, the ability to deal with complex information and handle multiple points of view; or are based on abstract materials like psychometric tests of aptitude, and aim for 'micrological skills' such as observation, classification and sequencing. Feuerstein's is an example of the latter, while the equally well-known CoRT programme of Edward de Bono is one of the former. There are many others less famous but, in some cases at least, more closely based on general research findings. Evaluation of effectiveness, however, is by no means easy. Many of these programmes are ill-defined or repetitive, while some have a kind of missionary zeal that may well help in propagation but militate against objective assessment. Virtually every evaluation, Adams found, included evidence of some gains, and some results are extremely positive; but in many cases adequate data do not exist and studies are flawed in design and control.

Bransford *et al.* (1986) distinguish two general research approaches in the teaching of thinking and problem solving: the first derives from studies of experts in particular fields, and emphasizes the role of domain-specific knowledge, while the second emphasizes general strategies and metacognitive knowledge, deriving more from cognitive theory. Bransford *et al.* feel that the latter approach has been too dominant, and that programmes of this kind could be strengthened by focusing more explicitly on domain knowledge. Rather similarly Glaser (1984) argues that effective learners are characterized by self-regulatory or metacognitive capabilities, such as knowing what one knows and does not know, predicting the outcome of one's performances, planning ahead, apportioning time and resources, monitoring and adapting one's efforts. These self-monitoring skills 'can become abstracted competencies when individuals use them in a variety of . . . tasks and several fields of knowledge'. Nevertheless, Glaser argues, they may be of less use in specific knowledge domains, and of more when problems in unfamiliar domains are faced. This of course is the old problem of transfer. Salomon and Perkins (1989) make a potentially useful distinction between 'low-road transfer' and 'high-road transfer'. The first depends on extensive, varied practice and occurs automatically when well-learned behaviour is triggered in a new context. The second occurs by intentional abstraction of something from one context and application in a new one. Such transfer can be either forward-reaching, whereby one consciously abstracts basic elements in anticipation of later application, or backward reaching, when, faced with a new context, one searches for relevant knowledge already acquired. Block (1985) describes a college level thinking skills course specifically designed to overcome the problem of transfer, by including three essential features: metacognitive skills, abundant real-life examples and exercises, and an emphasis on writing skills. An evaluation of this programme has not been published (personal communication).

Alexander and Judy (1988) however conclude that there are at any rate two undisputed findings from cognitive research over the last twenty years. One is that those who know more about a particular domain generally understand and remember better; the other is that those who regulate and monitor their cognitive processing during task performance do better. They present a set of 'hypotheses', which might be called tentative conclusions, since they are generally supported by the literature:

1. A foundation of domain-specific knowledge seems requisite to the effective and efficient utilization of strategic knowledge;
2. Inaccurate or incomplete domain knowledge (which may come from everyday experience) may inhibit or interfere with learning;
3. Strategic knowledge contributes to the utilization and acquisition of domain knowledge;
4. The ill-informed or unintelligent use of strategies can be detrimental to learning;
5. As knowledge in a domain increases, strategic processing is altered (i.e. becomes more sophisticated and effective);
6. Differences in the relative importance of domain-specific and strategic knowledge may be a consequence of the nature of the domain or the structure of the task to which they are applied.
7. Perceiving the relatedness in domain and strategic knowledge across tasks and across domains seems to characterize competent performance.
8. Motivational and social-context factors may impact the acquisition and utilization of domain-specific and strategic knowledge.

Consistently with much that has already been said, Prawat (1989) argues that successful learning involves (domain-specific) knowledge; strategy or skill; and what he terms disposition, which resembles the Marton/Entwistle analysis. Disposition is either towards performance – getting the job done, with learning a means to an end – or mastery – aiming to increase competence, become more knowledgeable or skilful. All three are largely a function of two important factors, organization and awareness, which it is the task of the educator to encourage. Thus in the case of knowledge, for example, organization calls for the presentation of key concepts which are carefully selected and have maximum potential for relationships with other concepts and wide applicability. Awareness should be fostered by encouraging students to articulate their own thoughts, discuss ideas and apply information.

A suggestion as to how cognitive learning theory could be closely linked to instructional prescriptions comes from Tennyson and Rasch (1988), who offer an instructional design model that 'focuses on the planning of a learning environment so that students not only acquire knowledge but also improve their cognitive abilities to employ and extend their knowledge'. They argue that two false assumptions persist: one that appropriate instructional methods are not available, and two that improvement in cognition occurs through some independent system external to the main curricular programmes. Their system is summarized in Table 1.2.

If some such analysis were to be generally accepted, it would produce a pattern of Higher Education teaching very different from the haphazard approach of today. However, Derry and Murphy, in the review already cited, conclude that although:

> there exists a wealth of empirical research and several good learning skills taxonomies to guide selection of objectives and design of training . . . we

Table 1.2   Model for the planning of a learning environment

	Acquisition of knowledge (storage)			Employment of knowledge (retrieval)	
Memory system components	Declarative knowledge	Procedural knowledge	Contextual knowledge	Cognitive complexity	Total cognitive system
Learning times	10%	20%	25%	30%	15%
Learning objectives	Verbal information	Intellectual skills	Contextual skills	Cognitive strategies	Creative processes
Instructional methods	Expository strategies	Practice strategies	Problem-oriented strategies	Complex-problem strategies	Self-directed experiences

found no integrated taxonomy that covered a full range of student populations and learning domains. The choice of which taxonomy to use and
which learning skills to train is a matter of selecting what is appropriate for
the student population, the training time allowed, and the type of learning
that is involved.

In other words it is still 'horses for courses', a conclusion reached also by Tobias
(1989), who agrees with previous research suggesting that, for example,
students high in general ability tended to succeed with instructions that offered
little assistance, whereas those of less ability profited when various forms of
assistance were added, such as advance organizers, demonstrations and the like
– perhaps not a conclusion that will surprise any who have taught a range of
students. There is a comparable difference, according to Tobias, between those
with low or high relevant prior knowledge. Similarly, students with constructive
motivation, that is preferences for learning independently with little anxiety or
defensiveness, tend to benefit from conditions that provide more freedom and
more challenge, that look to the learner to supply a good deal of the structure
and the specification of the task; whereas anxious or defensive students learn
better from instruction that is more clearly structured.

Orectic aspects

With this we approach the non-cognitive or orectic aspects of education. That
education should have aims beyond the imparting of factual information, or
even cognitive skills, was for long assumed without question. The idea informed
Greek practice of the classical period (Beck, 1964), which has seemed a model
for Western cultures; and mediaeval, church-based education (Leff, 1989); and
the nineteenth century public school tradition deriving from Coleridge and
Arnold (Bamford, 1960; Mathieson and Bernbaum, 1988). It is enshrined in the
Robbins Report of 1963, which still constitutes official policy on Higher

Education in the United Kingdom. In practice, however, little attention is now paid to such matters even though, as we have seen, students continue to think them of some importance. Bergendal (1983) points out that the dominant kind of knowledge is theory-based, propositional and cognitive; ideally it is seen as objective, independent of the world it describes, value-free and explicit. One of the problems with this is that there are, in fact, other equally legitimate forms of knowledge such as skills, experience and empathy. These have come to seem of less value, or even irrelevant, in Higher Education; even in the discipline of psychology to which, it can be argued, they are particularly germane (Radford and Rose, 1989). However this may be, another consequence, according to Bergendal, is that research takes precedence over teaching. And another, it may be suggested, is that those who teach are less interested in how and why students learn than in merely what they know, as exhibited in examinations.

Whatever the aims of Higher Education, there can be no doubt that other than cognitive factors greatly influence the effectiveness of learning; in particular motivation. As Dweck (1986) shows, perhaps not very surprisingly, research demonstrates that motivational processes affect (a) how well children can deploy their existing skills, (b) how well they acquire new skills and knowledge, and (c) how well they transfer these new skills and knowledge to novel situations. And there is little reason to doubt that this applies at any age. Entwistle (1988) found that students gave three main types of answer when asked what motivated them to complete academic work successfully: hope of success; fear of failure; or personal interest. Serna (1989) offers suggestions as to how teachers can make use of these motives through suitable reinforcement techniques.

Undoubtedly Beard and Hartley (1984) are right when they say that some students lack any motivation at all. They feel that these are usually either those who have been persuaded into Higher Education by parents or teachers; or those with personal problems; or those who are so extraverted in personality that they find solitary study unacceptable. 'But when a whole class seems unmotivated then the fault must lie with the teacher'. This seems rather sweeping, since it may surely also lie with, for example, the institution or the curriculum.

However, most students have some degree of motivation both to get along during their course, and to complete it successfully (though personal criteria of 'success' vary widely). Brophy (1987) offers practical guidance as to how the teacher may seek to improve motivation – again at school level but more generally applicable. There are three general strategies which should always be used, that is in each lesson: stress the value and relevance of school work to everyday life; show that you expect pupils to enjoy learning; and treat tests as ways of checking on personal progress. Then there are a number of specific strategies of which at least one should be used on each occasion, among them: explain why you find a topic or idea interesting; introduce topics or tasks in ways which arouse interest; create suspense or stimulate curiosity; make abstract content more personal, concrete or familiar. There may perhaps be some teachers at every level who feel that these are just the things they would do, if only they could discover how. Above all, Brophy says, teachers should spend more time and care in explaining the relevance and potential interest of each topic. This is no doubt true in general, but observation suggests it is neither sufficient nor even necessary for successful teaching.

Some of the outstandingly successful creators of motivation are to be found among sports coaches. Very high and sustained motivation is essential for competition at the top level, and coaches or trainers such as Fritz Stampfl, Arthur Lydiard or Percy Cerutty (athletics – Hemery, 1986), Cus d'Amato (boxing – Gutteridge and Giller, 1987), or Boris Breskvar (tennis – Breskvar, 1987) are exceptionally good at creating and maintaining it, as their protégés agree. Breskvar's account of the training of Boris Becker, whom he coached almost every day from the age of six for the next nine years, is a model of good teaching practice. It is clear that one common factor is the personal interest the athlete feels the coach has in him or her; and allied to this is a very exact matching of method, technique, schedules etc. to the individual. Of course such coaches often have the luxury of individual tuition denied to most teachers in Higher Education; nevertheless it is usually possible to attempt something along these lines.

That motivation is an individual matter is seen in some work by Piechowski and Colangelo (1984), who describe five dimensions of enhanced mental functioning or 'overexcitability', some pattern of which they think characterizes giftedness in different spheres. They are psychomotor, sensual, intellectual, imaginational and emotional. This is an interesting concept which might have wider application. It would, for example, fit well with the general idea which has become rather popular that successful learning is related to self-system and self-concept. McCombs and Whistler (1989) argue that the self is crucial in the development of autonomous learning. They maintain that all successful learning is in effect autonomous: it is 'an internally mediated, active, generative, and constructive process of attending, processing, and transforming information into both relatively stable and dynamic knowledge structures'. Human behaviour is basically motivated by needs for self-development and self-determination, and it follows that students are motivated by situations that: challenge them to become personally and actively involved in their own learning; are perceived as related to personal needs, interests and goals; present tasks that can be successfully accomplished; and allow for personal choice and control matched to age, stage and task requirements.

Many studies have shown that a positive self-concept tends to correlate with internal locus of control, the belief that the causes of success or failure reside in oneself rather than in external factors. In a very large study involving 27,718 American high school seniors, Keith, Pottebaum and Eberhardt (1986) found that internal locus of control had an important positive relationship to academic achievement. Self-concept had no direct relationship, but may have an indirect one since it is linked to internal locus.

Such an effect, general as it appears to be, nevertheless occurs in a particular culture, and the nature of this and how it is mediated must be important variables. At the anecdotal level, institutions with a very precise and explicit ethos clearly have significant effects: examples would be military academies and English public schools. Danziger (1988) gives many quotes from old Etonians, showing how there is both pressure and opportunity to excel. Institutions have been created more recently with the overt aim of fostering the highest achievement, in particular in the USSR and East Germany (Dunstan, 1978, 1987). Their success has been most observable in sport, as for example in the 1988 Olympic Games (132 and 102 medals respectively; 3rd, USA with 94; 4th, West Germany with 40). Dunstan describes how in such schools there is indeed recognition of individual abilities, but always subject to the needs of society. It will be interesting to see the effects of the current political developments.

2

From School to University

Kjell Raaheim

The following episode may serve as a partial explanation of how, some fifteen years ago, I came to undertake the writing of my first book within the field of students' learning.

After more than twenty years' experience as a university teacher, I was preparing the first of a series of lectures, to form part of an introductory course in psychology, philosophy and logic, compulsory for all new students in Norway. My intention was to start by introducing the subject, and by explaining the details of the syllabus. I suddenly realized that I was in the process of preparing a performance which, to some 300–400 students, represented their very first confrontation with teaching at university, without my giving this important fact any particular consideration.

What is a lecture like as an educational phenomenon? In what way does the role of the student as listener differ from the task of the pupil in the classroom? Is some activity expected of the student? Should he or she ask questions and take notes, or is the lecture theatre a place for passively receiving the benefits of oratorical display?

Admittedly these are questions of a rather trivial nature. But do they have to be asked again by each new student? Or rather: Is it necessary that the students, individually, spend a great deal of time in seeking answers to such questions?

On the occasion referred to I was given confirmation by my audience that no clear conception existed among them as to what a lecture was supposed to be, and what *they*, as listeners were supposed to do. The brief explanation I was able to give that time was far from being sufficient, but hopefully of *some* value.

What does the situation look like when it comes to the problems of changing over from going to school to becoming a student at the university? Is the situation today, as is often argued, especially difficult, since a greater number of young people seek higher education in many countries?

When I first began to look for relevant research findings I discovered that little had been done in my own country. I found that in Birmingham Wankowski had spent a number of years looking into the question of factors for academic success. His points of recommendation to schools and university, for bridging the pedagogical gap between those two institutions, are best explained by himself, and so I shall advise the reader to study what he has to say in other parts of this book. Here I only wish to present some comments on what I have found particularly important to Scandinavian academics, who are at present trying to improve the methods of tuition at university. Perhaps it is not unlikely that others would find the points equally important.

The question of students' goals

Wankowski has found that the more successful students are those who have a somewhat clearer picture of their future professional career than the rest. This is a finding that might puzzle the experienced university teacher who remembers the rather well articulated outburst of previous generations of students, towards more freedom to concentrate on whatever was found interesting and important, without considering an efficient way of training for professional roles.

Admittedly there are reasons to believe that student attitudes have changed over the last decades. The general care of today of not throwing away resources seems to have led to the awareness that time is also an important factor. So the student challenge is perhaps one of not throwing away any time on what is judged to be a fruitless enterprise and on what seems to be totally unrelated to future tasks. But in spite of this, as Jacobsen (1978) has reported, a more general aim of extending the world of knowledge still seems to be a popular theme for learning at university. Whereas students who had some definite goal in mind generally did better than students who were unable to give a clear statement of why they had entered university, a closer look at the results, on a particular course, would reveal that, if the content of that course was not seen as more or less directly relevant to future work, a student who had expressed some definite wish for an occupational role would tend to do *less well* than one who had simply stated that the reasons for entering university could be summarized as a general wish to learn more.

This particular motivational problem naturally leaves us with the question of who is going to make decisions where the contents of courses are concerned. I do not wish to enter into a discussion of this at the present point. But it is perhaps worth noticing that whereas only about one per cent of the new students of two decades ago hesitated when asked to list the subjects of their choice upon entering a Norwegian university, more than fifty per cent of today's students are found to be uncertain.

The use of lectures for larger groups

As can be seen from his own list of recommendations, Wankowski suggests that pupils in the sixth form be given an opportunity of becoming used to mass lectures and to be trained to integrate information gained from lectures and reading. At the same time he argues that a reduction in the size of audiences in lectures is needed at university level. These points in my view actualize the question of what is, normally, the purpose of the university lecture? Perhaps one would find that only a few teachers intend to act as substitutes for students reading the textbooks. Still there is reason to believe that comparatively few lecturers have a clear enough picture of the role their series of lectures might play in the sum total of learning activities of the students. Is it, for instance, possible to let a particular one hour of listening to a lecture somehow be tied to a given number of hours spent in reading some specified textbooks? Is it on the whole possible – and advisable – to let the students know how the lecture should be fitted into a more comprehensive instructional scheme? Or should we just keep on letting the occasional lecture play the role of a sudden and often unpredictable meeting of a subtle academic mind with the, as yet, less sophisticated members of the audience?

In my opinion lectures ought to be given a role to play that cannot, as easily, be played by other forms of tuition. Needless to say, if the teacher wants the students to attend, he must then also see to it that the role in question is one for which the students feel a need. But this ought not to be done in an artificial way. Some years ago, when I published some of the results of my experiments on the problem of students' attendance (see also Chapter 5), I received a letter from a senior lecturer of a Norwegian university. Having read that I had stressed the point that students would in fact attend lectures regularly, if only the teachers showed concern and presented the students each time with some useful information, he wanted my reaction to the following plan: As part of a regular course let there be some printed material for the students to read when they want to. But let there also be some gaps, by way of missing portions, in this material. So, if the students want to have access to the whole of the syllabus, they have to attend the lectures, where the master of ceremonies orally presents the missing links!

I had to explain that this was not quite what I had had in mind when arguing that the lectures ought to contain something that could not as easily be found in books! But the story seems to indicate that a need exists for a discussion among university teachers of the more fundamental part played by the traditional lecture in today's world of tuition.

Sometimes the argument is raised that when you have something like 500 students in the lecture room, there is not much hope for a fruitful teaching situation. So when Wankowski argues that a reduction in the size of the audience in lectures at university is needed, a number of teachers would tend to add that this is an absolute claim.

The situation in Norway is such as would normally give the university teacher who is running introductory courses in various fields a rich experience with large groups of students. Some courses are compulsory for all new students, so each year literally thousands of students, who are unfamiliar with university style lectures, find themselves in huge lecture theatres, where a group of 200 would be regarded as a small one.

I agree that new students, in particular, would profit from being taught in groups small enough to make possible a two-way communication. In Chapter 5

I shall even report some recent findings of experiments with small tutorial groups led by older students. But if the circumstances, financial or otherwise, are such as to put the lower limit of the number of students in a lecture at 250, it might be profitable to discuss the possibility of simply *doubling* the size of the audience, in order to spend the money thus saved on some other activity that might enhance the learning situation for the students. Sometimes, when the minimum size of the audience forces a lecturer into a one-man, or a one-woman show, the restriction on the audience is only one of a technical nature. If the lecture does not take the form of a courageous struggle to pass on information in a better way than does the well written textbook, and the teacher instead gives a demonstration of how some knowledge may be used to cope with the baffling, exam-like questions, it might be better to let into the lecture theatre all who are able to see and hear the things presented on 'the stage'. Admittedly such a stage 'show' must be preceded by some preparatory reading on the part of the students who should also be prepared, by some carefully worked out instructions, on how to 'follow a lecture'. An effort put into these instructions should result in an educational gain. In my experience, teachers often fail to discuss the general problems of lecturing till they are forced to do something by the size of the audience.

The importance of early feedback

Even if, in a number of courses at university, the student finds different forms of assessment, there can be no doubt that, to a large number of students, their own progress seems far more difficult to judge than it used to be in school. Also, when on a rare occasion some feedback is given, it has the form of a much more dramatic 'pass or fail' verdict than has been met before.

The need to know if one is 'on the right track', in the 'yet-to-be-explored' and perhaps not even altogether 'promised land' of university studies, is deeply felt by many new students. So when Wankowski says that the students ought to be given more frequent opportunities for evaluation of their progress, it might be agreed to, provided that the students do not feel that an 'extra assessment' is another hard burden to take on. Some experiments, later to be commented upon in more detail (see Chapter 5) might perhaps be worth mentioning here.

In the last fifteen years we have had the opportunity at the University of Bergen of investigating how various factors would influence the progress of students during their first year. As part of an experimental programme, optional 'test-examinations' have been arranged at certain intervals prior to the final, official one. The great majority of the students have welcomed this opportunity and, when asked, have put their names on the list of 'volunteers' to participate in this scheme. When, on occasions, the number of interested students has exceeded our capacity for marking the 'test-examination' essays, it has been decided to draw lots to determine who will take part in a test on a particular day.

We have found regularly that even when students are queueing up to fill the places of some friends who might be sick, on the next day, when the test-exam is taking place, perhaps fewer than three-quarters of the candidates turn up. Obviously not all forms of feedback work all the time. Even a 'test-examination' may evoke the fear and anxiety generally associated with assessment situations of the past. So although a student might feel the need of getting information on how he or she succeeds in coping with the challenges in academic work, the student might still hesitate in placing him- or herself in the position of being told.

We have tried to avoid the pitfall of turning the 'test-examination' into a 'recent memory test', or a test of the knowledge of the subject, by letting the students know in advance which parts of the syllabus will be drawn upon each time. But even so, the students would find themselves 'unprepared' to such an extent that, at the last minute, they decide not to ask for the bad tasting, if preventive, medicine of a low mark. And lecturers have very little to offer when it comes to the question of telling students what an academic discourse is all about, how they ought to prepare themselves or, in short, what it is like to study at university.

The feedback needed is not only one of how well the student has succeeded in reproducing some parts of a textbook. So even if the lecturer is tempted to assess the answers to questions in the test exam on factual knowledge only, he must be willing to *try* to give the students some information about their ability to take a critical attitude, to make fair judgements, and to give a balanced and mature presentation of the broader perspectives of a problem area. In my opinion universities might be facing an increasing challenge as far as these matters are concerned in the years ahead, since the number of new students with very limited knowledge of the academic world is increasing in many countries. In a number of cases it is not only a question of whether or not a given student makes the necessary progress within the subject chosen. It is also a question of whether his or her field of study is one that will turn out to be a sensible choice. In some fields we have a total absence of counselling arrangements that might, in some cases, prevent a student from going through years of hard work, only to find that the vocational consequences of the academic endeavours are quite different from what the student has been looking forward to.

The question of different types of assessment and the problem of reducing tension

Many attempts to improve the methods of tuition at university in recent years have resulted in near failure because the traditional types of examinations are still there, at the end of the road. This situation may vary as the autonomy of the university varies from one country to another. In Norway there have been some definite changes in the rules about university examinations. We have seen attempts at essays or research reports, prepared at home, take the place of the old fashioned eight, ten, or even twelve hours' sweat at the desk in the Great Hall. In some fields two or more students have been allowed to work together on their final thesis, and oral examinations have either been omitted altogether, or replaced by group discussions of some central questions from the syllabus.

Sometimes the students are allowed to choose between different forms of examination, and this reform seems to have been particularly welcomed, since students may differ in their preferences for demonstrating the results of their learning. Some students like the challenges of a written examination paper with a limited time at their disposal, and tend also to enjoy the atmosphere of an oral examination. Others, and this might be true for the majority of students, become highly nervous in situations where their performance on the day has important consequences for their future professional career.

As far as I know relatively few investigations have been set up to look into the improvements or changes in examination procedures. The question remains whether or not two weeks' work at home, say, gives rise to less tension than a one-day test of the traditional type. According to my personal experience, and judging from the examination *results*, a number of students seem to have great difficulties also in coping with a two-week task at home. Some of them are found to hand in essays, which both with regard to quantity and quality are quite comparable to the results of a ten-hour test of the traditional type. Admittedly one would doubt in such cases that the student has actually been working on his essay during much of the time allowed. But the important thing is that this does not necessarily mean that he has not felt the tension of the examination over the whole two-week period.

Meagre results and low marks obtained by the students who work within new examination systems might also be due to the lack of previous experience with these types of tasks. The writing of a 'semester', or 'term essay', as it is often called, needs definite instructions as to how to proceed. It seems to me that it would be more appropriate to present the students with an assessment situation which is equivalent to situations later to be faced in 'real life'. Then, there would be no need to prepare the students how to solve difficult theoretical riddles while sitting on an uncomfortable chair in some big, cathedral-like hall, *without* the aid of the natural tools — books.

The tension of examinations may perhaps be somewhat reduced if teachers were more explicit in explaining to students what is in fact expected of them since the clarity of the questions set on a number of occasions may leave much to be desired. It may rightly be argued that these are the problems which will not disappear even if the students are given a free choice between different *types* of exams. It is also difficult to prove that different types of assessment are equivalent, and there is no guarantee that the student will choose a type of examination that will turn out to be for him or her a better way of demonstrating the knowledge gained so far.

Maybe there is reason to believe that the situation at university will always be less 'fair' than the examination system in schools. At university the number of students taught in different groups will vary considerably, thereby making the basis for comparison of the effectiveness of teaching and assessment change all the time. The examination tasks set in university are often highly dependent on the individual lecturer's points of view and on his or her ability in formulating a question. Generally we have to do without the standardization and the stricter 'norms' used in various schools.

It can be argued on the basis of the factors mentioned above that in university assessments nearly all the rules of psychological testing are violated. Both the reliability of the examination results and their validity as expressions of knowledge and insight into a subject matter can be said to be highly questionable at times. How then are we to make improvements, when at the same time seeking to reduce the tension inherent in the assessment situation?

I do not wish to advocate the view that within university assessment we need a system that will give the individual student the place intended for him by the Almighty, provided he cares to work as hard as all the others. I would personally very much regret it, if the examinations at university were better specimens of *tests*, in the belief of providing the 'correct picture' of each individual's potential. Over the years we have taken some pains in trying to level out individual differences of both an economic and a social nature. A sharper distinction between people on the basis of intellectual abilities, therefore, can scarcely be said to constitute a worthy goal.

In my view the marks attained at university ought also in the future to be looked upon as *unfair*, in the sense that one should be aware of the fact that they might have been different under different circumstances. This means that one should understand that some coincidence might have occurred, that the candidate might have performed better (or worse) with another type of test, and that the marks, on the whole, only tell something about the situation here and now.

Some tension before exams is perhaps unavoidable, even if the students have the opportunity of deciding themselves in what manner they will demonstrate their knowledge or abilities. It is even conceivable that the tension might be increased by the very fact that one has to choose oneself, with the possibility then of making a wrong decision!

A greater opportunity for students to *work together* in the final exams should, in my opinion, be developed and I would like to mention some of the advantages of such a provision.

For one thing, the working situation in this case is the more natural one. In real life we are seldom forced to work alone in academic enterprises. Even professors seek help and advice from colleagues. Next comes the possibility that this would be a situation of less tension, since the individual student is not left with sole responsibility for the result. Furthermore, there is a chance that marks in this case would be seen as indicators mainly of the quality of the present *work* and not as signs of personal abilities.

As already mentioned, there have been some examples of students working together in written examination tasks in Norwegian universities. But rarely have we tried to let group discussions take the place of oral examinations on an individual basis, although in some fields this type of assessment has existed for years.

An oral examination situation where five to eight students take part in a discussion, may not seem to lend itself to an assessment of an individual student. Still, to some examiners, this situation may be regarded as highly satisfactory, if some necessary conditions are met.

It is important that the students are *trained* to work together as a group and to present their knowledge by means of a discussion of the topic chosen. Without some experience and skill in the art of letting other people have a word, the session might be a failure. And it is this very point that creates the most advantageous part of the arrangement. It is not a question – as is so often the case – of demonstrating one's own brilliance at the cost of others. A successful outcome of taking part in discussions depends on the ability to give others a chance of showing what *they* know.

Both students and teachers need to learn the variety of new ways of working together. As for the number of students who might profitably share a certain task, my personal suggestion would be that with *written* assignments, only in exceptional cases should more than two students work together, whereas in *oral* examinations five to six students would probably make a suitable team.

It might be objected that in such cases the odd 'not-so-bright' or partly uninformed student may be helped through by his fellow students. Here one could point to the fact that on the higher levels in the academic world we also have people with various forms of 'uncontrolled' accomplishments. And one could also add that in society there is a generally accepted rule of encouraging the able to help and support the less gifted ones.

A number of suggested reforms would no doubt increase concern amongst academics for deeper understanding of the learning processes *before* a certain kind of assessment takes place. An awareness by the teacher of his student's steady progress during the course should make the final examination less important. And generally, a discussion of forms of assessment should always take as its point of departure the particular nature of the course.

3

On the Pedagogical Skills
of University Teachers

Kjell Raaheim

It is likely that a number of people would react to this heading by suggesting that it is rather a question of the *lack of skill* where the university teacher's pedagogical status is concerned. Contrary to the case of teachers within almost any other field, university lecturers will as a rule start their career without any training for teaching at all.

It has been argued that the reason for this state of affairs is that it is taken for granted that a person who has the necessary qualifications for doing research – to fill a post at the university – will automatically be suited for lecturing. I am not willing to accept this as the whole story, at least not on the assumption that university teaching is equivalent to other forms of teaching activities. There is, however, the possibility that many would look upon the learning situation at university as something very different from what is found elsewhere in education.

We shall have a chance of returning to this matter in a later chapter. We have for a very long time heard stories with some sad consequences due to the insufficient educational skills of university teachers. They have given rise to serious discussions – and anecdotes. More recently we have had suggestions, particularly from student quarters, that pedagogical qualifications be given consideration when making new appointments. We also know that educationalists have offered courses for teachers at university level, without much success. As far as I can judge, the general picture is very much the same in a number of different countries. The courses are attended by very few and often only by those who least of all need to alter their educational practice.

We are often told that the concern about the lack of educational qualifications involves far more important issues than the practical skills of using audio-visual aids, or of talking clearly etc. This is *not* what courses should be all about. Rather it seems to be a question of learning to be aware of the individual and of group interactions with the lecturer and amongst students themselves. Maybe this is the reason why so many academic theoreticians hesitate to enter a course?

Let me try to ease the situation by some reflections on where the educational shoe starts to pinch.

My own first confrontation with teaching procedures at university took place shortly after my discharge from the army, where I had been exposed to courses for instructors in various disciplines. The relief I felt at being able, at the university, to choose subjects *myself*, was perhaps the main reason why I did not come to look upon the change in the learning situation as a problematic one. On the other hand, I could not fail to discover that in a number of ways the lectures at university were drastically different from what had been regarded in the army as basic principles of instruction.

Among other things this had to do with the attention of the audience. I had been given detailed information by the course leaders in the army of how the attentiveness would vary in a group during the 45 minutes of a lecture. And, moreover, there had been suggestions as to what could be done to counteract the influence of tiredness or boredom among the listeners, or those watching some demonstration. Now, among the lecturers at university, I noticed quite a few who never seemed to think of even catching the attention of their students in the first place, not to mention any action to heighten it at critical points. I must admit that, over the years of lecturing, I have myself sometimes let my own interest in a topic influence both my enthusiasm and the time spent talking about it. I have probably forgotten most of the relatively simple ways of securing the attention of a listener who was not attentive from the beginning. And I cannot, as an excuse, blame the fact that I was never really told what to do.

My disappointment as a new student was not, however, confined to the lack of attention in some lectures. In fact this was of minor concern to me personally, as I discovered that it was perfectly all right to restrict my attendance to those lectures I particularly wanted to follow. The annoying thing was that I sometimes could not get hold of the main points to which the lecturer was addressing himself. If his talk was accompanied by some demonstration of instruments or products, I would on occasions be completely lost. The lecturer would perhaps *hide* the objects in his hand, or stand between me and the things he wanted to demonstrate.

The interest the army takes in the question of whether or not the individual recruit has got a clear enough picture of the details of a weapon, say, cannot perhaps be compared with a university teacher's concern whether his listeners are catching every point. Still, much is likely to be gained if one considers some very simple rules such as always to hold small objects up towards the light, to turn them around, or to keep them at a distance from one's own body. Short remarks such as for instance 'Look here', or 'Listen to this', could be offered even if, as a general rule, the student is there, looking and/or listening.

As already mentioned, educationalists argue that university teachers need not learn how to 'write clearly on the blackboard'. Contrary to this, I would maintain that this is exactly what we need to learn *first*. It is conceivable that we shall have to start at an even more elementary level. I am thinking of something which the military course organizers never needed to worry about, namely *the attendance* at the lecture.

There may be a number of different reasons why, on a number of occasions, we find the student attendance to be following a rather fast declining curve as the term proceeds. But whatever reason is found to be most important, the fact remains that not even the most brilliant educationalist would have any impact on those *not* present in the lecture room. Admittedly, the importance of the problem of attendance varies with the areas of study and with institutions. But there seems to be a widespread belief that inevitably university teaching must be accompanied by this problem. Only in cases where the students' attendance is somehow of a direct importance for their 'pass' or 'fail' on a certain course does the problem seem to be taken seriously by teachers.

What are teachers and students like?

The question sounds probably more naive than intended. We have found that there is no short and precise answer to the question of what *groups of people* tend to look like when their members are observed individually. In the history of psychology, attempts at describing individuals on the basis of group assessments have ended in failure where the attempt to operate with just a few variables is concerned. The uniqueness of the individual generally makes the use of labels highly inappropriate, and in most cases these attempts have been abandoned. In most cases, but not in all. Within educational institutions such labelling still exists. Teachers often see their students as belonging to a small number of groups, whereas the students in many cases place their teachers into one, single category. And there is reason to believe that this holds true also at university level. The way students and lecturers perceive one another is characterized by a simplification not easily found elsewhere between adults.

At the University of Lancaster, Noel Entwistle (now in Edinburgh) conducted some extensive investigations on different questions of university pedagogics. Data were collected by way of interviews and questionnaires from more than 2,500 students from 21 universities and other institutions of higher education. More than 600 lecturers were also approached.

The investigations aimed at different objectives. One was to describe different learning strategies among students, and, if possible, to gain an insight into the question of study progress and personality. One asked the question of what are the different goals of students, both with regard to future work and to personality development and well-being. Of special interest in our present context is the student's statements of goals, which were seen to vary quite a lot. Students *are* very different, both as far as personality structure is concerned, and when it comes to views on what might be gained from studies at university. Whilst this is a finding that would scarcely surprise the reader, it is worth noticing that the teachers' conception of the students was almost without variation. Most teachers seemed to agree that there is a group of 'good students'. This group is rather small, as is another group, of 'poor students'. Whereas the 'good students' prove themselves early as future academics, the 'poor students' are seen as lazy and of low intelligence. The rest – the large majority of students – are seen by the teachers as belonging to one big group, the members of which do not seem to possess any particular noteworthy, positive feature. Only to a very limited degree did the teachers seem to be aware of the numerous, differing goals and interests expressed by the students themselves.

Since the seventies Entwistle has consolidated his insight in central factors of teaching and learning at university through a number of studies (Entwistle, 1981; Entwistle and Ramsden, 1983; Marton, Hounsell and Entwistle, 1984).

In Norway his early work sparked off a series of investigations at the University of Bergen. Also in this country university lecturers seem to have an oversimplified view of students, and vice versa. 'Teachers' and 'students' are normally seen as constituting very homogeneous groups of people. One might well be aware of deviations from the general picture, but these would probably be taken to constitute the exception that 'proves the rule'.

Entwistle's earliest investigations also seemed to confirm our assumption of what would be typical students' attitudes towards teachers. Most students seem to regard their teachers as members of a distinct group, where the common interest is to do research, and where an interest in teaching is almost absent. Students from different institutions, and of different subjects, all seemed to agree that most teachers were seemingly without any concrete goals as far as their lecturing was concerned.

The students were, however, able to point to *some* exceptions. The 'good teacher', although he or she is a rare thing, is a person with two distinctive characteristics: *enthusiasm* (for what he or she is teaching) and *concern* (for the students). Above all, the good university teacher is interested in the students, *as people*. This type of teacher tries to convey to the students an interest in the subject, by way of careful planning, and asking the question of how the teaching ought to be administered, as well as what its content should be at different times.

The 'poor teachers' – and according to the students those are in the majority at university – are all characterized by a *lack of interest* in students ('they do not care about students'). Their teaching seems to be aimed solely at detecting future researchers and thus runs the risk of being of little relevance to most students. The teachers also seem to ignore that there is a lack of communication between them and the students.

In a report, Brennan and Percy (1976) deal with the results of the early Lancaster investigation. They point to the fact that students from different institutions are almost unanimous in their criticism of their teachers, using nearly identical formulations. But although the teachers are thought of as being concerned only with what is relevant to examinations and assessment, many students are of the opinion that it is *the system* that ought to be blamed. Both students and teachers suffer from the system, the teachers being more responsible for its structure, though.

Brennan and Percy make another interesting point. If we look at how teachers feel that university teaching should present itself, we find a high degree of consensus between them and the students. Both parties argue that one must abstain from a one-sided stressing of the syllabus and mere knowledge acquisition. The teachers claim to be planning their lectures with the aim of stimulating the students' independence, flexibility and critical thinking. The way *they* describe a poor teacher more or less coincides with the students' description.

Judging from the interviews with the teachers, such a person is, however, a rare exception.

We might ask the question of what is the chief explanation for the negative attitudes, and the stereotyped descriptions students and teachers present of one another. Brennan and Percy point to the inconsistency between the teachers' *statements* of what must be regarded as sensible pedagogical behaviour, and their actual, daily pedagogical *practice*, and they emphasize that while teachers *say* they are not in favour of rote learning or of strict dependence on the curriculum and on mechanical routines, this is what they in their daily work stress the most. Much of the blame for this situation can perhaps be placed on the *working conditions*, under which the teachers have to operate: a lack of time, a shortage of resources, competition, and numerous committee assignments. These are all factors that often ruin both the pleasure of one's work and the best of plans for proper teaching.

This is all very well. But the fact remains that the relationship between teacher and students usually looks somewhat shaky from the start. Suspicion, or a lack of confidence, might be the result of a clash of basic interests that may differ in various ways – a clash which both parties may have experienced from time to time throughout their years at school. At university the teachers and the students *start* with a well established 'knowledge' of being on different sides.

Admittedly, this is to paint with rather broad strokes. Still, a mutual confidence does not seem to establish itself between teachers and students until the latter reach the postgraduate level. Now the two parties seem more alike, as far as insight into a topic of study is concerned, and it then seems to follow that a necessary basis for respect and co-operation may be found. A better knowledge of 'the other part' might do away with the fear that seems to exist, initially.

Are the goals of students and teachers after all more or less the same?

As already mentioned, Brennan and Percy report that a good deal of agreement exists between the *descriptions* of teaching goals at university. Teachers and students seem to agree on how 'the good teacher' organizes his or her teaching, and there is also agreement on the attitudes and intentions ascribed to such a person. When the daily pedagogical situation looks different, the reason for this might be that teachers find difficulties in following their ideals.

When they examine the data from their British investigations more carefully Brennan and Percy have some doubt about the possibility of shared goals. It appears that although both teachers and students stress the importance of 'criticism', 'enthusiasm', and 'tolerance', they seem to attach different meanings to the words. Students are, for instance, seen to complain that when the teachers ask them 'to be critical', this implies only the negative aspects of the word. They are encouraged to doubt the correctness of information, to challenge, and to tear up arguments. The students want to replace lost illusions by being creative, and by constructing new and better solutions to different problems. Also they object to the idea that 'criticism' is only to be held within rather strict professional limits.

That the students have goals other than entering an academic career is something that is often overlooked by the university teacher. The *variety* of goals is also such as would render a highly generalized statement of 'what students want' into a rather meaningless remark. Brennan and Percy find that there are signs that individually based goals *are* being recognized, for instance by allowing students to partly decide their own curriculum. However, the individual components seem to be very limited in scope.

It would, however, be wrong to give the impression that the British investigations leave us with a picture of only dissatisfied students. There are numerous statements to the effect that the time spent at university has been valuable. The criticism has been directed mainly towards the professional activities or activities related to the curriculum. On the whole, the teachers' demand for professional effort is considered too great, and seen as directed towards a too restricted acquisition of knowledge. In the students' opinion the teaching situation at university and that of pre-university schools may turn out to be quite similar, despite the fact that the university is generally looked upon as a unique centre for intellectual growth and the seeking of Truth.

Enthusiasm and consideration – how far would it take us?

According to the Lancaster investigations, a 'good teacher' may be characterized by such keywords as 'enthusiasm' and 'concern'. These are traits of a very general nature, but even so, we might do well in taking the students' opinions seriously, especially since there is so much agreement between the statements of students from different faculties and institutions.

The presentations of educational procedures are often very technical, involving complicated models of methodological structures and educational technology. Psychologists have often contributed to these pictures by evolving comprehensive theories of learning. In the Lancaster study we are left with some non-technical terms from everyday language, and I would like to take those terms as the point of departure for some comments relevant to the teaching situation in Norwegian universities.

Recently we have seen a growing tendency to let graded marks at the end of a course be replaced by a mere 'pass' or 'fail'. However, this arrangement has the drawback that when the students are no longer assessed by some examination test at the end of the course, the teacher is forced to rely exclusively on what he has seen of the student during the weeks and months gone by. He will be faced with the problem of having to assess students who have *not* had a regular attendance. If taking part in exercises and laboratory demonstrations is the student's chief way of showing his or her mastery of the subject matter, how much irregular attendance can be tolerated?

Admittedly these problems have been effectively dealt with for generations within some fields of study, as for instance in science courses based on laboratory work. What is new today in some countries is that forms of assessment, other than written essays, find their way into new fields, such as, for instance, psychology or social science. And then if the *choice* of assessment is left to students, how can a teacher be expected to watch a student's steady progress, if the student is not there to be watched? There seems to be no easy way out, since one naturally hesitates strictly to control attendance, when today more of the responsibility for the students' progress is left to the students themselves.

I have myself been confronted with this dilemma on a number of occasions, and have sometimes raised the question in a discussion with the students before starting a course. But what to me seems to be a problem is not automatically conceived in a similar way by the students, as will be clear from the following remark:

> There is no problem. If your contribution as a teacher seems meaningful to us, we shall be attending the course regularly. It is as straightforward as that.

On that occasion I tried to raise some objections, suggesting that probably 'the flesh is weaker than one tends to think', especially on a cold and snowy morning in the winter term. Does one not need, sometimes, an additional reason to get up in time?

Since the students were quite unwilling to see my point, I decided to keep my 'knowing better' to myself and silently accept the challenge. The results seemed to show that the students were right. When, because of the challenge to make a 'meaningful contribution' each time in my lectures, I put some extra effort into my work as a teacher, the students responded by a 100 per cent attendance. Admittedly the course was a rather short one, so the difficulty of keeping to the terms of the mutual 'contract' was not too great for either party.

In cases like this, teaching demands a great deal of consideration. Not just having to be correct or precise in what is presented, but also having to consider the audience, and to judge how to present the message in a way that it may be clearly understood.

A one-sided demand on the teacher to make the learning situation a 'meaningful' one is, however, somewhat unreasonable. The students should also be willing – and perfectly able – to make a contribution towards this aim. Speaking about the school system in Norway one may doubt that pre-university institutions have given the students any experience in this direction. Indeed, the lack of experience of personal contributions through agreement with the teachers is so pronounced that university students who, after some pressure from a lecturer, have promised to prepare a report for a seminar become 'ill', or simply fail to show up on the appointed day. Lecturers will sometimes describe this attempt to let the students share the responsibility for the success of a seminar as a sure way of *reducing* the number of participants.

A contribution to the tuition situation may, however, be given in more than one way. It ought to be possible to have regular discussions about the learning situation, and thus make changes while still under way. Teachers should encourage the students to let them know if something is too complicated or seems too elementary in relation to the previous learning.

If students are asked to state *the reason* for their absence – with an expressed aim of discriminating between illness and a wish to spend the time differently – two things may be achieved. In the first place there is the chance of revising a programme, to make a more perfect match with the students' interests. Secondly, one might in this way come to terms with the problem of assessment in cases where a regular examination is not to be held. Personally I have not yet met a student who was unwilling to give a reason for a half-hearted course attendance. And, in Chapter 4, I will discuss the possibility of using such procedures in systematically trying to improve the learning situation at university.

So far I have only been commenting on the question of the lecturer's *concern* for his students. The students did, however, also mention *enthusiasm* as an important characteristic as far as a 'good teacher' is concerned.

I have deliberately chosen to let my comments on 'enthusiasm' come second. *Without* some concern for the students, which may have resulted in a reasonable course attendance, it might be rather difficult to show any enthusiasm when lecturing.

Teachers will sometimes tell you how depressed and uninspired they feel when, towards the end of the term, the number of attending students has fallen to a mere third of the original number. If they also tell you that the reason for the falling off in attendance is, in part, that the students are preparing for some other examination, they will finish their series of lectures without losing face. It is, however, much easier to find ways of being enthusiastic when the lecture theatre is full of people, which makes you feel you have achieved your pedagogical objective, if only for once.

It may seem that enthusiasm comes as a natural *outcome* of a good reception of one's teaching efforts. But might not enthusiasm on the part of a lecturer be a necessary *condition* for a successful outcome of his teaching efforts? The students will often criticize the teachers for lacking enthusiasm and for presenting dull lectures, when they have no specific complaint about the professional standard of the lecture.

The question of how far enthusiasm *in itself* would really take us is a very difficult one indeed. One may argue that a teacher who is unaware of the fact that his favourite topic might be of less interest to other people, will soon lose his audience. This might perhaps fail to disturb him, as long as *someone* was there, to listen. He might also find comfort in the idea that it is only natural that very few would be gifted enough to fully appreciate his subject or wit. On the other hand, one may consider the possibility that a lecturer who is genuinely interested in his topic, and in letting others have a chance of sharing it with him, might often succeed in getting a full house throughout the season, even if, to begin with, a number of potential listeners would tend to think that the topic in question was unworthy of their concern.

Since I have no ambition in trying to formulate a 'final list' of characteristics of the good or successful university teacher, I shall make no effort to carry the analysis of enthusiasm and concern any further. Rather I prefer to stress the importance of a *combination* of the two, for successful co-operation between teachers and students.

It may seem that the teacher is always the one who carries full responsibility for the creation of a favourable learning situation, but it must be kept in mind that unless universities and other institutions of higher education provide sound basic conditions for co-operation between students and teachers there is little hope of a successful end-result.

Co-operation as the fulfilment of mutual contracts

Continuing the discussion of co-operation between the university teacher and his students, I want to focus on some minor details that may be important on closer scrutiny. I shall take, as the point of departure, an informal discussion I once had with a colleague from a university abroad, concerning the different educational problems met within the day to day life at university. Our talk was concerned with the question of how to ensure that students meet the time limits set for different types of written work and hand in their essays at a certain date, agreed upon on 'friendly terms'. My colleague told me that in his department the students were requested to prepare three comprehensive essays during one full year, as part of the requirements for a course in psychology. The problem much debated in the department was how to persuade the students to hand in their work to the lecturer without forever having to ask for more time, or simply failing to show up on the day agreed.

My friend told me that he had himself never had any problems of this kind in his own group(s) of students, but then he had perhaps more experience and more time than most of his colleagues. In any case he had chosen to be very careful in having the essay topics thoroughly examined in advance, and in arranging for some definite guidance to the students about the time they were expected to work on their essays. Last, but not least, he always *returned* the essays, with comments and a chance of discussing them, at a pre-set date, within about a week after their being handed in.

What we have here is a contract that involves specific contributions on the part of the teacher. It may seem obvious that it is advisable to let the 'feedback' come after such a short time. But it is also very important that the teacher himself keeps to the letter of the contract by returning the essays at the time agreed.

It is, of course, very difficult to tell whether or not the reason for my colleague's success with his students' essays is the one suggested. But it is worth noticing, I think, that the 'carelessness' of his fellow lecturers could be very easily detected from a look at their pigeon holes in the hall, where the essays of the students who *had* kept to the time limit were still to be found, at the time when he had already returned his with the necessary 'feedback' comments to the students.

Many of us will recognize ourselves in this situation, very busily trying to let 'first things come first'. To mark essays is perhaps not what we most like to do, and it is so easy to find a number of excuses for having to postpone it. Still, we might do well to give this task a higher priority, since it means so much to the students that we keep our side of the contract, and since the job has to be done sooner or later in any case.

More important than having everything done at a pre-set time is having a clear enough contract set up in an atmosphere of mutual acceptance. An 'agreement' on time, which is reached by the lecturer writing a certain date on the blackboard, will probably be very difficult to keep. If this is an example of how *not* to do it, it is also wrong to believe that all problems are solved once an agreement has been reached after some discussion, in a seminar. A strict time schedule is indeed very difficult to meet in academic work, especially when the students have limited experience with the work set and few sources of help and guidance as they go along.

It may seem that we now attach too much importance to a problem of a rather trivial nature. It might be objected that the most natural solution to the problem would be to state simply that time limits and rules are there to be kept, if chaos is to be avoided.

My answer would be that we are here touching upon problems of great importance to both lecturers and students in many departments. It is not just a problem concerned with shorter essays. In Scandinavian universities it is often found that major theses – in some areas of studies – would tend to engage a student in work *for more than a year*, after the time when, according to the official time table, he or she ought to have graduated.

We have argued that, at least as far as Norway is concerned, pre-university schools seldom prepare the students for individually based studies, where the student has to decide for himself, not only on which topic to concentrate, but also what line of approach to take and at what speed to proceed. As mature individuals university students are expected to do many things that nobody *orders* them to do. Still, even when students are seen as 'grown ups', it is as well to remember that adults also fail to keep to some prescribed modes of behaviour. We postpone things, tend to forget what is unpleasant, time-consuming or boring and sometimes set out on ventures that other people would prefer us to leave alone.

This may as a rule all take place in situations where we don't have to share with others the responsibility for our actions. But the situation becomes very different where there is a contract involving other people. The fulfilling of contracts and acting according to mutual agreements is usually secured by numerous laws and regulations in society.

The tuition at university must have its point of departure in a co-operative situation, where lecturers and students meet as equals, as far as the responsibility for the performance of certain tasks – within certain time limits – is concerned. Maybe it is the teacher's extra responsibility to have the students looked upon as mature partners. This may imply that the teacher cannot allow himself to delay the marking of essays, say, to a day when he feels like it, but it may also imply that his reactions ought to be different from a mere raising of the eyebrows, if a student does not show up at a seminar, where he or she had promised to be one of the main participants in the discussion. With an equality between the partners, the lecturer's presence should not be more obvious than that of the students.

Must we learn how to teach at university?

To raise this question is to step into the lion's den. Two issues may be discerned here: What is needed by way of educational training? And, how should one go about it? I have been visiting a number of universities in various countries, in order to study the educational programmes offered for new members of staff. I have found that there is a lot of experimentation and a great variety of courses. An interest in these questions is most readily seen in the specially engaged educational experts and in students who suffer most from the unsolved problems of tuition.

Around Europe the picture is remarkably similar, particularly when it comes to the question of how to evoke interest in taking a course amongst those who are judged as lacking in pedagogical skills. There are as a rule optional courses for newly appointed lecturers, as well as for senior members of staff. The courses are given sometimes by educationalists within the institution, and sometimes by experts from an institution elsewhere. In both cases it is found that among the lecturers who choose to attend a course the majority already possess some formal training and also show interest in the day to day problems of education. The teachers for whom the course is really set up are found to be in the minority amongst the course participants.

It has been repeatedly argued that if more prestige were given to educational qualifications, university lecturers would be more willing to make more effort to increase their proficiency in teaching. The view has also been advocated that if researchers were really shown the intriguing problems of education, they would not hesitate to become involved in research and problem-solving in this area also!

Personally I hesitate a little in following these lines of reasoning. Challenges are plentiful already, and most of one's energy is likely to go into the solving of problems within one's own area of research. Also I feel that there is a need to start by discussing, a little bit more seriously, what would be the main objectives in raising the pedagogical standards amongst researchers. Perhaps it can be agreed that the university teacher has before him not only the task of presenting to the students a reasonable introduction to the knowledge and skills within the various fields but, he must also guide the students in mastering certain methods and techniques for *developing them further*. The research process as such is seldom set up as a separate topic for teaching, although within most subjects there may be courses in research methodology. It seems obvious that the academic staff at university have a definite experience with a variety of procedures for research, which ought also to be handed over to new generations of students at the undergraduate stage.

Having said this, it seems that researchers, when lecturing, behave as if *all* of their students will become future workers in the academic field. They tend to forget that the great majority of students of today will take up jobs of all kinds *outside* university. We are, perhaps, left with the dilemma of deciding to what extent we shall behave as school teachers, and to what extent we are merely to follow the routines of a research worker, in an institution that produces new insights in some fields of study.

Professional educationalists and other external 'experts' cannot contribute much when it comes to the specific routines of research within a particular field. But the research worker himself may sometimes be unable to present his way of working as part of a course in methodology. It is not inconceivable that it is more a question of passing on *attitudes* and '*life styles*' closely connected with the work. Some of the more technical ways of procedure might be explained in detail within a teaching situation, but in many ways the researcher should be looked upon as a *model* craftsman, whose 'peculiarities' may sometimes be well worth observing. Heretical as it may seem to look upon the academic worker in this way, at the present time, we must be aware of the fact that the problems of higher education are of a rather complex nature.

If we accept the idea that a researcher is in part acting as a 'model' for the students in a given field, it follows that the 'full picture' of what academic work is all about can only be found by watching the whole group of researchers in that particular field. Whilst one member of staff may be 'admired' for his thoroughness, persistence and systematic way of working, another may become a source of inspiration when it comes to enterprise and 'creative fantasy'. 'Research' implies a vast variety of different activities, and progress is not attained in the same manner within all areas of study.

It is certainly worth discussing how the students may profit both from the systematic course programme and from the far more incidental manifestations of the researcher's personality. Today, the old picture of the master, addressing himself to a small group of youngsters in the shade of a huge tree, might perhaps be replaced by that of a 'research jungle', where large groups are let in, to find that it is very difficult indeed to establish any contact with the older ones, who are there already, and often following paths which are impossible to detect.

With such a colourful picture I mean to suggest that the qualifications for research, possessed by the various members of staff, must be demonstrated, in contacts with the students, and established as a result of an organized programme of guidance or tutoring. Seen within this framework, there is still a claim on the members of staff *to learn* (or to get used to, or to accept) *to teach by acting as an example.* And this implies that researchers must be willing to make contact also with students who are *not* heading for a future career in their own laboratory. But since the number of students in most fields is so much greater today than it used to be, new ways of coping with the problem of contact must be sought.

Nothing we have discussed so far removes much from the statement set forth in the beginning of this chapter: that university lecturers generally leave something to be desired as far as pedagogical skills are concerned. What I have stressed is that the skills in question are of various kinds, and that some of the skills are of a nature that makes it unlikely that they can be obtained through a training course within a short period of time. On the other hand, I am of the opinion that there is also the question of bringing about an improvement in such simple tasks as using a microphone or writing in a clear hand. How to use audio-visual aids of different kinds may probably be taught in shorter courses. But then again, what are we to do if only very few lecturers are willing to accept the invitation to follow a course?

Wankowski is probably right in suggesting that successful students (and future academics?) may often be seen as fitting the description of an introvert personality. As such they (or rather we) may have a strong dislike for having to practise – for training purposes – in front of assessors. A number of courses are in fact arranged in such a way that the participants may have a chance of actually trying out different techniques or procedures.

What then, if we have to reckon with not only the shyness of the participants, but also their unwillingness to accept the educational 'expert' as one who can really grasp the particular nature of their problems of teaching, since he is an 'outsider' in the sense that he is not a professional mathematician or biologist?

Maybe the time has come to discuss the possibility that we shall have to accept the personality of the academics, and arrange the training period for the new members of staff in such a way that the problems of tuition are taken in small steps, at departmental level, having the young lecturer *gradually* take over the different tasks of teaching from an older colleague, carefully chosen perhaps, not because of his or her age, but because he or she has shown that a younger member of staff would benefit from acting in a sense as an understudy.

Only a few of the older professors would perhaps be suited for functioning as models for younger members of staff, where a proper way of going about the different tasks of teaching is concerned. And they might be thought to be more competent in some fields than in others. But since one would probably agree which procedures have been the most successful in the past, and since a teacher might be reluctant to demonstrate to others the different ways of *failure*, we would perhaps not run the risk of having too many models of the less successful approaches to teaching.

In my experience being 'two on the job' would often come as a welcome arrangement even for the experienced lecturer, who would perhaps find that the students respond well to this type of learning situation. I have tried the technique, both with smaller groups of students, and in larger lecture rooms, where 150 to 200 students have been present on such occasions. If normally a teacher has difficulties in making the students comfortable enough to dare to ask questions in such a large audience, the presence of *two* lecturers, who may be disputing with each other when difficult problems or vague statements are presented, would sometimes ease the situation sufficiently to make the students willing to take the stand. If the professor says he does not understand what his colleague is talking about, it may help the students to admit that they also have difficulties in grasping the full meaning of a given statement.

As far as the individual lecturer is concerned, more frequent use of work in pairs would often reduce his feeling of loneliness and anxiety, which can so easily be an outcome of a confrontation with the challenges of a 'one man show', especially perhaps when the group 'out there' looks a not too friendly crowd. It ought, therefore, to be comparatively simple to have the lecturers accept this kind of arrangement, even if in this way they have to double the amount of time spent with students each week!

You learn as long as you teach

In Norwegian the word for (you) 'live' is (du) 'lever'. And, then, when the word for 'pupils' is 'elever', there is only a small step to turning 'You learn as long as you live' into 'You learn as long as you have pupils'.

A teacher who is (again) reminded of this state of affairs is expected to react with a friendly smile. Very few people would, I should think, regard the statement as a proper way of summing up the benefits of the schoolmaster's trade. And, yet, there is reason to believe that the teaching of others is a reasonable way of guaranteeing that you will still be learning something yourself.

In fact, Wankowski's technique for helping students with learning difficulties is built upon the principle of self-learning by the 'teacher' who is, in this case, the student who is asked to explain to the counsellor what are the basic problems or the tricky parts of his subject of study.

It may not work all the time. But there is the possibility that systematic attempts to clarify an issue, for the benefit of other people, may lead to a deeper understanding on the part of the person who is in the teacher's role. As a teacher you might perhaps only become a tiny bit wiser, each time you teach. But then again, if you teach others often enough, you may in the end have learnt a lot.

It is, perhaps, not all that easy to explain why this is so. In an attempt to make it a bit more clear how the teacher may come to profit from sharing his knowledge with others we shall take tuition at university as our point of departure.

A number of lecturers at university would very much like it if they were excused where the teaching of first-year students is concerned. Rather they would prefer to meet their teaching obligations by talking to graduate students. Then they might concentrate on important details, which might form part of, or somehow be related to their own research efforts. However, from time to time one is simply forced to meet new students.

When there, in front of you, is a large number of totally new students of the field, you simply cannot place any importance on some details of your subject. Rather you ought to present an overview of the field of study, indicating some important connections between various sub-topics and perhaps also giving the students an idea of the development within the field.

It is during the preparation of such a presentation, and also perhaps, during the presentation itself, that one may sometimes realize that strangely enough one is 'discovering' new things about a subject matter with which one is very familiar indeed. In an attempt to clarify a complicated issue, in order that the new students would be given a chance of grasping its nature, one may gain some new insight oneself. By pointing to various ways of looking at a problem you may come to 'see the old truth in a new light'.

If one is fortunate enough to have kept the almost childish curiosity and the enthusiasm related to a discovery or the disclosing of another secret one may, even in the role of a senior professor, come to amaze the students by exclaiming 'I had really no idea before I came here today of what I am telling you now'.

Admittedly, in a case like this, you are faced with the difficulty of getting the students to see that what you have just said does not simply amount to a confession that you have failed to prepare for the lecture in a proper way. If you *do* succeed in convincing them that they are witnessing an important part of academic knowledge production you have, at the same time, fulfilled an important obligation as a teacher, namely that of letting the students in on the secrets of the trade. At school it was mainly a question of obtaining the knowledge which the teacher had already. At university it is a question of discovering ways of organizing knowledge, such as would make it possible for the student – or the teacher – to somehow proceed to a level of deeper understanding and increased knowledge at a later stage.

It takes time before a new student realizes that even the most experienced professors still are themselves (somewhat advanced) students of the field, and not someone who knows – or *ought* to know – the correct answer to all the questions within the syllabus. But sooner or later the student must be taught that 'to study' means something different from 'going to school'.

4

The Need for the Development of Study Skills

Kjell Raaheim

Psychological tests and prediction of academic ability

The question of how to assess young people's opportunities in a university setting is raised on occasions when the number of new students seems to be increasing beyond the capacity of the institutions of higher education, or when a certain institution is faced with a reduction in its financial means. About a generation ago one witnessed in Scandinavia attempts to make arrangements for the use of psychological tests to determine, *in advance*, who would be fit for the intellectual problem-solving activity at university. Today one can sense that the faith in psychological tests has, to some extent, been lost. However, there are still voices to be heard advocating the view that *some* kind of selection procedure must be found, and also that there is today an increased demand for such procedures, since society has itself become, increasingly, more demanding and complex.

It is my firm belief that very little can be gained by using tests to assess intellectual prerequisites of some general nature for the university studies which have not yet been entered upon by the one being tested. The following points will perhaps elucidate this view:

(i) *Psychological tests are of little relevance outside the situation in which the tests are taken*

A psychological test may be seen as something different from the everyday procedures of assessing knowledge and skill, and different also from the various kinds of examinations in school and at university. The test procedure is – like other scientific experiments – a highly regulated, standardized affair. The situation under which the testing takes place is such as to make the conditions as equal as possible for all who take part in it. If it is a question of the so-called 'intelligence testing', one tries to unveil the more or less 'naked' abilities, which are held to be functioning also in everyday life, but are there, to a large extent, 'wrapped up in the clothes' of motivation, interests, personal experience and self evaluation.

If one is to make predictions, on the basis of the results of a test, about the future performance of an individual one must look for an equally standardized situation. Normally this situation obtains in school where a student's examination marks are compounded in a similar way as the scores he may receive in a test. School marks might be predicted with a reasonable degree of success on the basis of test results. But the relationship is far from being perfect. Even at school there will be room for 'disturbing factors' like varying enthusiasm and differences in the work load taken on by the pupil. In everyday life, predictions of success made on the basis of psychological tests are extremely poor, although psychologists sometimes behave as if the opposite was the case. And when it comes to the question of the development of study skills, there are data to indicate (see also Chapter 4) that an initial test tells little about later performance. A closer correspondence between the results of consecutive tests might, however, be found if, using another assessment test, care is taken to keep to the highly standardized and specialized problems or skills, at the cost of broader tasks which would demonstrate insight and understanding. I would hope that in academic life there will be a greater interest in the latter type of achievement than in the production of neat test results.

(ii)   Tests of achievement at the time of entering university coincide with the students' stages of development that may vary with individuals

In the area of intellectual development one is likely to find considerable individual differences which might be due to maturation. Since very few students can be said to have reached the peak of their intellectual performance when they enter university, initial testing may be of little value for prediction of academic achievement. As is the case with tests of personality factors, tests of academic achievement before entry to university will have a rather low predictive value mainly because of the uncertainty that will always exist about the *course* and the nature of development in every individual.

As mentioned above, the introduction of some kind of 'entrance test' has, in fact, been discussed at Scandinavian universities, despite the fact that a number of people would agree to the points previously mentioned and despite evidence from studies abroad.[1] There is still the feeling that one should do *something* to ensure a reasonable selection of candidates, particularly in fields like medicine and psychology where the profession later to be taken up by the students is one that makes great demands on them, e.g. where the responsibility for the welfare of other people is concerned. Psychologists in Scandinavia seem to have been confronted with a special challenge, since they are the ones who have suggested the application of tests for the selection of candidates in various fields of non-academic life. Their answer seems to be that a university course in psychology, in addition to providing the necessary *knowledge*, ought also to contribute to the development of personality and to the formation of certain attitudes, professional and otherwise. If this is so, the majority of students might be regarded as *becoming* fit for a professional career in psychology; all as a result of experience gained during the extended course in this subject.

Similar arguments might also be offered in other fields of study. In a great number of cases there will also be the problem of finding criteria of assessment, since obviously the final outcome of a course of study at university is, very often, unrelated to a particular professional role in society.

(iii) Human performance is not dependent on ability factors only

Even if there were psychological tests that could be used to assess factors of ability which remained stable over time, as well as factors that were of importance over a wider field of activity, an admission procedure to university based on such tests would still be of restricted value. As already mentioned above, the 'naked' abilities derived from psychological tests are operating in a situation where the test administrators have some control over the motivation of the subjects taking the test and of their ways of working with the tasks presented. Naturally some subjects would tend to put more energy than others into the attempts at task solution. But the enormous differences that exist in everyday life when it comes to ways of coping with problems are greatly reduced in the artificial situation of testing in the laboratory of the psychologist.

I have no wish to deny (see also above) that the results of ability tests are often found to correlate with success in schools, where performance is assessed in a way that is similar to the procedure in a psychological test. But even here, in school, we find examples of performance that are drastically different from what could be expected on the basis of test results. From my own experience as a consultant at a rehabilitation centre in Norway I recall a case where a young boy whose test results indicated mental retardation succeeded in talking himself into being accepted for a course for car mechanics, and demonstrated to all who thought this to be an impossible venture that a strong enough motivation can work miracles. The explanation of success seemed to be related to the boy's habit of nailing wall charts of engines and/or parts to the ceiling above his bunk, where he spent hours before going to sleep in examining – studying – their details.

I can think of few schools where a motivation like this would not take a pupil a good part of the way. When at university a student may start with a prescribed amount of schooling behind him, and so the question of his abilities might be looked upon in a more relaxed way. Naturally the freedom at university also implies the freedom of doing next to nothing. And what a student thinks his or her chances are may, to a large extent, also determine his or her success, or failure. But then, once more, we are left with the question of motivation rather than skill.

The question of who would be fit for studying at university can, of course, only be answered if we know what it means to study. Little may be offered by the laboratory studies within the psychology of learning to clarify this issue. In everyday speech 'to be studying something' comes close to 'hesitatingly examining and reflecting upon some matter, about which some uncertainty or doubt exists'. If this 'definition' is adopted where learning at university is concerned, I am tempted to conclude that 'everyone' is fit for studying. But then, to save the reader from thinking of the strange consequences this would have, I should hasten to add that within present day universities, life is not such that 'everyone' would survive.

Having been trained as an experimental psychologist the author regularly makes attempts to see if there are data to support a point of view, in particular when it seems to be at variance with what is commonly held to be the truth. About a decade ago there was the opportunity, at the University of Bergen, of performing a rather unusual experiment. Among a number of people who were anxious to see what university studies were about, but who were lacking (by far) the qualifications needed to be allowed, in a normal way, to enter a course at university, a group of about fifteen 'subjects' were recruited for a particular experimental exercise. The question was whether or not these people would in fact be able to pick up the necessary 'study skills' during a one-term course in psychology.

To be able to assess the 'academic skills' of the subjects, initially and as the course proceeded, the 'experimenter' (the lecturer in this case) asked the subjects to hand in essays at regular intervals during the term. After a normal lecture a session of discussion was held each week. Here the lecturer tried to explain to the subjects how such questions as those met with during the lecture were normally dealt with in an academic discussion, and how one ought to go about it when writing an essay about the topic. Each week, then, the students would get a topic to write about at home. They were instructed to try to follow carefully the rules which had been explained to them.

During the first few weeks about half the students seemingly had come to the conclusion that university studies were not, after all, for them. In any case they stopped attending the weekly lectures. The remaining subjects, upon inspection, did not turn out to be in any way 'superior' as far as formal education was concerned. Rather it seemed to be a question of motivation, since in fact rather strong demands were placed upon the subjects each week. So much of what was going on was totally outside their previous experience. No diploma or any other formal qualification would be a result of the course, and with the subjects having ordinary jobs during the day and the lectures taking place after working hours, it is likely that the subjects who withdrew simply came to the conclusion that they could spend their spare time more profitably and in a less demanding way by doing something else.

The first few essays handed in by the remaining subjects also left the experimenters (Raaheim and Raaheim, 1982; Raaheim, 1987) with serious doubts as to the possible success of the lay students. There seemed to be such a lot of things about which the subjects were totally ignorant. They did not seem to understand how one could possibly be interested in arguing about subtle differences of opinion among scientists living in the last century, they did not see why or how one ought to make one's own contribution to a discussion about complex problems, and they seemed also to be in difficulties when trying to choose proper terms in which to express themselves, to mention some of the most important problems faced by the subjects.

Towards the middle of the term a few more subjects had to leave the group as a result of obligations at work. To the remaining half a dozen subjects the experimenters were able to give even more personal advice than had been done before and also more detailed comments on their essays each week.

Gradually, but very slowly at first, the essays improved. But eventually the subjects seemed to have discovered the trick. Since the rules had been specified to them in a way rarely done at university and perhaps also since they came 'from the outside', so to speak, not having already more or less automatically adopted a way of expressing themselves in essay writing, the subjects of this study seemed to be more conscious about every step to be taken. Towards the end of the term a few of the essays became remarkably good, reminding the lecturer of essays of a type normally only produced by students after a full three term course. The final test of the achievements of the subjects was performed, then, by letting the subjects take part in the ordinary examination at the end of the term, with their essays smuggled in between those of the ordinary students without the examiners knowing anything about the experiment.

The experiment was a success in so far as all the remaining students passed the examination. Two of them had marks well above the average for the group of normal, full-time students. Nothing very sensational perhaps came out of the experiment other than a clear indication that even with people who, because of formal schooling, are totally unfamiliar with the rules of academic discourse, a specially arranged course may be all that is needed to teach them the necessary skills.

Which cognitive processes may be developed?

This is, of course, a question of such a general nature that a simple answer cannot be found. I would, however, like to comment upon it, while at the same time trying to build upon some empirical findings.

If the process of learning generally is looked upon as a problem-solving activity, studying at university naturally implies coping with tasks of a high degree of difficulty. Now, problem solving might be described as consisting of different phases or stages, where the demands on one's cognitive abilities may vary in nature from one stage to the next. For each stage, however, we might ask the question: 'to what extent will it be possible to influence this process so that the individual will profit from some particular type of experience?'

Faced with a situation where some routine type of activity is of little help, the first step towards solution could be said to be that of *formulating the problem*. It is not only a question of discovering that *some* challenge is there, in front of you, although it is of vital importance to become aware, in the first place, that you cannot proceed as if nothing has happened. For your success in dealing with the situation, it is necessary to get the clearest, or most precise, picture of the nature of your difficulty. We may assume that *some* people are better than others in quickly discovering what is really the matter. While they soon have their 'diagnosis' ready, others have but a vague idea or feeling that 'something is wrong', without being able to pin-point the root of the difficulty.

Individual differences aside, is it conceivable that we all, given the appropriate training, would be able to *improve* our ability to formulate a problem precisely?

In an experiment (Raaheim, 1964) a number of students were presented with a practical construction problem which had to be described in writing. Half of the subjects were given some short, additional instructions to start their attempt at task solution by (a) determining, as precisely as they could, what was in this particular case 'the missing part' and (b) trying to replace a given implement found to be missing by using other objects at their disposal. The reading of these extra instructions did not take more than ten seconds, after which the subjects of the Experimental group had one minute to reflect on what they had just read. They were then presented with the actual problem situation, as were the members of the Control group, who had not been given any suggestions as to the general, or the proper ways of organizing their thinking.

The results showed that in the Experimental group the number of solutions of the problem was 50 per cent higher than in the Control group. Admittedly the experiment and its result must be subjected to a somewhat more searching analysis in order to unveil some of the deeper mysteries of the working of the human mind. But even if the impact of the outcome of this experiment on the general theories of cognitive psychology might be a little dubious, it shows that, for educational purposes, there is benefit to be received, even if in part this may be due to motivational rather than cognitive factors.

A precise diagnosis of the nature of the task difficulty will always be important for problem-solving behaviour. It is, however, easy to see that the impact of the diagnosis on the ultimate solution will vary from one situation to the next. At times the 'therapeutic phase' (point (b) above) is easily handled when, granted a correct diagnosis, the procedure towards the task solution is relatively straightforward. At other times it may be more difficult even with a precise diagnosis. Often enough in everyday life we are faced with situations where it is relatively easy to tell what is wrong, but where it is highly difficult to pin-point possible ways of solving the problem.

Whether or not a given person will engage himself in task *solution* – once the nature of the problem has been made clear – is a question that depends on motivation and access to appropriate resources. Educational procedures, therefore, must involve considerations of both of these background conditions. Whilst it is likely that much is to be gained by training people to use suitable aids and implements, the influence of motivational changes may be thought to be of the greatest importance. In an experiment, Nielsen (1971) found that the problem-solving efforts of students varied systematically with what he called 'task courage', a concept different from 'level of aspiration' in that it refers to a person's real confidence in attacking difficulties of various types. Whether a student did in fact master a given task was dependent, to a large extent, on his or her *conception* of its difficulty, relative to what he or she had previously stated to be one's own 'level of mastery'. By manipulating the *descriptions* of the tasks – as easy, of average difficulty, or difficult – the experimenter succeeded in equivalently varying the percentage of solution.

Within both the 'diagnostic' and the 'therapeutic' phase of problem solving one can distinguish between *divergent* and *convergent* thinking. Divergent production is taken to indicate a production of ideas, which may take as its point of departure some concrete situation, but where flexibility and fantasy lead the thought process into different (divergent) channels, such as to form a basis for the original constellations of ideas. By 'convergent thinking', on the other hand, one refers to those ways of reasoning that lead to a concentration on, and an adherence to, a particular end result, as for instance a particular solution to a problem.

In the last thirty years psychologists have been trying to assess people's varying 'abilities' of divergent production. A long series of unconventional 'tests' has been made up to investigate 'creative fantasy' rather than 'intelligence'. The traditional intelligence tests have been regarded as placing too much weight on convergent thinking, asking of the subject the one and only 'correct' answer on each task presented. The new tests, on the other hand, are said to invite the subjects to show abilities which may be of more importance in today's world: originality, flexibility and fantasy.

Guilford's *Uses for Things*, which is a well-known example of the new tests, presents the subjects with the task of suggesting as many ways of using a given object as possible. An individual who is not able to find more than one way of using an object – suggesting that a *brick*, say, can be used for housebuilding – may well be considered as having little fantasy. A greater production of ideas might be said to be demonstrated by a person who suggests *additional* ways of using the brick, such as having it replace a paper weight, or using it to help keep a car in its position, when parked on a steep road, by placing the brick behind one of the wheels. Psychologists, who have conceived these new tests as easy ways of assessing *creativity*, are, in my opinion, running the risk of being mistaken (see e.g. Raaheim, 1984). But there can be little doubt that both divergent and convergent production play important roles in intelligently using one's past experience in problem solving.

The question of whether it is possible to increase easily people's output in the production of ideas, by some educational procedure, is, however, of greater concern at present. And if the answer to the question turns out to be affirmative, one may well suggest that motivational factors are of great importance, perhaps to such an extent as to make the notion of 'abilities to create' a highly suspicious one. But again one might be satisfied by the improvement in the competence whatever its cause may be.

We can do little more than merely suggest an answer in the present connection. Experiments have been conducted (Manske and Davies, 1968) to find out if some short instructions would be influential, as far as people's 'ability' to suggest uses for things is concerned. When the subjects *were asked to* present 'wild suggestions', their proposals were quite different from what they suggested when the instructions were to present 'practical' ways of using an object. Admittedly one may feel justified in objecting that this is nothing more than stating that people (naturally) are likely to do what they are told. Yet, one might argue that the educational implications of such a statement are worth reflecting upon.

The student as the architect of his fortune

We may look upon the university as an educational institution, where the subjects of study are numerous, where the conditions for tuition are highly unsatisfactory at times, and where the teachers often seem to be lacking even the most elementary forms of tuition skill. But we may also look upon the university as a place of work, where representatives of different professions meet, not only to bring people of varying subjects together, but to have people who are established research workers co-operate with younger people, who have not yet decided which field of work they will choose as their future career. Regarded in this light, the problems of higher education may be described as those of having the students take the full responsibility for their own educational development, and of having to discover, in their own good time, that something might be learned from contacts with research workers, who neither seem to have the necessary qualifications to teach, nor to be willing to organize things in such a way that effective learning may take place.

Wankowski argues that rather than trying to improve the selection procedures at university, one should make a point of increasing the students' chances of learning. He finds that the majority of those who have difficulties in the initial phase of their studies are students who have somehow *lost* their ability to learn effectively. It is likely that this is, in part, due to the fact that the students continue to work according to the pattern they adopted in school. Wankowski maintains that there is reason to believe that two thirds of the students are unaware of the effect their previous routines of both school and homework have had on their learning process.

The 'academic freedom' is what the students have to face from the moment they enter university. What we have found in Norway – when taking a closer look at students who have difficulties in adjusting to their new freedom – is that sometimes a whole term passes by before the student has managed to get through the first chapter of an introductory text book. I think that most students should be able to take full responsibility for their own progress, and to do so within a relatively short time. But this can perhaps only take place when we, as teachers, stop behaving as if all students already had all of the skills needed for effective learning when they first enter university. Sometimes we are perhaps all too eager to demonstrate that our own lectures are more brilliant and useful than the textbook read by the students. The consequence of such an assumption may be that the student might think it highly improper to ask for help, or advice, since he might feel that he is making queries about lectures rather than asking for help in coping with the material read in the books. That the students do in fact need some help in organizing their reading can be judged from the great demand for written summaries, reviews and hand-outs prepared by lecturers.

If we look upon the university as a production plant of knowledge, it follows that the students – being in fact the most important producers of tomorrow – must be given a thorough description of the most efficient ways of producing their goods. No industry would have a reasonable chance of surviving if newcomers, under training, were simply given the necessary tools, without any instructions on how to use them. But, at the same time, even an apprentice who has an excellent introductory programme, should not hope that everyone among his experienced colleagues, by being a good craftsman, will also be an efficient *teacher*. The apprentice might do well in *watching* his older colleagues, in order to pick up the odd trick of tackling a difficult problem.

There is, of course, more to learn at university than what is officially taught by lectures. But watching the various activities of the different members of staff is today obviously more difficult than it was years ago, when the number of new students was relatively small. There is also reason to believe that in some fields of work little can be gained by merely looking at others practising their skill. Yet, I would like to argue that something would be gained, were we – as teachers – more willing to encourage the students to take part in activities other than sessions in the lecture rooms.

Teachers often object to this and suggest that 'the good student' is supposed to find his way around himself, without a special invitation to join in at research seminars. In this case there is nothing left to do but to admit that life in general is just as hard to come to terms with as the university jungle, and that one might just as well start fighting, every man for himself, right away. Or perhaps it is possible to find ways of easing the tuition situation without too much effort from the teachers?

When people 'get to know each other' it often happens that certain qualities of their characters appear which may not have been seen to begin with. A research assistant may for example be able to point to conciliatory traits of his pedagogically 'unskilled' professor. Qualities not so easily discovered in lectures or seminars might have shown themselves in published articles, or in daily conversations and contacts arising from the research work. What would be gained, then, if there were, generally, better contacts between colleagues of all categories – teachers and students – at university?

Any suggestion of how to make contact between an established research worker and lecturer, and the individual members of a group of two hundred freshmen, say, is likely to be considered a worthless idea. But what would happen if the general scheme of tuition was built up in the same way as research work, so that the graduate students, tutors, and research assistants function as links in a chain between the newcomer and the more distant figures of academic staff?

As already mentioned, learning at university by watching others was probably less difficult a generation ago, when the number of students was relatively small. The students' knowledge of the peculiarities of their lecturers sometimes helped them to realize that *one* professor was someone who expressed himself best in his writing, whereas another had the ability to give precise, verbal accounts in reviewing a field of study without, perhaps, having done any important research himself. One member of staff could be seen as an original and enterprising researcher, while another was a particularly well-informed contributor to the already well established directions of study tasks. Perhaps with better channels of communication, a student could profit from such knowledge, even today.

Today students often challenge their teachers to describe precisely the ultimate objectives of their lecturing, and to make clear the connection between different parts of the total programme within a field. Students also want to know more about the research activities undertaken by their teachers, as well as about their ideas and ideologies. Sometimes the university teachers may get a feeling that students today are more interested in pedagogical questions than in the more fundamental topics of research. And finding themselves being constantly reminded of their pedagogical shortcomings, the teachers cannot perhaps be blamed for wanting to see the return of a time when the message was more important than the manner in which it was conveyed.

The student challenge of today is perhaps a natural side effect of the general situation in society, where everyone has a greater opportunity than before of influencing his or her own working conditions. But part of the student criticism may also be a result of a greater confusion about the situation of tuition and its relation to their future career. Only a minority of the 'apprentices' who can learn by watching the process of producing knowledge will later take up a position within the academic field of work. Perhaps it is not totally out of place to point to the finding of Wankowski and others (Jacobsen, 1978) that students who know more precisely what is likely to be the occupational outcome of their stay at university are more successful as far as study skills are concerned.

Note

1. A mammoth national study of 9,395 university entrants out of a complete 1968 cohort of 27,315 sixth formers in 619 schools in England and Wales were surveyed, by a specially designed test of Academic Aptitude, by the National Foundation for Educational Research in England. The results were a complete fiasco as far as predictions of the final degree results were concerned: 'The data provide no valid base for the introduction of a system of threshold criteria for university selection'. (Choppin *et al.*, 1973).

5

The First Examinations at University

Kjell Raaheim

One may argue that there are two types of difficulties facing the student when first setting foot in the university: problems related to 'academic freedom', and problems of learning how to lead an 'academic discourse'. As a teacher one soon becomes aware of the latter type of difficulty. The results of the first examinations often show that the ability to handle a scientific problem by intelligently analysing it leaves much to be desired. When factual knowledge seems to be present to a reasonable degree, the art of *discussing* a problem seems to be under-developed in a large number of cases. The teacher may, however, be less prepared to give an account of his students' difficulties with *academic freedom*. He has himself, perhaps, had little difficulty in planning an academic career. And so it may take some extra fantasy to become aware that a number of students may get a feeling of despair and great uncertainty, when after years of highly regulated school life, they are asked to set the course of their learning process themselves. Admittedly entering the university has had an intoxicating effect, to begin with. The freedom feels good at first, even to those who later wake up to a reality of hopelessness. But, since there is reason to believe that most students have *some* difficulty in getting things sorted out, the teacher might perhaps do well in trying to look closer into the problem.

Brennan and Percy (1976), in their summary of the Lancaster investigation stress that students of almost all faculties agreed that there is *a lack of concern*, on the part of the teachers, for students 'as people'. It does not matter whether this impression is real or imaginary. As long as this *feeling* of being left to oneself exists amongst students, one should take action to try to do something about it.

Some fifteen years ago I launched a series of empirical investigations at the University of Bergen, Norway. I took, as my point of departure, the results of the Entwistle study. My first aim was to get a picture of the reasons behind the high rate of 'dropping out' from the non-compulsory lectures in the introductory course in philosophy, logic and psychology: a course leading at that time towards what is in Norway called 'Examen Philosophicum', an examination which is necessary for the continuation of studies at university.

Looking at the graph of students' attendance at lectures in psychology

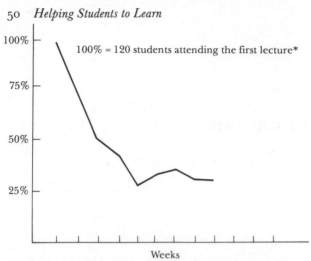

100% = 120 students attending the first lecture*

Weeks

Figure 5.1   Attendance in a lecture group in psychology – autumn term 1976
*The number of students attending the *first* lecture of a series is taken as 100%. This means that if the attendance is *increased*, the percentage will go above 100.

(Fig. 5.1), I wondered if the shape of the curve might be the outcome of students' impressions of lack of concern among the lecturers. It is possible that the drop in attendance was, in this case, partially due to the fact that this series of lectures formed an additional offer to students who were attending the regular introductory course in psychology, and that the number of students in the group (N = 120) was too large to make this offer look like a beneficial extra support. Still many lecturers will probably recognize the problem of attendance outlined by the curve as one they have come across themselves at times.

A dividing of the students into a number of smaller groups is in itself no guarantee of an increased attendance. But what if the teacher tells the students that their presence *is* – after all – of great importance to the lecturer and that it is also interesting for him to learn something about the reasons behind a possible absence?

In our first investigation programme we asked the students if they would be willing to co-operate in a scheme for improving tuition, by stating the reason(s) why they had been absent on a given occasion. Were they absent because:

   (i) of illness, or unable to attend for other reasons?
  (ii) they had an express wish to spend the time in a different/better way, e.g. by being left to themselves, or reading some other parts of the syllabus?
 (iii) 'it just so happened'?

The curve in Fig. 5.2 is based on the attendance in a group where the number of participants at the outset was only half of that of the first group, but where, in addition, a list of names was passed around each time, for the students to list their presence and the reason for a possible, earlier absence.

Since nearly all the students are there all the time, there is not much to be gained by analysing reasons for absence in this particular group. Still, we might like to know whether the enormous difference between the two groups is a result

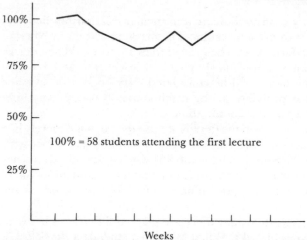

100% = 58 students attending the first lecture

Weeks

Figure 5.2 Attendance in a group under experimental conditions

of the 'new signals' from the teacher, or is merely what can be expected with a smaller group. Further experiments did show (see Raaheim and Wankowski, 1981) that *both* the group size *and* the new strategy of the lecturer might be of importance in securing a good attendance at the lectures. We also have data to show that the increase in attendance was not simply due to the fact that names were now taken down each week.

I am also presenting the curves of attendance in order to underline my opinion that it is wrong to think that poor performance, at the first examinations at university, is merely a result of a *general* lack of motivation amongst students of today. In my view both failing attendance and meagre examination results may be due to some *specific* factors, against which some specific action might be taken. So far, it seems possible to conclude that, at least as far as the wish to learn is concerned, very little effort is needed to awaken interest if it has indeed been dormant.

A reasonable degree of attendance might be thought of as a necessary, but by no means a sufficient condition of success at university. Table 5.1 is set up to

Table 5.1 Attendance and examination results of a group taking an introductory course in psychology, 1977

	N	Mark	No. failures
Present on every occasion throughout the term	8	2.55	0
Absent once: 'Illness'	7	2.77	0
Absent a few times: 'Wanted to spend the time differently'	19	2.93	2
Absent a few times: 'It just so happened'	10	3.12	1
Irregular attendance	13	3.12	2
Totals	57	2.93	5

illustrate this point, rather than to indicate a particular relationship between lecture attendance and examination results. The marking system in Norway allows for an accepted performance to be graded from 1.0 to 4.0. When marks between 1.0 and 1.5 mean 'extraordinarily good', or 'excellent', and are very seldom used, anything up to 2.5 will be considered 'very good'. An 'average mark' in social sciences is probably in the neighbourhood of 2.7. Anything above 4.0 means failure to pass the examination.

Leaving the reader to reflect upon the details of this table, I would merely like to draw attention to the fact that we have here – as is nearly always the case with the introductory courses – a result which, on the whole, must be said to be rather poor. It is often argued that this is but an indication that many students of today are 'less gifted' or 'unqualified' for studies at university. I myself, however, have some objections to this.

Upon inspection one might find that there are marked differences between the results of different types of tasks. When an essay demands a *description* of factual knowledge the students often have much better results than when an essay asks for a *discussion* of a question which in itself may not be altogether very complicated. When asked to write about the coefficient of correlation (What does it tell you, what are its limitations?) a group of new students ($N = 174$) received an average mark of 2.55 (which, according to the Norwegian system, is nearly a 'very good' mark). Contrary to this the average mark among students writing about intelligence (trying to discuss whether or not this is a *general* ability) turned out to be 3.11 ($N = 362$), by far a more 'discouraging' result.

Results like these might be taken to indicate that the necessary *motivation* to do well is there, among new students. However, among the students of today, a large number must perhaps be regarded as partly *unsuited* for the task of leading a proper academic discourse. Or is it more correct to state that a number of students of today are, in part, *unfamiliar* with the style of intellectual performance asked of future academics – due to the fact that students are today recruited from 'non-academic' environments to a greater extent than was the case before? In order to throw some light on these questions, a training programme was planned for students in the first year at the University of Bergen.

The solving of intellectual problems: Experiments with test examinations

Research results in the area of human problem solving have convinced me that insight into a situation, as far as intellectual tasks are concerned, is built upon past experience that may vary with the background of individuals. If problem solving is looked upon as a handling of unknown, or rather *deviating* elements, in an otherwise familiar situation (Raaheim, 1974, 1984), a necessary condition for solving intellectual problems would be that not all of the major features of the situation represent completely new challenges. There is reason to believe that the human abilities, constituting what we refer to as 'intelligence', would play their most important part in situations *where the amount of unfamiliar factors is of a moderate size* (see again Raaheim, 1974, 1984).

There is probably an agreement that an individual facing mere routine tasks would be able to succeed by repeating some well known patterns of reaction. But it is perhaps a little more difficult to appreciate that what may be needed, in situations where completely new challenges dominate the picture, is a determined, but at the same time unprejudiced, search for *new* information, rather than an intelligent reflection upon some well established knowledge.

To suggest a conclusion of relevance to our present concern: the first attempts at solving the new and unfamiliar intellectual tasks at university must be considered as an unreliable basis for making predictions as to future success, as far as the academic performance of the student is concerned. The good results obtained, when the first-term tasks are of a well known type (as with the exercise where the coefficient of correlation was to be described), suggest that students generally cannot be considered 'unmotivated' or 'stupid'. There is reason to believe that differences in results between tasks reflect differences in important background factors.

In a number of studies at the University of Bergen students have had an opportunity to take part in *test-examinations*, which have had the form of training sessions in essay writing. The results of these attempts at taking part in an academic discussion have been assessed in the usual way by an external examiner.

As mentioned in Chapter 2, the students have been found to welcome the opportunity of getting some early feedback on their attempts at writing a scientific essay. At the same time, the nervousness connected with exams – even in a case where the result 'does not count' – has been found to lead to a substantial number of students being absent on the day. On the other hand the outcome of these experiments with training sessions must be looked upon as highly interesting: for one thing, our suspicion that the student's first few steps on the road to an academic career are not always a reliable source of information about his subsequent walking speed, was given some confirmation. In five different sub-groups of students, where the number of participants varied from about 20 to about 60, we found the following correlations between the results of the first test-examinations and the official examinations held a few months later: 0.13, 0.36, −0.05, 0.12, and 0.50. Furthermore, *the distribution* of the marks at the time of the first attempts at writing an 'academic paper' repeatedly has been found to indicate much greater variance among the students than is found at a later stage in their academic career (see Raaheim and Wankowski, 1981).

The development of academic skills in a short-term perspective

As I have already argued, it takes some time before the new student is able to adjust to the world of academic discourse and simply to get started with the work. If we are right in assuming that each student faces the challenges at university with his qualifications varying because of background factors, rather than due to his 'inherited abilities', it is only natural that the performance of the students, after repeatedly taking part in test-examinations, would become more alike and at the same time show some improvement.

It has been found that the average result of the *first* (test) examination is roughly the same irrespective of time spent (weeks or months) studying a subject in the course of the first year at university (Raaheim and Wankowski, 1981, p. 93). So when the first examination met with by the students is the official one at the end of the term – or the half year – one ought not to be surprised if, on the whole, the results leave much to be desired. On the other hand, we have also repeatedly found that the participation in *training sessions* in the form of test-examinations leads to a significant improvement in examination results. In one particular study (Raaheim and Manger, 1983) a group of first year psychology students – who also had the opportunity of taking part in 'tutorial groups' led by a graduate student – were offered participation in altogether three text-examinations prior to the official examination. The effect upon the outcome of the latter of participation – on a voluntary basis – in tutorials *and* different numbers of test-examinations is illustrated in Figure 5.3.

The figure shows that in this case a very close correspondence is found between participation in tuition activities and examination results. Among the students (N = 56) who choose *not* to take part in tutorials and test-examinations only about 30 per cent pass the final examination. This is in contrast to the students of the two groups with total (or almost total) participation (N = 13 and 26, respectively), where nearly everyone succeeds in passing the examination.

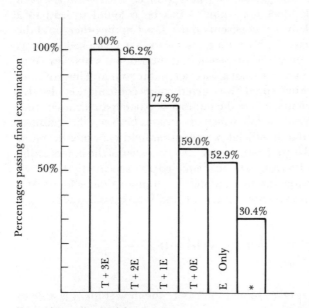

T = took part in tutorials
E = took part in test-examinations
*Did not take part in either tutorials or test-examinations

Figure 5.3   Effects of participation in tutorials and test-examinations

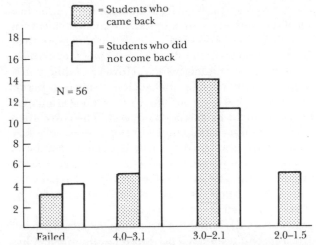

Figure 5.4   Students in different performance groups and their appearance or non-appearance for another test

(As for the number of 'very good' marks it was found that among the 56 students who did *not* take part in the tuition activities referred to, only two students (4 per cent) had such a mark, as against 8 students out of 13 (62 per cent) in the group with *full* participation.)

Clearly enough motivational factors are at work here. Yet the university lecturer who decides to be less concerned with the rate of failure among students who *refuse* to take part in the tuition offers provided might still be pleased with results like these.

Motivational effects of test-examinations

An opportunity to practise essay writing – whether it is called test-examination or not – might seem a valuable means of preparing the students for a successful handling of examination challenges. One ought, however, to look into the question of possible *negative* outcomes of such a test programme. What about the students who initially perform so poorly that the feedback given, however kindly worded, necessarily amounts to a signal that 'this simply will not do'?

If you have a situation where the students are given the opportunity of returning for a second test, it is possible to get some idea about this. In Figure 5.4, the results of a test-examination among new students taking a course in psychology at the University of Bergen are presented in such a way as to show to what extent students with *different* results did in fact come back for a second test.

Students who were unable to pass the first test seem as likely to come back for a second attempt as they are to withdraw from further tests, whilst students with varying marks seem to follow a pattern which suggests that those with a good mark may be found again in the second and the third test. A close scrutiny of attendance records shows that, whereas the majority of students with rather low marks do not come back, *all* of the students with marks above 2.0 do in fact turn up a second (and possibly a third) time. Admittedly, this is nothing more than could be expected on the basis of the laws of 'positive reinforcement' or similar, differently formulated laws of learning and motivation. However, while this is so, one ought not fall into the trap of believing that such a result is of minor importance, since, after all, the good marks are attained by the 'good students', to whom a hearty welcome back might be extended anyway. The correlation between the results of the first two test-examinations in this case is only 0.22 (non-significant). (In a similar study at a later date, with an outcome similar to that of Fig. 5.4, a correlation of 0.07 was obtained.) Three students were seen to come again in the present study, despite the fact that they did not get a 'pass' the first time – or maybe *because* of that? Their results on the second test were the more remarkable: 2.7, 2.0, and 1.8 – well above the average.

We have seen that a good result on the initial test is accompanied by a greater probability of attendance on a second test than a poor result at the start. It has also, repeatedly, been found that the level of performance is raised with each test (see again Raaheim and Wankowski, 1981 and Fig. 5.3 above). Continued participation in the test programme ought therefore to mean an increase in skill – or some progress as far as learning is concerned. When, at the same time, we know that the correspondence between initial performance and later results is next to nothing, we might conclude that what the student *happens* to get out of an initial attempt, might be of great importance to his future career. We might even risk an assumption that, when we say students get good marks *because* they are academically competent, we might simply be saying that the student *becomes competent* (partly) because of a good mark at the start! And so, in a discussion of the use of marks in schools and university, we might argue that we ought to look for a way of getting rid of the poor marks only.

Sometimes the tendency among students who have got poor marks to begin with, of refusing to sit for a second test-examination, may be reduced if, instead of a mark, there is a prefabricated list of good and not-so-good sides to an essay ticked off by the lecturer for each individual essay. When feedback is given in this way, it might just be that a student feels less inclined than when a mark is given, to believe that he himself is of poor quality. In any case, anything that might bring about the idea that even a very talented student might, sometimes, produce an essay far short of perfection, would come in handy as far as the motivation to try again is concerned.

It has even been demonstrated that a remedy does, in fact, exist against the rather strong tendency of avoiding test-examinations altogether, to the extent that one does not show up even on occasions where one has asked specifically for an opportunity to take part. By an arrangement of tables in the examination hall that allowed for sub-groups of students to sit together, the author succeeded, apparently, in making each individual student feel obliged to come along with the others, once he or she had signed up for the test. In any case, now, for the first time in my career, there was a full house with a test-examination on the programme.

Who can tell the students precisely what to do?

When during the fifteen years of experimentation at the University of Bergen, with test-examinations and other training sessions, we have found that students do make great improvements after a rather short period of time, the greatest effect seems to be that of a reduction in the rate of failure to pass examinations. The percentage of 'very good' or 'excellent' marks has not always been found to be markedly different in an 'experimental group', from what has otherwise been found with the ordinary tuition procedures. In one particular year (autumn term 1978; for details of experiments, see Raaheim and Wankowski, 1981) we succeeded in having 895 out of a total of 904 students pass the first term examination in psychology, which equalled a one per cent failure, as against about 20 per cent as the 'normal' rate. It was even found that none of the nine students who failed had, in fact, taken part in the training programme. Still, whereas the participation in test-examinations led to an increase also in the number of 'very good' marks *during* the training period, there was *not* any clear sign at the official examination of a similar increase in promising end-results.

Similarly, if a closer look is taken at the examination results of *all* the students of the training experiment referred to in Figure 5.3 (see above), it is found that *unless* a student is seen to have been a member of a tutorial group – in addition to taking part in test-examinations – the chances of him having a very good mark are negligible.

A 'very good' mark (2.5 or better) at the end of the first year course in psychology is, at the University of Bergen, an absolute condition for anyone who seeks to be enrolled in the extended course towards a licenced psychologist's degree in Norway. So, at the School of Psychology in Bergen the teacher who wants to make provisions for extra training sessions for students may feel confident that he or she will have no great problem in securing a group of highly motivated students for the 'experiment'. In later years, then, the author has had the opportunity, yet again, of conducting a series of studies to look into the preconditions for (noticeable) improvements as far as the percentage of good marks is concerned.

Two different approaches have been tried out as a means of improving the students' chances of a satisfactory examination result at the end of the first year. In the final term before the exam, the students have been offered some extra training, *either* by taking part in a specially arranged programme (of essay writing and detailed work assessments) administered by an experienced lecturer, *or* by entering a study group, consisting of about 5 to 6 students, monitored by the experienced lecturer, but otherwise led by a student who had him- or herself been sitting for the same examination not too long ago.

The results of the two training procedures have been found to be strikingly different. In the (larger) group led by the lecturer only marginal effects have been detected, towards an improvement in examination results. With the participants of the study groups the following results were found: The rate of failure was only 6.5 per cent, as against 23 per cent among students not taking part in study groups of this kind. The number of 'very good' marks equalled 48 per cent among participants, as against 26 per cent for the non-participants.

It should be emphasized that all the students had an equal opportunity of attending lectures and seminars and, in short, of taking part in all normal tuition activities. The students who were recruited for participation in the specially arranged study groups were recruited in a random fashion.

There seems to be a definite limit to what can be obtained by 'normal teaching procedures' as far as examination results are concerned. At the University of Bergen attempts have been made to include among the regular offers to the students such things as test-examinations and tutorial groups of various kinds. Still, as long as the person who is there to explain to the students how learning problems ought to be attacked, is one who has himself or herself come a long way in the field of study in question, there is, perhaps, little hope of the words of advice hitting the right spot. As a teacher you may not be able to point out the direction in which a given student may see the light, if you cannot remember, or somehow conceive of, the situation of darkness in which this particular student finds himself at the moment. And so, it must perhaps be left to a fellow student to tell him precisely what to do, just now.

6

Success and Failure at University

Janek Wankowski

Why some students succeed and some fail

When in 1964, following recommendations of the 1963 Robbins Report on Higher Education, the University of Birmingham took up the challenge to investigate problems of student wastage and failure and gave me the task of investigating educational aspects of this phenomenon, I began my exploration by testing and evaluating four major assumptions. These assumptions were derived from the general theory that human learning, spontaneous or formal, is a continuous process of regulating behaviour with reference to future events, anticipated in the light of past experience (Kelly, 1955).

These assumptions are:

(i) That the individual student's readiness to learn efficiently at university may depend, to a great extent, on his habitual disposition derived from past experience of learning and projected into the expectations and assumptions about learning in the future.
(ii) That continuity of success is more likely to be maintained if the learning and teaching conditions at university are as satisfying to the individual as were his educational experiences in the past.
(iii) That difficulties and failure may be more likely to occur when the conditions of learning and teaching appear, to the student, to be different, unfamiliar, bewildering and therefore contrary to his habitual expectations.
(iv) That notwithstanding these basic habitual acquisitions from the past, many students may succeed in adopting new and efficacious ways of dealing with the conditions of tuition at university if they have clearer professional and social goals, and if they are of a certain temperamental disposition which is less likely to interfere with the readjustment of their habits of work and attitudes.

Consequently, the objectives of my random sample inquiry concerned with the educational aspects were as follows: (a) to examine, as fully as possible, students' habits of learning and their attitude to the teaching situation at university and at the earlier levels of formal education and (b) to relate various 'factors' elicited by the analysis of information obtained from this enquiry to achievement in degrees.

Findings and operational prescriptions

The data, resulting from two probes by structured interviews, administration of several questionnaires and a scrutiny of formal records of students' progress, may appear inadequate to throw much light on the complex problems arising from the decisions of hundreds of uniquely endowed and uniquely formed young persons to enter into equally complex and unique tuition transactions at university. Added to this, the time when these young people embark upon their academic career is also a most difficult period of transition from an obvious, but seldom acknowledged, dependency on home and school, to a seemingly free and independent but actually often a lonely limbo of academic existence; a state of repressed apprehension, disillusionment and ineffectiveness, mingled with the unexpressed hopes and joys of exciting opportunities (Erikson, 1971; Kiell, 1964).

However sincere the intentions to go along the well grooved paths of research procedure – to select the issues, to see what affects what, to make observations, to control experiments, to derive inferences, to present cautious conclusions and to formulate further hypotheses – there can be little doubt that such intentions are far from being realized by this study. The difficulty, for the reader, may stem from the popular assumption that the learning activity of students can be regarded as amenable to a pin-point scrutiny whilst it is, essentially, a part of the entire dynamism of life. The whole process is continuous, historical and hierarchical, reflective as well as ongoing, constrained as well as goaded by the experiences of the past, drawn into a flight of hope as well as overshadowed by the restraining tyranny of the future commitments.

It is for these reasons that centrally conducted surveys of learning difficulties of students cannot possibly provide more than an outline of general inferences typical of group phenomena. Experience of individual tuition, clinical contact or any other person-to-person dealings soon shows that inferences drawn from group phenomena dissipate in the maze of other, more pertinent influences discerned in such transactions. Individuals are vastly different from the collection of their characteristics expressed as a group statistic. Consequently the central research findings in education might be more useful for inducing sensitivity towards problems of interpersonal transactions in tuition than in offering operational prescriptions. The pressure for such prescriptions is however so persistent that the researcher must yield to the call for concise statements of what might be done to increase students' efficiency in learning.

In order to offer such a list of prescriptions it is useful to recall the general inferences from the survey, which was designed as a combined project of research and counselling and the findings from both these activities are included in drawing up these inferences. Moreover, since students' difficulties at university seem to be linked with the pre-university experience in tuition it is more appropriate to deal with the prescriptions under two headings: one dealing with the pre-university level and the other with what should be done at the university.

The findings of the survey suggest an overall impression that success at university may tend to be associated with:

(a) personal confidence and a feeling of competence in learning
(b) hopeful but realistic projection into the future occupational and social roles
(c) emotional stability
(d) temperamental tendency towards introversion
(e) relative independence from teachers
(f) a tacit acceptance of the curricular and work demands arising within the structure of tuition.[1]

Obversely, academic failure seems to be associated with:

(a) lack of personal confidence (or with an overcompensation for this disposition resulting in too much confidence)
(b) fearful and unrealistic projection into the future including occupational and social roles (or an overcompensation resulting in phantasy-bound planning, or an overt rejection of planning ahead and in repudiating of achievement)
(c) emotional instability characterized by a tendency to overact in social and in learning situations by either a complete social withdrawal, or a too eager desire for participation (or in sudden swings in either of these directions resulting in refusal to approach tutors when in difficulties, or again in an undue demand for support, guidance and attention)
(d) temperamental tendency towards extraversion which, at its extreme and in a learning context, makes for preference for speed rather than accuracy, for unreliability and poor concentration in boring tasks, for preference in dealing with people rather than theories[2]
(e) dependence on teachers and other significant figures
(f) feelings of disenchantment and an overt rejection of the curricular and work demands arising from the structure of tuition (or with an overcompensation of this tendency resulting in a too rigid interpretation of such demands and an inability to adapt readily to changing milieux of academic activity).

When problems of academic competence are examined from the angle of affective influences in learning (in contrast to the cognitive standpoint) the temperamental dispositions under points (c) and (d) subsume the remaining areas. It is easy to discern that emotional stability as well as the tendency towards introversion may contribute substantially to personal confidence and to a feeling of competence in academic studies. Emotional instability and a tendency to extraversion are likely to result in a loss of personal confidence as well as a loss of academic competence. The consequence of persistent anxiety is a phantasy-bound style of existence where concrete efforts or action are substituted by wishful thinking; an extraverted preference for interpersonal relationships and the need for constant challenge, stimulation and 'feedback' may induce great dissatisfaction with boring theoretical and stereotyped routines of tuition at any level of education.

Thus, the most general rule for operational prescriptions for schools and for universities should, on this analysis, be aimed, in the first place, at a considerable reduction of learning anxiety and of its most obvious overcompensatory tendencies.

Pedagogical gap in transition from school to university

Academic over-compliance, rigidity in learning styles and undue dependence on routines and teachers are often inadvertently induced at the pre-university levels of tuition (particularly in the sixth form) and no less inadvertently denied by the more detached modes of tuition at university.

(i) What happens in the sixth form

It seems that, as things are, a great deal of learning anxiety is very skilfully accommodated in the sixth forms, if indeed not unduly masked to the point of inducing an illusion that an individual is a competent and autonomous learner. This state of affairs is often brought about by the apparent ease of survival in the front ranks of academic attainment at school. It is but little realized by the teachers and by the educators in general, and certainly very seldom by the student himself, that his survival is due largely to the protective structure of tuition. Here the teaching and learning procedures had their clear objectives – the public examination requirements. The well planned, systematically presented and frequently tested set of factual knowledge was copiously and almost instantaneously reinforced by a ready feedback from the teaching situation. The proximity of teaching staff and emotional support derived from keen supervision and from parental influence at home tended to accommodate anxiety, oversensitivity, self-doubt and depressive tendencies, creating a firmly established illusion of competence and autonomy.

The same conditions of interpersonal relationships in tuition, the frequent and insistent demands for work and home exercises, build up the confidence of pupils with strong extraverted tendencies (Malleson, 1972). These scholars, whilst not anxiety ridden, are essentially 'reality bound' and the reality of the tuition pressures helps them to succeed in a structured situation of academic work in the sixth form.

(ii) What happens at university

It is only when such scholars meet the largely impersonal routines of teaching at university that many of them lose their nerve, their confidence and their ability to persevere. Here the objectives of learning must be established by the students themselves. The teaching material, vastly increased and in far more numerous subjects of study, must be organized into some order of priority for exploration and learning. The exercises and working papers, in some areas of study, are scarce or their execution largely unsupervised. The palpable consequences of learning, the 'feedback' from the teaching situation (Peel, 1956), occur at rare intervals.

The student who was trained to depend on others has to learn how to learn by himself. No wonder his plight seems great, his dissatisfactions manifold; his susceptibility to failure has been exacerbated out of all proportion by the very system of tuition which was designed to make him an independent learner. Clear teaching objectives, proximity of support from teachers and availability of 'feedback' from tuition are the most distinct pedagogical features of the sixth form. The same features are very much less distinct at university.

This is only a very generalized impression and must not be taken as implying a complete absence of supportive aspects of tuition which, no doubt, exists in many areas of university studies. But, if general prescriptive recommendations are required, they must match the equally generalized picture of reality rather than the particular and sporadic features of university tuition.

(iii) What could be done at both levels of tuition

Perhaps the most readily implemented solutions of the problems of transition from school to university would be for the schools to prepare their pupils for the impact of the most unsatisfying features of university tuition, and for the universities to continue, at least initially, to provide supportive tuition to which the students were so habituated at school. Drastic changes in tuition methods may tend to induce greater anxiety in the less emotionally stable individuals. They are the most vulnerable section of the student population and their numbers are considerable.

Thus, in order to help students to adapt more easily to the tuition patterns prevailing at university they should be given some foretaste of these methods at the sixth form level. Obviously, in the present system of educating the sixth formers mainly for excellence in public examinations the measure advocated below would form only a marginal aspect of the preparation for university entrance. Some effort to acquaint the prospective students with what may lie ahead should, nevertheless, be made.

This process of preparation should not be made by precepts or by telling the sixth formers what they may encounter in university tuition: such instructions will not help much. The preparation should be active and exercised over a long period of time if it is to be effectively integrated by the pupils. Talks and freshers' conferences are not likely to have much effect as means of training for the hardship ahead.

Preparation at the sixth form level: an interim measure

It would, so it seems, be necessary for a time to introduce a part-course in every GCE 'A' level subject, run on the lines of tuition prevailing at university. The underlying strategy of such a course would be to help the sixth formers to learn how to learn, largely by themselves, to organize their learning on the basis of mainly expository tuition.

A 'pre-university training course' should involve experience in being instructed by means of large-audience lectures (mass lectures), and in being taught by teachers who are keen on research and deep exploration of their subjects and who would be less involved in the day-to-day progress of their pupils than other sixth form teachers. The 'feedback' from tuition should be considerably diminished: work assignments less frequently assessed, marked or commented upon.

Generally, in areas of the curriculum assigned to such a 'pre-university training course', the sixth formers should be given less opportunity of knowing how they fare in their learning whilst, at the same time, they should be trained how to become more skilled in self assessment of their own progress. Large numbers of topics and sub-divisions of subjects should be introduced in order to diffuse effort and attention in learning, revising, etc. The volume of information should be drastically increased and the contents aimed far beyond the requirements of external examinations.

Some aspects of the 'Advanced' level subjects should be taught by teachers from other schools. This would reduce the opportunity of post-lesson contact and provide experience of greater distance from the key figures in tuition. The necessity for pupils to read, explore and organize their own search for information from books and publications should be stressed. The objectives of teaching various subjects (now clearly outlined by the 'Advanced' level syllabus) should not be made so readily apparent to the sixth form pupils. Pupils themselves should be encouraged to develop their own points of integrating and interrelating their information with reference to some objectives which may be academic or practical.

Skeleton strategy for training how to contain academic learning anxiety

A skeleton strategy of such a course of preparation for university studies at the sixth form could be summarized as follows:

(a) mass lectures as a means of disseminating information

(b) less frequent contact with teachers who actually give such lectures

(c) limited 'feedback' from the teaching situation and training in self-assessment as pupils learn to organize their studies

(d) encouraging pupils to construct their own objectives in learning and to integrate information, gained from lectures or reading, round some points of interest (objectives may be academic or practical)

(e) occasional guidance by means of tutorials with teachers not involved in mass-lecturing

(f) assessment by internal examinations and by extended essays and dissertations.

Prescriptions to moderate academic learning anxiety at university

Whilst in the sixth form pupils should be exercised in the less structured and less 'teacher-dependent' routines, so as to give them a foretaste of tuition at university; once here they should be taught, at least to begin with, in a more 'teacher-dependent' manner.

Such methods should include:

(a) a reduction in the size of audiences in lectures and, generally, less reliance on mass-lectures as a means of disseminating information

(b) more frequent contact with tutors who actually teach the subject in lectures

(c) far more frequent correction and appraisal of the submitted work and exercises

(d) more clearly formulated objectives of tuition in each subject as well as clearer objectification of the entire course of studies

(e) frequent attempts to point out the inter-subject relationships in the given course of studies

(f) more frequent attempts to discuss with students the career implications related to the course of study (encouragement to use the facilities of the University Careers Service)

(g) more encouragement given to students to discuss their specific learning difficulties as soon as they arise, with tutors, or with other members of staff who can give time to such discussions (personal tutors, educational and psychological counsellors)

(h) a greater variety of approaches to teaching even within the same subject of study

(i) varied methods of assessment and examination which should be clearly explained and made well-known to students: some options as to the methods of examining should be given to students

(j) attempts to reduce examination stress by:

    1. holding examination sessions, supervised by departmental teachers, in familiar surroundings within departmental premises

    2. varying the time of examinations (holding examination sittings in

different departments at different times of the academic year) in order to minimize the seasonal build up of mass apprehension (collective panic) amongst the anxiety-prone students

3. allowing students to re-sit examinations as many times as may be administratively possible
4. allowing students to re-sit only those papers in which they failed and not, as is a practice in some departments, to re-sit whole groups of papers irrespective of successful work in some of them
5. preparing parallel examination papers in order to have reserves for use by students who miss some specific examination sessions
6. spacing examination sessions to allow for a reasonable break between papers (if examinations became the responsibility of each department and were organized and held in departmental premises the difficulties of the central examination timetabling could be avoided)
7. use of tape-recorder examination techniques for students whose reasoning under stress may be less subject to 'emotional blocking' when they *talk about solutions* to problems than when they have to *write about them*; facilities for typing examination tapes should be provided.

Prescriptions for tuition and research

(i) Tuition

More generally, if learning efficiency is regarded as an outcome of successful performance during learning tasks, the feeling of success is inherent in the teaching situation, and it is at this level that its restoration ought to be attempted when students enter university.

Thus, the teaching transactions and consequently teaching methods should be such as to match – at least initially and until the student is able to stand on his own feet – the deeply ingrained habits of previous learning. It is commonplace for a well trained teacher that each new teaching endeavour must be preceded by an evaluation of what students already know in the given field of study. It is, unfortunately, seldom recognized that this evaluation must include the manner and the nature of the students' past learning styles. Some individuals can proceed to master new things and to develop new styles of learning eagerly and without apprehension. Many others will cling to the old, well-grooved, paths: 'familiar therefore safe' is the prevailing refrain of their lives, and compulsive conservation of their styles of learning a more natural tendency than exploration. Although university education would fail its purpose if it did not foster an independence of judgement as well as independence in organizing students' own work, the process of academic emancipation should be gradual if it is not to be destructive.

Tuition should therefore be tailored, at least to some extent, to the needs of individual students being, for some, more demanding, more extending their natural curiosity and far more encouraging to proceed ahead of the main stream of studies, and for others, a little more circumscribed and gently graded to their own, less ambitious, flights of academic exploration. Tuition should also be meaningful in terms of students' deeper academic interests and their professional aspirations.

Their problem of reducing student wastage, through action at the level of teaching, is very much in the forefront of the new thinking about university tuition. The need for training university teachers is recognized and, sooner or later, more energetic steps must be taken to encourage all prospective teachers to take up some formal studies in this area of academic activity.

(ii) Research at tuition level

Research and studies in tuition methods should be more frequently conducted at department and course levels. The facilities of any study assistance service, if available, could be extended and used by tutors engaged in such projects.

Perhaps one of the most effective means of encouraging research at tuition level would be to introduce higher degree studies of educational problems generally and of tuition methods in particular, in specific academic disciplines. Such on-going, departmental research, conducted by one or two post-graduate students, could become a subject of lively discussion in departmental common rooms, providing fertile ground for exchanges of views and critical appraisal of tuition procedures. It would, at the same time, encourage some students in every department to think seriously about professional training should they contemplate an academic career.

Notes

1. Educational tractability – a concept suggested by G. G. Stern – is perhaps the most neatly generalized label, if not in itself a prescription for academic success: 'In so far as it combines elements of both intellectuality and submissiveness, this dimension is of intrinsic interest to the educator. Reflecting interests in academic activities coupled with orderliness and conformity, this factor seems likely to be specifically associated with academic achievement. Persons high on this factor are not likely to be original or creative; they are however likely to accept directions readily and be educationally tractable' (Stern, 1970).
2. As succinctly summarized by Furneaux: 'The extreme extravert prefers speed to accuracy, tends to be unreliable and is poor at tasks which demand prolonged vigilance under boring conditions. On the other hand he is very flexible. His primary orientations are social and he greatly prefers dealing with people than working with things. It is the inter-personal element in any situation which holds his attention' (Furneaux, 1962).

7

Disenchantment, a Syndrome of Discontinuity of Learning Competence

Janek Wankowski

How disenchantment comes about: differences in the mutual support between students and teachers at school and at university

There are, in my experience, as many causes for academic failure as there are students and teachers. But there are also themes of dysfunction discernible in each individual's inability to learn effectively in a new setting of formal tuition at university.

I have tried to observe such dysfunctions and found that attempts to discern general patterns provided me with conceptual frameworks of the difficulties encountered by my students. Thinking about their problems in terms of themes, however tentatively held, helped me to adjust my tuition to their individual needs; encouraging my students to discern such patterns helped them to re-establish their competence in learning.

Here I shall try to discuss only one such theme under the heading of the syndrome of the 'disenchanted elite'. I should like to propose a thesis that disenchantment amongst some students arises from a sudden discontinuity of learning competence on entering university.

Briefly, the situation at school seems to be like this. Teachers train individual pupils how to pass external examinations through mastery of the subjects as reflected through the examination structure. The loyalties and their concomitants - the emotional and economic 'payoff' for both teachers and pupils – are derived from the same source: the number and the quality of the GCE 'A' level certificates (Hajnal, 1972). The pupils sense the nature of this mutual commitment and many, particularly in the relatively small classes of the sixth form, feel extremely secure and successful as scholars and as individuals in their own right. They are often shocked beyond all measure when the same 'payoff' elements of tuition transactions are absent from the vastly different university situation.

The first loyalty of a university teacher is essentially 'cosmopolitan' – a loyalty to the 'reference group' of other academics, scattered throughout the world, but working in the same field of research (Hatch, 1972); a fraternity of interest invested in the subject of study (Medawar, 1972). The lifeline of academic existence is mutuality with other researchers and scholars in the field; the tangible currency of mutual respect is the number of publications. Their appreciation of their impact on the given field of research constitutes the emotional, if not the economic 'payoff'. The quality or the number of students' awards are inevitably the secondary currency of the emotional satisfaction of their tutors. There exists, no doubt, a great deal of feeling of dependency on students who provide stimulus and the 'raison d'être' for resources and thus for academic inquiry, but an interest in their day-to-day progress becomes a matter of constantly nagging self-discipline; as such it may belong to those regions of the mind which lie largely beyond the 'pleasure principle'.

Furthermore, the mutuality of support at school between teachers and pupils occurs in moments of tuition, whilst at university it is probably seldom the case. The highest level of emotional satisfaction for tutors – their reward for academic enterprise – occurs in the moments of research activities, research reporting and by the exchange of research information. The chief motive for academic enterprise thus tends to lie outside the ambit of tuition. For students such feelings of academic satisfaction might occur at tutorials and seminars but there can be little doubt that even in this close contact they instantly discern the lower 'payoff' elements from those they experienced at school. The student is expected, in this scheme of earning academic awards, to become an independent learner. Many, not unnaturally, respond to this encouragement towards independent study and, progressing from strength to strength, begin to learn to judge the fruits of their own academic labour. But many are clearly not prepared for this lonely toil, in spite of being trained specifically for independent learning.

The summary of the considerations of how 'disenchantment' comes about can be made as follows: academic competence at school may be regarded as an outcome of successful performance during learning tasks – a currency of emotional satisfaction which sets up expectation of a future success which, in turn, enhances performance.

With many pupils – if not with most – this 'deposit account' of competence and a charge of optimism is not self-perpetuating and dissipates with an absence of success in performance. This is particularly so if the successes in performance were obtained in any highly selective, but also very stereotyped educational milieu where the 'chosen few' (Furneaux, 1961) are subject to the process of 'pedagogical hugging' which inflates promise.

When in a different milieu of tuition at university the charge of promise does not seem to help in bringing about an instant success, many of the more anxious individuals panic and produce the syndrome of the 'disenchanted elite'. This syndrome is a natural outcome of an over-institutionalized tuition in the over-selective environment of secondary schools, particularly in the sixth forms (Musgrove, 1971).

What kind of person may become prone to disenchantment?

It is the more highly emotionally sensitive individual who is likely to show the syndrome of the disenchanted élite. There are, however, some fortunate people who are not likely to be unbalanced by the transition from school to university. George Stern labels them, most aptly, as 'educationally tractable' (Stern, 1970). Liam Hudson's 'yielders' might also fit into this category (Hudson, 1970).

It is, I think, worthwhile to spend some time in discussing a few problems of their presence amongst academics.

(i) Constancy of learning behaviour

However skilled the process of pedagogical conditioning in the 'sixth form', the expected constancy of learning competence is shown only by a small section of students. I can illustrate this phenomenon by examining the relationship between the GCE 'A' level grades and degrees, and by regarding the correlation coefficient of this relationship as an index of constancy of learning behaviour at two successive levels of formal tuition (Wankowski and Cox, 1973).

The overall correlation coefficients for both males and females are persistent but small ($r = 0.29$**[1] and $r = 0.24$ not significant, respectively). They are, in themselves, an indication of an over-inflated expectation of the benefits of a selective process for academic education, crowned by the sixth form tuition. (This data pertains to the final position of the random sample studied by me, after six years when all students had completed their courses of study.) The trends revealed by this study have been confirmed by analyses of the two successive yearly intake of students (Holder and Wankowski, 1980).

When, however, the relationship between GCE 'A' level grades and degrees is examined with reference to temperament, as assessed by Eysenck's Personality Inventory, the effects of constancy of learning behaviour between two milieux of tuition alter drastically. A considerably higher correlation between GCE 'A' level grades and degrees occurs amongst stable introverts (phlegmatics): an $r = 0.51$** for males and an $r = 0.52$* for females, whilst the coefficients of correlations for the other three typologies (the stable extraverts, emotionally labile introverts and extraverts) become not significantly different from zero. Thus it seems that young people of a phlegmatic disposition display a considerably stronger tendency to preserve the constancy of their learning prowess, as reflected by their marks in the matriculation examination and in the grades of their degrees, than their colleagues of a different temperamental make-up who tend to show greater variations between their academic attainment in schools and university.

Two points are worth commenting on in this context: (a) if there is still, amongst educationalists, a tendency to emphasize the fact that school matriculation grades, and all that goes with them, are still the most significant predictors of success in higher education, they must consider the possibility that it might be only a small proportion of the student population (the phlegmatics, for instance) who contribute to this trend and who, at the same time, mask the still more impoverished relationship between attainment at two successive stages of education; (b) that the notion about the statistical phenomenon of 'restricted range' (Parkyn, 1967) which is said to diminish the effects of association between grades and degrees, because the students are already highly selected by 'ability', should perhaps be revised when temperamental dispositions of students are taken into consideration.

(ii) The successful student

A sketch of an academically successful, phlegmatic student, emerging from my studies and from my work as a teacher, could be as follows: a relatively independent and versatile learner, readily adopting new ways of tackling his problems of learning as they arise. Unruffled by demands, pressures or lack of them from the tuition side, he is tolerant, though not uncritical, of his tutors and friends. Ready to put up with inconsistencies and petty regulations of departmental or campus administration, he weaves the outside pressures through the well-established programme of his inner confidence, certain that with enough work, good luck and not too deep an involvement with the demands of academic life, the time of graduation will come and pass, as yet another landmark of pleasant toil, on the way to other hopeful expectations.

There are thus some fortunate people who are not likely to become so easily susceptible to institutional 'enchantment' which might enslave them by its structure, however benevolent. Subconsciously they have learned how to stoop to conquer. To fit snugly into things as they are is to gain complete mastery in the end! But to claim that such people are many, even amongst the most successful, is to be unreasonable. A very interesting study, though not moderated by a standardized psychometric test, was done by Fazakerley (1972) at Manchester Polytechnic which demonstrated that the amount of help a student received depended on whether he/she was labelled non-conformist (unacceptable) or conformist (acceptable) rather than on levels of academic ability; the conformist received the help.

(iii) An unsuccessful or a weak student

Presenting a sketch of some attributes of the 'academically vulnerable' student I would say that, prone to impulsiveness, he enters university with little idea of how his decision fits into the pattern of his future endeavours and suffers a shock of disorientation at the beginning of his studies. From this he seldom recovers. Here an ambivalent feature of his temperament is immediately apparent: depending greatly on support, response, and stimulation from other people, particularly those in authority, he is not prepared to approach them when in distress. This reluctance is not at all helpful to his tutors who would be only too ready to take more notice of his initial loss of confidence (Kipnis, 1971). His work patterns, style of study and preparations for examinations are very haphazard (Wankowski, Reid, Raaheim and Jacobsen, 1984). His study hours are generally shortened by preoccupation with extracurricular activities. Temperamentally he tends to be rather extraverted and anxious; egocentric, excitable, impulsive, exhibitionist and sociable. It is not surprising that other studies of unsuccessful students seem to support this picture. He is also described as lacking self-reliance and self-control, persistence or tenacity of purpose (Saenger-Ceha, 1970).

Such an array of adjectives seems to be very negative and portrays a profile of a difficult person. But since these temperamental qualities are but an outcome of his life-long struggle to achieve an equilibrium of emotional existence and since his habits of behaviour have, in the past, solved even his academic problems he needs to be understood rather than rejected.

How to reduce the impact of disenchantment

I do not know to what extent I have succeeded in conveying my view of the syndrome of 'academic disenchantment' as a reaction to an unfulfilled promise of competence, derived from previous institutional comfort – largely a subconscious process of self-conditioning within a specific milieu, which 'programmes' the mind with a set of inferences, untried by wider experience.

I would not, of course, claim that the vicissitudes of this syndrome are the only causes of student difficulties – there are obviously many, many others. But I would not hesitate to state that, from my experience, emotional disenchantment, arising from an initial academic and social disorientation on entering university, is one of the most important factors in student failure. I would at the same time like to suggest that a great deal of disenchantment could be reduced and moderated by skilled and enterprising tuition.

The problem is, of course, when and how to do it; certainly not by another bout of academic selectivity, nor by a handbook on what to do, or by preaching, precepts, or mass 'teach-ins' at freshers' conferences, but more likely through the recognition that it is the accumulative effect of self-conditioning at school which builds up a mountain of difficulties in a different milieu of tuition at university; and, consequently, that it is by a process of levelling down this mountain that some measure of really independent competence, not unlike that displayed by phlegmatics, may be won at school, and some of the shaken academic confidence be restored at university.

Universities were aptly described as 'research establishments with students' and, as long as they remain in this position, they should project this image very clearly to their prospective students, warning them in no uncertain terms what lies ahead in the period of transition.

The student who has learnt to depend on others has to learn how to depend on himself. No wonder his plight seems great, his dissatisfactions manifold; his susceptibility to failure exacerbated out of all proportion by the very system of tuition which was designed to make him an independent learner. In order to help students to adapt more easily to the tuition patterns prevailing at university, they should, as suggested before be given some foretaste of these methods at the 'sixth-form' level.

Note

1. The degree of probability is shown by an asterisk: * $p < 0.05$, ** $p < 0.01$, *** $p < 0.001$.

8

On the Vagaries of Students' Motivations and Attitudes to Teaching and Learning

Janek Wankowski

Reflections on the phenomenon of students' wants

Students' attitudes to teaching and learning at university are most likely to derive from their *wants* and, consequently, from their expectations of how their *wishes* are to be met or fulfilled on entering an institution of higher education. But human *wants* are extremely difficult to assess and still more difficult to predict.

With students things are even more complex and difficult for, in the period of late adolescence (most of it prolonged artificially by the formal dependency of schooling), the young individual is very much concerned with the problems of self-identification, i.e. with establishing a new, independent relationship with his peers and with the adult world. At such times the most prominent common feature of individual wants is to cherish the freedom of *Separateness* and of *Self-interest* most of the time and of *Togetherness and Others' Interests* for the remaining part of the time. Attempts at separateness must, at that time, be regarded as the primary theme but *self-mastery through the mastery of others* is undoubtedly its concomitant refrain.

If, at this point, I were asked to seek the basic behavioural laws governing such 'socially related individuality' of each person, I would try to discern them amidst the many ways in which humans learn to *master the world around them*. And if I were asked to describe what any individual seeks from any institution he happens to join, I would start by speculating on what kind of *mastery* or *competence* he is trying to derive from such an institutional foundation. Thus, in response to the problem posed by the title of this chapter I would say that students' attitudes to teaching and learning at university would derive from their desire to increase, to reaffirm, to gain or to find *skills, mastery* and *competence to cope with their world*. The fact that such skills happen, allegedly, to be of a so-called 'academic' nature does not exclude them from the generality of this human tendency (Wankowski, 1980).

But here instant provisos come to mind: (a) a student's world, with which he wishes to cope competently, may be largely imaginary. His adolescent feelings of powerlessness are only too readily transformed into impatience of unapplied ideas, which provide a wide scope of images of an obstructing or a compliant world. And (b) with most students their attempts to gain academic competence will be largely based on their styles of maintaining their competence at school. Both these intervening influences must be kept clearly in mind when thinking about students' attitudes to tuition and learning at university.

Components of learning competence

However imaginary we think the students' world may be, their academic competence, proved by the school examinations, must appear to all of them as very real (has not this reality been stamped with the official seal of the public examiners?) and, as such, it must give rise to an expectation of continued success. Consequently the style of learning, which has enabled such a student to maintain his competence at school, must be, logically, regarded as a model for successful learning at university. But, if we reflect that this style of learning has been developed and perfected, over long years, in some *very specific tuition milieu at school*, we cannot possibly grant that it will prove efficacious in any other, particularly in the very different circumstances of teaching at university. Ingrained habits of competence cannot possibly be expected to dissipate overnight on transition from one milieu to another. Competence in learning is a part of the competence in living, and thus a part of the individual's mental, moral and physical health. The world would be a far crazier place than it is, if its precarious stability did not depend on the comforts of habitual dealings with the contingencies of life. Thus, in order to understand what kind of expectations and attitudes students bring with them, when they enter university, it is necessary to ponder about the more outstanding features of their school learning particularly those of the sixth form which, as I said before, is, misleadingly, popularly regarded as preparing directly for the exigencies of advanced academic studies.

The most important components in developing the learning competence in school are, to my mind, the significant figures (parents, teachers and important friends) and the inter-reaction between them and students. It is quite possible that the nature of this 'social transaction' of tuition and learning may be considerably coloured by the temperamental dispositions of both parties. An initial attempt to explore these factors has been made within the scheme of my surveys and I will describe them briefly.

(i) Significant figures as sources for the security for academic exploration

If we agree that a healthy personality is really 'a person in relation to other persons' (MacMurray, 1961) and that these most important 'others' were, in childhood, parents or other adults, rather than peers, we must assume that the most important components of learning to live in the world and of learning to live at school are adult 'significant figures' – the main reference points of behaviour, the sources of comfort or discomfort, approval or disapproval, rejection or protection.

Students, or people in the state of seeking competence in general, might accept or repudiate the regard of older or more powerful 'others' but they will inevitably cast such figures in the role of parent substitutes. Teachers at all levels of education are cast in such roles and it is futile to deny this. The more uncertain an individual is of his own competence or strength, the more tenaciously he will seek the approval or disapproval of significant figures. If, for reasons of deep aversion (imaginary or real), an anxious person cannot cast *people* into such guiding roles he will turn to ideologies or religions, and if these are not suitable he will invent his own ideological props. Healthy personal competence demands a solid point of reference and academic competence is no exception to this rule.

Thus, the first thing for the university teacher to remember about his students' deeply rooted attitudes is that, whether he likes it or not, he is very likely automatically cast into the role of being 'in loco parentis', not by the pronouncement of pedagogical rules or customs but by the habitually established, subconsciously elaborated programmes in each student's mind. The next thing to remember is that at the stage of adolescence (and, indeed, with a great many people throughout their lives) parents become, often *simultaneously*, largely suppressed targets for all dissatisfactions, attacks, repudiations, envy and derision as well as equally severely suppressed objects of demand for endless rounds of comfort, support, source of skill and other supplies of semi-magical 'omnipotence'. It is these mixed feelings about parental (and hence teachers') 'stupidity' and 'power' that unconsciously endow all 'significant figures' with an exaggerated importance whilst the young individual is learning to be a competent person. Most people, and particularly the more anxious ones, can seldom be expected to shed this, largely imaginary, 'love–hate' relationship.

Generally, true to the deepest psychoanalytic insight, most of us are 'endeavouring to make a world around us which will be suitable, if not appropriate, for the relief of our tensions created by the emotional pattern of our early life' (Berg, 1957) and since the earliest tensions were experienced with reference to adult 'significant figures' they have undoubtedly contributed greatly in laying down an indelible programme for dealing with the world. As Freud wrote (1949):

> The long period of childhood during which the growing human being lives in dependence upon his parents, leaves behind it a precipitate, which forms within his ego a special agency in which the parental influence is prolonged.

This attitude of dependence on 'significant figures' is expressed very clearly, and very frequently, in the individual therapy of remedial tuition and counselling, as well as in the supervision of academic research and theses. I tried to get a glimpse of this phenomenon in an experimental context and looked at it in the random sample studies (Wankowski and Cox, 1973). One point is worth mentioning here. The examination of students' impressions about their earlier education elicited references to 'significant figures' such as parents or teachers who were mentioned in connection with success or failure, changes of interest in specific subjects, or in connection with feelings of confidence or difficulties at school. It was hypothesized that students who made more frequent reference to teachers or parents might be those whose learning behaviour was more 'people-oriented' and who might, in consequence, become 'teacher dependent'.

The influence of 'significant figures' such as teachers is obviously crucial in any transaction of tuition, as all early learning is structured with reference to other people amongst whom adults are of the greatest importance. This was confirmed by the statements made by the random sample students where 80 per cent made *spontaneous* references to teachers as significant people who had a positive, i.e. helpful, or a negative (frustrating) influence on their scholastic progress in primary or secondary schools.

When the statements of the most successful (Honours Class I) and the unsuccessful students were examined, there appeared to be no difference between the frequency of reference to *school teachers* in a negative or in a positive context. When, however, both these types of statements were linked, on the assumption that a 'teacher dependent' scholar might be prone to remember teachers' influences in any context, positive as well as negative, an interesting trend emerged.

When the 'school teacher dependence' ratio was calculated from these statements for students in classes of higher and lower achievement in their degrees at university, a higher ratio was apparent for groups of students in the lower achievement range. The *overall* correlations between the 'school teacher dependence' scores and degrees do not however suggest any significant linkage, though an additional factor analysis suggests strongly that, in the male population, high 'school teacher dependence' scores are linked with high emotionality, whilst in the female population high 'school teacher dependence' scores are linked with high extraversion. This trend appeared to be strongest at the extreme polarities of populations which, at the most successful degree level (Honours Class I), includes mostly science students who tend to be introverted (less people-oriented), whilst amongst the least successful (withdrawals) the predominant characteristic is that of extraversion (more people-oriented). This trend seemed to be obscured by other factors in the middle range of the population and the breakdown by personality and by faculty showed that this indeed might be the case. A considerable negative correlation ($r = -0.5^*$) between the 'school teacher dependence score' and class of degree obtained amongst stable and introverted females who tend to do better at university when they are less 'teacher dependent'. Analyses of responses of science students revealed that a similar, negative correlation obtains between 'the school teacher dependence' score and class of degree amongst males in physical sciences ($r = -0.36^*$), suggesting that an ingrained *habit of dependence on teachers in schools might be linked with lower achievement at university* in this particular area of study.

There is also a positive, though not quite significant, correlation between degree achievement and 'school teacher dependence' score amongst male students in the arts faculty. This might suggest that in this area of study, male students who were more 'teacher-dependent' at school might have an easier passage at university, perhaps because the arts faculty teachers, being themselves more 'people-oriented' (extraverted and anxious), might understand their students better than teachers in the science faculty; they might be less detached and more supportive, etc.

An interesting feature emerged from correlating 'goal orientation' and 'teacher dependence' scores of the random sample when it was divided into groups of degree achievement. A high, positive correlation ($r = 0.63*$) was found in the group of male students who failed and withdrew from university. Perhaps, in these cases, it is their undue reliance on 'inspiration' from teachers in schools that becomes a source of disenchantment at university (Wankowski and Cox, 1973).

(ii) Personality and temperamental disposition

However great the controversy about the value of studies of personality, their importance to clearer understanding of human behaviour and of human wants, wishes and fancies cannot be disregarded (Entwistle and Wilson, 1977). If we allow ourselves to be patient with only one approach to this extremely complex field of psychology, we might get a glimpse of how much such studies may help us to think a little more clearly about students' attitudes to learning and tuition.

Without detracting from the unique endowments of every individual, as well as from the unique transformation of these endowments through learning, we can nevertheless find some themes of similarities in behavioural tendencies of certain groups of people. We can attempt to classify behaviour on various 'personality trait' continua and to predict that, on the whole, person 'X' will tend to be more cheerful for most of the time whilst person 'Y' will remain predominantly in a mood of relative gloom.

My own investigations of students' problems as well as of the general problems of human learning have been enhanced by the use of personality measurements. I have found that, in spite of all their shortcomings, these measurements are strongly and persistently related to various aspects of the learning behaviour of my students, my counselling clients and other samples of populations who participated in my studies.

I think that these insights might be helpful to our quest for greater understanding of our students' attitudes to us and to our ways of teaching, as well as to our own understanding of the ways we may see ourselves as their teachers (Holder and Wankowski, 1980).

I will now present some of my analyses of students' educational attitudes, as related to the personality traits of extraversion and emotionality (Eysenck, 1965) and to the joint effect of these traits classified into four temperamental dispositions of Stable Introverts (Phlegmatics), Stable Extraverts (Sanguines), Anxious Introverts (Melancholics) and Anxious Extraverts (Cholerics).

Anticipating, perhaps unnecessarily, a great deal of scepticism and aversion on the reader's part to such classifications, I will ask them to bear with me for a few moments, and to bear in mind Huxley's classical way out of such a dilemma when he said that:

> All systems of classifications tend in some measure to distort reality; but it is impossible to think clearly about reality unless we make some classifactory system.
>
> (Huxley, 1937)

When personality traits of extraversion and emotionality are included in the analysis of relationships between variables, the complexity of influences conducive to success or failure at university becomes very great indeed.

First, there are significant relationships between admission grades and extraversion. Second, there are significant relationships between degree achievement and emotionality and extraversion. Third, personality traits of emotionality and extraversion are related to students' choices of subjects of study. Fourth, temperamental influences in choices of subjects of study are also linked with the success and failure phenomena in some departments and courses. Fifth, temperamental influences are also visible in analyses of sub-samples of students who attend for counselling. Sixth, there are clear discrepancies between the numbers of students of different temperamental dispositions gaining first class honours degrees. Seventh, temperamental disposition is linked with the 'lie' detection scale included in Eysenck's Personality Inventory. Eighth, temperamental disposition is linked with the syndrome of early disorientation in academic studies. Ninth, temperamental disposition is linked with the manner of study, preference for methods of tuition, preparation for examinations, attitude to teachers and opinions about schools from which students came (Wankowski and Cox, 1973).

A study of students' attitudes to tuition and learning in the sixth form and at university was carried out as part of the random sample investigation. A questionnaire pertaining to the sixth form tuition was administered in the first year at university, whilst a similar questionnaire about university tuition was administered during the second year. It seemed essential to obtain some picture of attitudes and habits of study at these two levels of learning and to assess, if possible, the degree of change. It was possible that students' readiness to change habits of learning might affect performance at university, particularly as the tuition methods in the sixth form are very dissimilar from those used at the university.

For example, the random sample investigation shows the persistence of the 'dictation' method of teaching at this most advanced level of secondary education, designed for the purpose of preparing young scholars for university studies. The survey shows that in Britain at least *one teacher in five* might be using this teaching procedure in the sixth forms; in some subjects this proportion might be as high as *one in three* (e.g. physics, chemistry, geography). As far as I can ascertain, dictation is not used as a teaching method in universities (Wankowski, 1974).

The statements made by some random sample students about this method of tuition are quoted to illustrate the point:

'Dictation 100% of the lesson'
'90% of lesson – dictation of notes'
'Dictation mainly'
'Almost entirely dictation'
'Entirely dictation – even methods how to carry out experiments were dictated'
'Dictation straight from textbooks, most of the lesson'
'100% dictation of notes to be re-written as fair copy for the next day'
'Blackboard and 100% dictation of notes as teacher wrote them down'.

The conditions and manner of study during the second year at university were also investigated. The trends of association of students' responses with personality or motivation factors became far less clear-cut than those shown in the sixth form investigation. The passage of time and experience in adaptation to the varied and very much more complex problems of academic life may have contributed substantially to the dissipation of such trends. Some traces of old adaptations did however remain.

An examination of the sixth form effects suggests that, for the female students, choice of GCE 'A' level subjects is affected mainly by extraversion. (Those who state that they took up their 'A' level subjects on advice of other people tend to be more extraverted ($p < 0.05^*$.) The more anxious female students tend to prefer discussions rather than lessons as a medium of tuition ($p < 0.001^{***}$) and work for examinations as the mood takes them ($p < 0.05^*$). They tend also to be critical of their schools (would not send their children to the same schools as they themselves attended) ($p < 0.05^*$).

Male students of a more highly emotional disposition tend to transcribe notes from rough to neat copies (compulsive systematizers) ($p < 0.05^*$), are not satisfied that their 'sixth form' education has prepared them for university studies ($p < 0.001^{***}$), and, like the highly emotional females, are generally critical of the schools they themselves attended (would not send their children to those schools) ($p < 0.05^*$).

An examination of attitudes to study and tuition at university suggests that higher emotionality amongst female students tends to be associated with a feeling of inadequacy (coping inadequately in their second year work) ($p < 0.05^*$) and hesitancy to approach tutors when in difficulties ($p < 0.05^*$).

Amongst males, higher emotionality seems to be associated with feelings of inadequacy in work during the second year ($p < 0.01^{**}$). The more highly emotional students would hesitate to approach tutors when in difficulty ($p < 0.05^*$) and tend to be more haphazard in their work ($p < 0.01^{**}$) than the less emotional ones. A haphazard style of work is also significantly affected by high extraversion ($p < 0.01^{**}$). Higher emotionality is also associated with the routine of transcribing notes from rough to neat ones ($p < 0.05^*$). There is a nearly significant (p < 0.10) tendency for the more extraverted students never to use prescribed reference books in their studies.

Generally speaking, emotionality is a more powerful influence in shaping the style of learning and acquiring attitudes to tuition at school and at university than extraversion. It seems, on the one hand, to induce persistent states of uncertainty about work progress, hostility to schools, apprehensions about contacts with teachers, compulsive and ritualistic methods of formulating records and learning and, on the other hand, it makes for haphazard methods of study and preference for less formal contacts in tuition.

In order to check these interesting trends in a different population sample, similar questionnaires were administered to 151 Post Graduate Certificate of Education Students (Kwiatkowski, 1973).

A very similar picture to the trends found in the random sample emerged from this exercise. The following observations were made:

> Emotionality is significantly correlated with lack of system in work and generally with the feelings of not being able to cope at university, the effect being particularly strong for females. The wish to become more systematic, the absence of ideas about future goals in life, as well as the tendency not to use reference books whilst studying and revising is also linked with emotionality.
>
> Extraversion is correlated with an unsystematic approach to work, with a liking for tutorials and with the student's confidence in being able to fulfil his wishes; this effect is particularly strong amongst males. For males the feeling of being able to cope with university work is also correlated with extraversion.

These pictures reinforce the common sense observations that style of coping with problems at hand are often linked with temperamental dispositions. A greater understanding of this relationship should lead to considerable improvements in pedagogic procedures. It was of interest to my colleagues and myself whether these trends could also be detected amongst pupils in schools. We were particularly interested in the problem of the disruptive influences of high emotionality in shaping the styles of learning and in developing ambivalent attitudes to academic (i.e. largely theoretical) studies at the pre-university level. Our research was supported by funds from the Norwegian Research Council and by a small personal research grant from the Faculty of Education in Birmingham. It involved 451 upper-secondary students in Norway and England (including a small sample of the USA scholars). It confirmed, at significant level, that study habits tend to be related to traits of personality. A briefest summary of the first order factor which emerged from the analyses is given as Table 8.1. The analyses are obviously related to the main objective of this book and can serve as palpable points of illustration and discussions about teaching and learning. I will return to this theme in my last chapter. The full analyses can be found in Wankowski, Reid, Raaheim and Jacobsen, 1984.

The main feature of this exercise in analysing study habits and their link-age with personality seems to be the striking similarity of the responses of

Table 8.1   Summary of the first of the three factors (principal components) in the national samples of boys (a) and girls (b)

Boys	Norway n = 92	England n = 68	USA* n = 28
Factor 1	Disorganization, irresolution, neglect and procrastination, high emotionality, not easily acquiescing with social norms	Disorganization, irresolution neglect and procrastination, high emotionality, and high extroversion, not easily acquiescing with social norms	Disorganization, irresolution, neglect and procrastination, high emotionality, not easily acquiescing with social norms

Girls	Norway n = 128	England n = 61	USA* n = 13
Factor 1	Disorganization, neglect, procrastination and worrying, not easily acquiescing with social norms	Disorganization, neglect and worrying, high emotionality	Disorganization, procrastination, unsystematic approach and worrying, high extraversion

* The very small number of boys and girls in this sample calls for extreme caution in interpretation of factor analysis.

the scholars from three countries. This similarity is important considering the differences in national educational traditions, curricula and school organization.

The underlying factor seems to be the common sense generality of behaviour and attitude to academic work whilst in the final stages of secondary schooling. And that, in spite of some discrepancies in the mean values of personality traits of extraversion and neuroticism, the Norwegian boys and girls produced the lowest average scores on extraversion and neuroticism followed, respectively, by the higher average scores of the USA sample and by the still higher scores of the English sample; the Norwegian population being more introverted and stable than the English one, their mean scores differing quite substantially on both these personality traits, the USA falling in between.

The Eysenck Personality Inventory included in these studies has been adapted and used extensively in all these countries and can be regarded as relatively culture free. Thus, it seems that the generality of attitudes to work and study discerned across the national samples is not much affected by the possibly quite substantial emotional differences in temperamental dispositions of the scholars. When faced with the prospects and pressures of academic work their responses seem to be uniform rather than discrepant, suggesting that the generality of basic human learning behaviour may be regarded as a safe base for summarizing and reflecting on the value of this exercise.

Thus, assuming that the school boys and school girls in all three countries behave in a similar way vis-à-vis their academic work, we can bear in mind the most simple model of behavioural adaptation borrowed from ethological psychology.

All learning tasks however simple or complex can be solved basically only in three ways: direct attempt to master them (fight), avoidance of going near them (flight) and cautious examination by trial and error (careful moving towards, or examining cautiously the problem – *a tentative study*). These three main tendencies seem to be most particularly illustrated by the collection of study habits derived from the responses of the boys' and girls' samples as revealed by the factor analyses.

Remembering that academic learning tasks must appear as rather far removed from the immediate needs, wishes and fantasies of adolescents, we should perhaps grant that, unless some subject of study or task at hand fits snugly into the wishes and fancies of the young, they must appear as rather superficial preoccupations. Thus, it is not surprising that the strongest factors (Factor 1) snowball into a litany of negative habits which would be characteristic of the 'flight' method of adaptation to the imposed, or partially even self-imposed, demands to work and to learn systematically.

Dodging the issues in any way at all becomes the first underlying tactic, when the spur of fear and worrying seems of no avail. The fact that at least one in every three boys and girls seem to adopt this tactic speaks of its pervasive nature. It is, of course, by no means certain how pervasive it may be, for the 'fight', 'flight' and the 'examine cautiously' tactics might vary from one subject, or an area of study, or a task at hand, to another. The survey by one questionnaire cannot illuminate this problem any further. But the interpretation of the cohesion of this factor, gathering into itself the most typical range of 'defence mechanisms' against anxiety of failure to be masterful, cannot be easily disregarded.

The 'fight' tactic can be characterized by the association of habits which turn worrying (fear of failure) into a positive spur to fight on, and thus to gain mastery over the pressures of work, when work and perseverance become a positive, reinforcing agent in academic survival. The 'examining cautiously' tactic can be characterized by a set of habits whereby conscious and relatively fear-free appraisals of pressures and work demands are made, and 'adaptive compliance' stratagems are assumed. This adaptive compliance (a knack of advantageous adaptation) is probably most beneficial to survival amidst work pressures. It may, in itself, tend to reduce fear of failure to a minimum, so that risks can more easily be taken by not always behaving as a scholastic 'Stakhanovite worker', and work assignments and dates of submission can be occasionally dodged, in order to indulge in some more exciting pastimes with a free conscience.

Having indulged in these 'ethological' interpretations of the results of the exercise in study habits we can conclude that it might be of great interest to find out if the 'facts' and 'factors' derived from this study are real when related to academic survival at the next stage of education – in the universities. Or, better still, if a greater awareness on the part of academic teachers of how students respond to the demands made on them, would enhance their pedagogic skills and make their own and their students' study more mutually satisfying. If student learning strategies are 'minimally adaptive' rather than 'maximally efficient', what does this suggest about the kind of curriculum model we should assume when we propose to improve student learning and what kind of pedagogic procedures would be most likely to maximize students' competence in self-teaching?

Dynamics of circularity of personal, social and educational influences

Having looked at the attitudes of students entering university we may be tempted to try to separate them into those which might be called 'social and personal' and those which might be called 'academic and occupational'. But such a division must be regarded as very superficial, since personal and social competence is very often bound up with work or skill competence. This inter-relatedness can be illustrated by another exercise in the Birmingham surveys.

There can be very little doubt that miseries and dissatisfactions with social life will generally throw an adolescent, or even an adult student, from the path of successful academic progress. It is only in cases where such miseries are, by sheer luck or chance, sublimated by compulsive academic work that their influence might become advantageous in promoting learning competence, or in establishing obsessive academic commitments, popularly acclaimed as true academic motivation of 'learning for learning's sake'.

My reading, and my experience as a remedial teacher, have given me some grounds to assert that social difficulties and insecurity are often associated with students' inability to do justice to academic work at university. But these associations are by no means simple. An illustration from a special sample of students who withdrew prematurely from university in 1968 may corroborate this contention.

Possible causes for withdrawal of a sample of 170 students, who left university in 1968 without obtaining a degree, were indicated by tutors on a specially constructed list. The list comprised several areas of reasons for withdrawal such as motivation, learning, teaching and social factors. Analyses showed that 80 per cent of students in this sample, who were known to have been *disturbed by social factors*, experienced learning difficulties. These trends were checked by examining the responses of 69 students from the same sample (44) who completed a similar questionnaire, and comparing their responses with those indicated by their tutors. The first relationship between the 'socially disturbing' factors and the difficulties in studies was confirmed, but another set of trends was also observed: *difficulties in learning* were clearly linked with *inadequate motivation*[1]: 90 per cent of students who were inadequately motivated experienced difficulties in learning. Moreover, *inadequate motivation* was associated with *dissatisfaction with teaching methods*: 75 per cent who were inadequately motivated were not satisfied with tuition.

Motivation seems to be a very persistent link between all manner of influences contributing to success and failure at university. Since it is not a unitary tendency it cannot be properly assessed, predicted or too readily evoked by any special tuition routine or method of approach. But since its theme weaves so clearly through the maze of other influences in learning, its impact should be appreciated by people involved in tuition.

However much confusion has been caused by this attempt to survey and to describe students' attitudes and influences in academic learning, and however pale and unformulated the concepts of such influences, and however inadequate the analyses, one feature has been clearly and simply quantified in the Birmingham surveys: *over 80 per cent of the random sample students have ascribed their ease over their difficulties in pre-university learning to the influence of their teachers.* Allowing for the persistence of habits, attitudes, dispositions and, above all, hopes and expectations set by previous experience, is it not reasonable to infer that this important influence may be equally strong when students come to university?

Many educationalists and administrators concerned with higher education still talk and think about learning and teaching in terms of the two concepts of *nature* and *nurture*. The GCE grades and the Degree awards are usually regarded as the most obvious manifestations of the student's native endowment. The reader might, very rightly, object that I am making an inadmissible simplification, but all I will do to defend this contention is to say that, from the experience of ten years' sales of the University of Birmingham Educational Counselling Unit publications, papers and reports which have the term 'admission grades' or 'GCE's in their titles are invariably the first to run into second editions – so strong is the lure of the well-ingrained concepts which are still used in coming to terms with the complexities of educational phenomena!

All I was trying to do was to draw the reader's attention to the fact that by using only two or three more concepts such as personality traits of *extraversion*, *emotionality*, *motivation* or *teacher dependence*, the scope of speculative thinking about problems of tuition and learning becomes spectacularly greater. The didactic power of the multifactorial approach in exploring the nature of human learning behaviour lies not in what relationships it reveals, but in suggesting how many other influences may remain unaccounted for. And this, to me, is the most useful lesson which is helpful in my work as a remedial teacher at university.

I cannot judge how much empathy or aversion this way of presenting to the reader my glimpses of students' attitudes has evoked. I know that to stray from the straight and narrow paths of the purely cognitive considerations implies the necessity of dealing with the *affective* concomitants of learning and, worse still, with the interpersonal transactions of tuition of which the emotional strains and stresses are an inevitable part. Yet we cannot, I think, avoid the commonsense inference that teaching and learning are mostly, if not wholly, transacted in and through social situations. Temperamental dispositions, and attitudes, and their concomitants of motives and goals, are all relatively stable habits of behaviour. They are all established within the context of the social transactions, and success or failure in learning is an outcome of the nature of such transactional relations. Social transactions always involve strong emotional undercurrents which are at any given moment extremely complex. It is this complexity which often frightens even the most persistent analyst of learning behaviour, but a total disregard of emotional influences in learning leads only to static resolutions of educational problems which will tend to fit a limited number of people and create wastage and attrition amongst many.

In touching upon influences of attitudes and dispositions in learning, it is necessary to remember that we are dealing with delicate issues impinging on the totality of each individual make-up. This totality includes past, present and future orientation rooted, most probably, in the bio-physiological imprints but never separate from the sets of habits which, in turn, were established through experiences of life. Success or failure at university is, by implication, success or failure within a certain social context. It is a social phenomenon and must continue to be examined as an outcome of a social transaction.

Note

1. Assessed as future goal orientation (Wankowski and Cox, 1973).

9

Assisting the Individual Student with Study Difficulties

Janek Wankowski

Theoretical standpoint: the individual as a self-teaching agent

It is interesting that the most recent data on student wastage in British Universities reveals a very similar league of attrition to the University Grants Committee's table in 1968. It seems that nothing much has changed in this respect in Higher Education in the UK. Attrition in Scottish universities remains very high and causes renewed concern, as mentioned in Chapter 1. Recently, the University of Scotland standing conference has launched an official enquiry into this problem conducted by the Executive Secretary (personal communication, 1989).

I hope that readers will not expect any tight therapeutic prescriptions for dealing with the highly idiosyncratic difficulties of their students. The infinite capacity of the brain ensures that man is indeterminately determined; yet, at the same time, an individual is also an obstinate slave to his habits of acting and thinking which, once set, provide inevitably an indelible programme for any future exploration and learning. Since no conditional response is ever erasable, the principle that 'disposition selects stimuli' obtains in any learning process, and dispositions to cope advantageously with one kind of learning milieu might not necessarily be conducive to coping with another, particularly since the most discrete aspects of learning at school and at university are vastly different. It is only to be expected that the ways of learning skills practised at school may become completely unacceptable at university. New learning to cope must take place, and this might have to happen against the background of obsolete or counter-productive habits.

The issue is further complicated by the fact that the time of a young individual's life assigned traditionally to the pursuit of higher education is also a time of intense moods and swings of attitudes. Most young people are affected by them, some very slightly, some moderately and some very severely. The adolescent's 'identity crisis' is lived through amidst acute conflict between the 'need for devotion' and the 'need for repudiation' (Erikson, 1971).

My experience of remedial tuition in schools and at university has taught me to regard human learning as largely an activity of self-teaching. But not only that; it is a ceaseless attempt on the part of the individual to teach others round him how to respond to his whims, fancies, wishes and needs; in a word, an effort to manipulate the world around him to his own advantage in the first place and, perhaps, to the advantage of others in the second. Borrowing from Wordsworth's and Freud's precepts that 'the child is father of the man', I came to regard the individual learner as a teacher of himself and of his teachers.

The convenience of my approach becomes apparent when you reflect that whilst placing the ball of the tuition game in the student's court, it leaves the teacher – the more experienced and hence the more responsible partner – still the vital member of the learning dyad. This is where, in my view, the crux of tuition rightly belongs when we consider that during the process of upbringing, the traffic of mutuality (Erikson, 1967) goes both ways from the mother (the significant figure) to the child (the pupil) and from the child to the mother; both partners of mutuality enjoying the benefits of the social transactions. Such a view is supported by considerable experimental evidence (Smith and Cowie, 1988).

At the same time, perceptive educators recognize that there is a point of balance between the forces of socialization and the individual's demand for autonomy, and it is at that point that the mutuality of respect is won or lost. I learned this lesson in the earliest days of my teaching career when I realized that when I wanted to teach some of my more reluctant pupils arithmetic or reading they, in turn, wanted to teach me to leave them absolutely alone! Having, with due respect for their autonomy, recognized this point of resistance (a point of mutual pressure) there was only one thing to do: I tried to help such pupils to learn arithmetic and reading by structuring tuition in such a way as to give them the opportunity to teach themselves. The results of adopting such an approach were usually very successful.

Another advantage of my theory – in my work as a student counsellor – is the obvious convenience of turning the tables upon the student who, if feeling trapped in his commitment to academic studies, imagines that his plight, his pangs of conscience and his inner anger, are solely due to the social pressures around him. I find that, sooner or later, in the progress of remedial tuition, the student himself realizes that it was also his own skill and joy in manipulating his teachers and his home environment that have contributed to his self-imprisonment within the framework of inflated scholastic competence. A discussion of the emotional concomitants of learning successes and of learning failures at school soon leads to a reflection of how the student himself managed to teach his teachers and his parents to provide him, copiously, with the tokens of emotional support.

The word 'counselling' carries a connotation of dispensing advice and this is the last thing I would do in order to help somebody; my function is more as an assistant in studies, or a remedial teacher. An admission that learning difficulties can emerge at this level seems to reflect sadly upon the highly selective preparatory system of schooling as well as on the system of tuition in higher education. The accepted label of 'counsellor' and 'counselling' seems to be less of an irritant for administrators and teachers in schools and universities. Its inappropriateness, or ambiguity should not, however, worry anyone who feels like making use of this service. It is one of the basic principles of a 'counselling' process that it is tolerant of all apparent verbal contradictions. Helping a person to become an efficient, self-directing learner is not an exercise in dialectics. It is not words that matter in understanding the nature of disorientation, loss of confidence and the ensuing depression, but the shades of hope, fear, joy or despair which may underlie words and actions in counselling transformations.

Predictive prescriptions: who is likely to lose learning competence at university; reactive depression and loss of academic competence

There is, of course, no way of predicting which individual student will fall a victim to the loss of academic competence, but a few informed guesses about general trends can be made. My investigations and counselling work in Birmingham suggest that susceptibility to high emotionality and, consequently, greater proneness to reactive depression, can be regarded as a most powerful influence associated with academic failure. How this tendency comes about and how it should be interpreted I leave to the psychological theorists and experimenters. My main concern is what to do when a person who comes to see me seems to be clearly in a state of losing his competence to keep up with his studies. And the state of such a person is so closely fitting Seligman's (1975) paradigm of helplessness that it is useful to quote him:

> What kind of events set off reactive depression? Failure at work and school, death of a loved one, rejection or separation from friends and loved ones, physical disease, financial problems and growing old. There are many others, but this list captures the floor.
>
> I believe that what links these experiences and lies at the heart of depression is unitary: the depressed patient believes, or has learnt, that he cannot control those elements of his life that relieve suffering, bring gratification, or provide nurture – in short, he believes that he is helpless. Consider a few of the precipitating events: what is the meaning of job failure or incompetence at school (*or university* – italics mine)? Often it means that all of a person's efforts have been in vain, that his responses have failed to achieve his desire.

Having long tried to cope daily with people, young and mature, suffering from reactive depression who come to me when they themselves seemed to have ceased to cope, I endorse Seligman's every word. But I would add a rider: 'learned helplessness' is often exacerbated, beyond belief of a casual observer, by sheer though deeply suppressed envy that others can cope and control their way towards the achievement of their desires, whilst the helpless sufferer has lost all hope to be as successful as others whose fun, achievements, joys, thrills, goods or skills he secretly resents.

Loss of coping power, or helplessness, and the ensuing depression can be regarded as a state of paralyzing fear, not unlike that of an animal freezing when surprised by a predator which, by inducing a state of apathy, slows down the more dangerous, desperate reaction. Looked at from this angle, reactive depression is to me a safety valve, just hissing its first cloud of steam! It is, in a sense, a good thing, like the experience of physical pain, which sounds a warning bell against further damage to the organism. It must not however be disregarded by those who themselves, being at the time in a more fortunate state of not feeling helpless, may bring relief to the sufferers by helping them to regain the competence to cope with not coping.

Much of the reactive depressions of the young students is just that, and their demand for being instructed (for this is what they seek in the first place) in the skills of coping with academic work is, more often than not, a demand for guidance in coping with life. This is, of course, seldom admitted even to themselves and, if it is presented through an image of helplessness in formal learning, it is far easier to accept on that plane, if only to begin with. That a recovery of competence to cope with academic work often spreads to recovery of competence in coping with other problems of life and vice versa, I have no doubt whatever. The 'transfer of training', I noticed in my earliest years of teaching even the youngest ones in schools, occurs on the level of attitude. It is really a transfer of confidence in learning: 'if I can do this, surely I can do another difficult thing'. The learning of a dead language like Latin, or ancient Greek, had this effect on generations of scholars who had to knuckle down to it under the fear of overt punishment, derision by teachers or friends or, worse still, withdrawal of esteem by the world which continued for centuries to regard it as a prestigious skill. If one could endure learning a largely useless ancient tongue, one could learn other useless things and perform useless tasks to please the world.

Success, even in a useless task – and much of the academic learning often is, or at least appears as such – is addictive in proportion to the size of an inferiority complex known now as poor self-image. And poor self-image is undoubtedly the basic component of modern neuroses developed in the pursuit of the 'jet-set'; the pursuit of academic degree is, of course, a major part of this vogue.

An attempt to restore the lost competence of young people who fall into a state of helplessness should aim at moderating their temperamental or habitual acquisitions, but it is not an easy task. I find that the process of untying their emotional knots, which form a part of their style of life and learning, is easiest when an approach is made from the bases of their most meaningful experiences of learning in school. Keeping to the scheme of examining and of discussing the idiosyncrasies of learning difficulties helps the client to recognize which of his learning (self-teaching) routines and procedures helped him at school and where his satisfactions lay. From this he is soon able to spot the gap in such experiences in the tuition milieux at university.

The most obvious shortcoming of university tuition is the lack of feedback from the teaching situation. This vital element of efficient learning is noticed by most students – not only by those susceptible to academic disenchantment; over 70 per cent of the Birmingham random sample students complained that they were not satisfied with the assessment of their work in the first year of studies (Wankowski and Cox, 1973).

There can be little doubt that much of this profile of students at risk would also fit very neatly into the framework of factors comprising Eysenck's typology of emotional instability, where low self-esteem, unhappiness, anxiety, obsessiveness, lack of autonomy and guilt can be easily recognized as underlying the attitudes of a great many 'academically weak' students. Excessive extraversion, with its components of activity, sociability, risk taking, impulsiveness, expressiveness, lack of reflection and lack of responsibility also has its share in the undercurrents of these attitudes (Eysenck and Wilson, 1976). In fact the most succinct description of people who are likely to be successful, or to have few difficulties in their passage through the neat and narrow strictures of academic demands, has come to us from William James. The passage is as follows:

> Some persons are born with an inner constitution which is harmonious and well balanced from the outset. Their impulses are consistent with one another, their will follows without trouble the guidance of their intellect, their passions are not excessive and their lives are little haunted by regrets. But there are others whose existence is little more than a series of zig-zags, as now one tendency and now another gets the upper hand. Their spirit wars with their flesh, they wish for incompatibles, wayward impulses interrupt their most deliberate plans, and their lives are one long drama of repentance and effort to repair misdemeanours and mistakes.
>
> (William James, 1890)

It is the second type who seem to fit my overall findings and impressions from years of counselling, whilst the first type fits those who are usually found amongst the great majority of the most successful students. I think that Eysenck's experimental work on personality – particularly in the area of the temperamental characteristics derived from the orthogonal arrangement of the two personality dimensions of emotionality and extraversion – neatly confirms the acuity of William James's observation.

Having said this, I must, on the one hand, immediately make a correction for the majority of young people who are most likely to form the bulk of the distribution between these polarities; yet, on the other hand, I must add that my studies of the random sample, controlled carefully by two entire intakes of students at Birmingham, strongly suggest that high emotionality – as measured by the psychometric tests – is associated with a high risk of ill-success in academic studies. When, for instance, in the random sample, the emotionality scores of students at risk (those who suffered setbacks and those who did not complete their courses) are scrutinized, 67 per cent of them have above average scores on emotionality; 45 per cent falling into a very high score category. Generally, as I mentioned before, a high level of emotionality appears to be a more powerful influence in shaping the styles of learning and in acquiring attitudes to tuition at school and at university than extraversion. It seems to induce a state of inner dissatisfaction which is perhaps best illustrated by a desire to become a 'changed person' – a trait not prominent amongst stable people.

My observations and 'measurements' of levels of emotionality amongst students coming for help in educational counselling also confirm my overall research findings, as seven out of every ten students tend to have higher than average emotionality scores.

The personality data for these studies were obtained from students who completed Eysenck's Personality Inventory when they took part in the surveys of the cohorts of all freshers, or when they were involved in other investigations as part of the control exercises for the random sample enquiries, prior to coming for help to the Educational Counselling Unit. Normally, personality tests were *never* used by me in connection with my counselling work, as I consider this practice as being harmful and unnecessarily disturbing to the progress of pedagogic and counselling assistance. Personality tests, used in short-term encounters, tend to introduce an element of distrust. The student suspects that the helper (the counsellor) is looking for information which the student does not wish, or is unable, to communicate.

Being, however, very familiar with these tests, which I used for over two decades as practical teaching aids in my courses on 'Individual differences in teaching and learning', I found it helpful to employ personality paradigms in my counselling work. The tests were taken with a battery of other psychometric instruments by more than one hundred students in each academic session. They were marked, analysed and discussed as part of the course work in lectures, tutorials and seminars, as well as in individual supervisions of numerous research projects, essays and dissertations. My claim of familiarity with the EPI scales can also be supported by the fact that I have used these personality tests in most of my researches involving over 13,000 individual students. I have used this knowledge sparingly but advisedly in my daily psychological and pedagogical practice.

Making a note of my impression of every student who showed pronounced traits[1] of very high or very low emotionality and extraversion helped me considerably in my thinking about their predicaments and in assisting them in developing their own styles of self-teaching. I began this routine in the late seventies and have, by 1986, collected data on 508 students who came to see me. The results of this exercise were as follows: 353 students of both sexes (69.5 per cent) had been placed as tending to be high on emotionality and 155 (30.5 per cent) as tending to be low; 429 students (84.5 per cent) were placed as tending to be highly extraverted and 79 (15.5 per cent) as tending to be introverted. Although these data, coming from my observation of each student in counselling encounters, cannot, strictly speaking, be as objective in the same sense as ones obtained from the well standardized inventory taken by the cohorts of freshers, yet the results from the formal testing, and from my subjective assessments, are mutually supportive.

The 'quadrangle analyses' of these data in four clusters of temperamental dispositions has also shown strong similarity with the trends obtained from my other studies. The largest cluster obtained in the 'emotional-extraverted' quadrant comprised 287 students (56.5 per cent) whilst the smallest in the 'stable-introverted' one comprised only 13 students (2.5 per cent). The remaining two clusters, the 'emotional-introverted' and the 'stable-extraverted' comprised 63 students (13.0 per cent) and 142 students (28.0 per cent) respectively.

This distribution is again similar to the trends emerging from my other studies. A large proportion of students who experienced difficulties in adapting advantageously to new milieux of tuition showed very clear tendencies to strong mood alteration (Eysenck, 1970). They tended to be disorganized and undependable, yet easily disciplined by their own effort or by others; to be dependent on rules and obsessively tidy, yet impulsive and compulsively restless; to be changeable, yet obstinately persistent; to be lovable and aggressive, dominant and submissive – a real hotch-potch of swings towards extremes of extravagance and parsimony. Altogether a different sort of people whom I came to regard as the changers of the world, whom it would be well worthwhile to study, if only for the purpose of understanding how they learn to function competently in one formal educational set-up and to malfunction in another. And, consequently, how to help them, should they require such a help, in making their way through education with less stress and upheavals for themselves and others. That such a

Figure 9.1 Organization of correlations between selected traits
W. D. Furneaux, from sources reported in Eysenck (1970).

Table 9.1   Number and percentage of male and female students from the 1965/6 and 1966/7 cohorts of freshers who attended for educational counselling, categorized into four groups of temperamental disposition*

		Extraversion		
		Low n %	High n %	Totals n %
	High	44 (36.7)	34 (28.3)	78 (65.0)
Emotionality				
	Low	21 (17.5)	21 (17.5)	42 (35.0)
	Totals	65 (54.2)	55 (45.8)	120 (100.0)

*These students were tested formally in their first week at university, as members of the two cohorts of yearly intakes numbering 3,020 students. Division into four quadrants with reference to the mean scores on Emotionality or Extraversion of the total group of 3,020 students.

help could easily be incorporated in the ordinary pedagogic practice by most teachers I have no doubt. But of this later, in Chapter 11.

Meanwhile, in order to sharpen the picture of the trends described above let us look at Tables 9.1 and 9.2. (For the more clear and succinct summary of the four temperamental dispositions see Fig. 9.1, a chart of correlation between selected traits of emotionality and extraversion.)

We must, however, beware of inferring that emotional lability, seen as anxiety, is a largely maladaptive feature in academic education, for it has very precious advantages. If it is considered as an outcome of greater lability of the nervous system, it must be regarded as a most necessary factor in initiating and in maintaining the exploratory activities which should clearly be beneficial to academic work. Emotionally highly labile subjects are known to be poor habituators to repeated stimuli, but superior to emotionally stable people with

Table 9.2   Number and percentage of male and female students attending for educational counselling categorized into four groups of temperamental disposition, as estimated by impressions at the first two interviews*

		Extraversion		
		Low n %	High n %	Totals n %
	High	66 (13.0)	287 (56.5)	353 (69.5)
Emotionality				
	Low	13 (2.5)	142 (28.0)	155 (30.5)
	Totals	79 (15.5)	429 (849)	508 (100.0)

*These estimates were based on observing very highly pronounced traits of Emotionality and Extraversion, i.e. at the extreme polarity of these traits. As such they do not include the mid-range trends as contained in the classification in Table 9.1. This is an important distinction to be borne in mind when comparing the two tables.

respect to attending to and processing information (Katkin, 1975). Such a propensity, if translated into the dynamics of socialization in a new tuition situation, would probably prevent many of the emotionally labile individuals from responding positively to the unfamiliar and hence frightening environmental pressures and conditions. It may also, by the same token, push anxious individuals towards initial alienation rather than towards acceptance of the new tuition environment. But it must be remembered that since, figuratively speaking, their frequent 'standing on the sidelines' in the game of life sharpens their perceptual sensitivity, it can help them also to become more discriminating. Also, because alienation is always painful, some ways must be found to compensate for the discomforts of odious tensions arising from this state. The anxious individual may be amenable to sensitive and sympathetic tutorial help, particularly through the medium of some skill where he can prove his competence and raise his self-esteem. I do not wish to expand on the theme of therapeutic procedures designed to encourage the more anxious students to moderate their nervousness through an involvement in academic studies; a separate book should be written on this topic. Perhaps it might be just as well to bear in mind that a tendency to high nervousness as well as to high extraversion may often be a spur in the 'creative malady' of outstanding people (Pickering, 1974). It is, I submit, a mark of excellence in teaching to enable students to convert their desperation into inspiration.

However useful it may appear to have a generalized theory of learning – if only a sketchy model of working theory, or of the still more generalized picture of students' susceptibilities to failure and of their prospects of success – when it comes to meeting a real person in distress in one's room much, if not most, of this theorized and over-intellectualized structure falls apart. And rightly so, if only out of respect for the numerous idiosyncracies left out of any generalized model of behaviour and, if only out of sheer personal honesty in admitting that individuals are never like the streamlined daleks of psychometric regressions. There is also the unavoidable factor of time which urges us towards improvisations in the face of emergencies created by the unnecessary pressures of tight academic work schedules and the histrionics of students relating to such departmental milieux. I am firmly of the opinion that personality tests and other psychometric tools are still far too crude to serve as tools of predictions for the purpose of dealing with problems of individual students. Having, as a consciously planned exercise of some twenty years' duration, cured myself of the phantasy of solving problems of educational selectivity by applied psychometry, I have learnt that good, perceptive teaching can more than compensate for the shortcomings and blunders of selection. But it is undoubtedly through the study and application of psychometry that I have become a more perceptive therapist and teacher. Psychometric models based on theories can be very useful, if held tentatively and flexibly.

Individuals have, as I said before, so many degrees of freedom in their manner of adaptation, in the course of manipulating the world around them to their own purpose, that it is safest to regard everyone as unique. This unique and idiosyncratic pattern of adjustment to the conditions of past and present learning/teaching situations calls for individual treatment when students find themselves in difficulties. They must be given individual help in an atmosphere of relaxed co-operation in reviewing patterns of efficient and inefficient learning. This is particularly important in cases of severe distress when anxiety about personal and academic problems has reached a stage of reactive depression.

But there again, we must not forget that the milieu of tuition and learning in each department and course depend on the equally idiosyncratic fancies, habits, styles of life and 'defence mechanisms' of the tutors. It might be true that each department may tend to have its specific climate created and maintained by the personalities of tutors, who, not unlike students, tend to congregate round specific areas of academic studies. It might even be possible to assess and to describe some 'hues and colours' of such climates, but such an assessment is not likely to render any clearer picture than the usual broad spectra of other sociometric and psychometric surveys of group phenomena (Reid, 1979). The principle of uniqueness in teaching styles and in relationship to other people applies to tutors as well as to students. And while, from departmental studies of students' personality, we can anticipate that the individual student's alienation from tutors and colleagues might follow from the mismatching of temperamental disposition, the interpersonal and social relationships can be played differently in each department, and indeed in each course. Thus, for example, it would be entirely foolish to assume that, following the example of the chemistry department where, in the male population, the students who failed tended to be rather unlike the majority of their colleagues (Batty and Wankowski, 1974) an individual student's difficulty in his physics course may also be associated with his temperament not matching the group image of his colleagues' temperament. In fact the matter is far more complex, since actually the greatest loss of physics students, who, as an overall trend, tend to be of a melancholic disposition, i.e. moody, anxious, rigid, sober, pessimistic, reserved, unsociable and quiet, occurs precisely amongst the more melancholic individuals who tend to fail at the rate of 1:7, as against the overall failure in the department of 1:12, whilst the smallest rate of failure in physics (1:38) occurs amongst the phlegmatics who tend to be passive, careful, thoughtful, peaceful, controlled, reliable, even-tempered and calm.

I call this example of advantageous adaptation by phlegmatic physicists a social psychodynamic of the 'body phlegmatic feeding on the body melancholic'. But it may not be only a phenomenon of advantageous adaptability. The art of 'taking the rough with the smooth', without undue effort or stress, may yet prove to be largely a matter of the biochemistry of neuronal transmission. The Vicar of Bray might have been a person of phlegmatic disposition.

The problems of advantageous adaptation on transition from school to university are very real. In my work as a psychologist dealing daily with students in difficulties, I seldom see stable and introverted students (phlegmatics). They can obviously find their own ways through the idiosyncratic jungle of academic demands, pressures, and expectations, through their knack, so well described by Emmanuel Kant, of 'persevering in their objectives whilst appearing to give way to others' (*Anthropologie*, 1798). This facility for adaptation or the lack of it cannot, to my mind, be disregarded in thinking about who amongst students is likely to maintain, or to lose, learning competence at university.

Tuition and educational counselling as a help to re-establish academic competence

I should perhaps state that no extraordinary skills are needed for 'educational counselling'. I have never yet found a student who could not be successfully assisted in his difficulties by his teachers in his own area of study *provided the teachers were familiar with the basic principles of learning theories and their pedagogical application*. Since, however, a great majority of university teachers are not professionally trained in this respect, it is not surprising that they so often fail in giving effective help to students who have difficulties.

My approaches to this work are basically those of a tutor – my shortcomings are obviously those of not being versatile enough to be knowledgeable in all areas of university studies. A perceptive and professionally well-trained and experienced tutor in each area of study would, no doubt, be a thousand times more effective than any layman like myself – but this is another story which I do not intend to elaborate here.

Assuming that an individual's learning is essentially a process of self tuition as well as that of teaching the tutors to respond to his efforts at self-teaching (to give guidance and to facilitate feedback, if not, occasionally, also some encouragement), I must now proceed to ask myself how my client arrived at the stage of learning competence at school. To answer this question I must try to build up a picture of his self-teaching habits. I do not, however, think that a very comprehensive picture of the aetiology of past competence and failure is necessary at any point of remedial tuition which takes place in counselling.

The whole purpose of the exercise is to enable a student to realize that he did proceed within a certain self-structured framework and that, with a more conscious effort on his part to re-structure his self-tuition at university, his learning competence may be restored.

I find that the best way to re-construct the picture of past competence is to examine the history of schooling. I begin, usually, with the mid-school career of what was happening up to the 'O' level stage. I have found that a recall of the earliest stages of schooling evokes considerable resistance, whilst recall of the sixth form experiences tends to be overdrawn with wishful thinking, fear of admitting a mistaken commitment to an area of study, and undue rationalization. My method of examining the history of schooling is based on an assessment of emotional attitudes to all subjects of study. I encourage the client to relate how he *felt* about his subjects and his experiences of learning and tuition rather than what he *thought* about these matters.

From the examination of the mid-school experiences we move to early schooling, searching for material of early pleasure, and/or evasions, linked with elements of attitudes to teachers, schools, subjects and activities. By now the resistance about 'childish' stages of learning is far less, and good ground is gained for teaching students how to label their emotional concomitants of the more advanced learning (self-tuition) in the sixth form and at the university. It is surprising how resistant some young people are to admit that they disliked certain school activities, subjects or teachers. They seem to assume that it is not 'academic cricket' to admit that they loathe many things connected with academic work.

An examination of the sixth form tuition and learning procedures is a more precise exercise. More detailed analyses of feelings and attitudes are carried out in the counselling dialogue since the areas of studies of the GCE 'A' level subjects bear a more direct relationship to the university course.

Another important point of this exercise is to enable students to perceive more clearly the similarities and differences in the tuition routines in the sixth form and at the university (Taylor, Reid and Holley, 1974). Allegedly, sixth form education is designed to meet the requirements of university tuition. My carefully considered view is that the incompatibilities between the two systems are so enormous as to make the problems of transition more, rather than less, difficult.

The formal scheme of assessment of the emotional attitudes to tuition experiences gives more than a picture of the areas of 'love subjects', phobias and aversions. I try to note the themes of the more pleasurable experiences of learning and feedback from tuition. I note shades of enthusiasms, hesitations, regrets, hopes and exasperations which might have contributed to the habitual style of the individual's learning.

A great deal of material about a client's relationship with his family, siblings and friends becomes available for discussion in examining learning and tuition styles. This is extremely useful information, for many students encountering difficulties in studies suffer from painful confusion, guilt and resentment vis-à-vis their nearest and dearest. Very often their resistances to learning and tuition are either a new tack, or an extension of the 'shadow boxing' with their imaginary, or real, points of pressures from home. Although these factors of interpersonal dynamics of behaviour are, at times, the prime causes of study difficulties, they do not need to be given the first role in the transaction of remedial tuition (counselling). Keeping close to the problems of academic difficulties and helping students to do something about them lets out a great deal of steam from the cauldron of adolescent resentment, self-hatred, anger and fear of commitment. A great deal of pent up aggression and, consequently, guilt can be displayed in discussing matters pertaining to difficulties of revision, or essay writing, or attitudes to departmental regulations, in the *neutral atmosphere of counselling*. Attempts to manipulate the realities of learning and re-structuring self-teaching provide well-defined objects for displacement of frustration. Cooler reappraisal of tuition structures in departments sets useful limits of resistance to the outside world, and strengthens the 'capricious' and often 'fragmented' ego – all within the legitimate and, on the whole, desirable framework of mastering academic work. Very often, I find, a successful restyling of self-tuition restores confidence and moderates the more exaggerated features of the emotionally charged intra-psychic and interpersonal conflicts with family or friends.

To me, discontinuity of academic competence is essentially a syndrome of 'work neurosis'. I try to treat it as such, through the medium of work. Erik Erikson's insight into this problem is worth noting (paraphrasing in brackets is mine):

> In the treatment (educational encounter) with young people ... it is impossible to ignore what they are busy doing or not doing in their Work Life or in their unofficial avocations. Probably the most neglected problem in psycho-analysis (educational psychology) is the problem of Work, in theory as well as in practice. ... Decades of case histories have omitted the work histories (educational histories) of the patients (students) or have treated their occupations as a seemingly irrelevant area of life ...'
>
> (Erikson, 1959)

This contention is shared by Anthony Ryle, who also perceived the need to treat students' difficulties within the framework of their tuition and learning structures.

> up to now ... attention has been focused upon the intra-psychic factors in the student which can interfere with his capacity to survive or to make use of the environment and opportunities provided by the university. Faced with a student in difficulty, however, it is important that one should ask not only what, in the history or personality of this student, has predisposed him to this problem but also what, in the experience offered by the university, has provoked this difficulty or what might have prevented its occurrence. Questions of this sort are relevant when one is thinking about the many students who under-achieve or drop out without the operation of major neurotic factors in their personalities, as well as when one considers those with neurotic dispositions.
>
> (Ryle, 1972)

The main underlying principles of therapeutic procedure in individual counselling of students are very few and very simple. I regard counselling as a process of fostering relationships between two or more people in which the person who feels worthless learns to feel worthwhile. And the worthwhileness is derived usually from mastering some skill. Educational counselling aims at restoring the mastery of learning how to learn to live with oneself and others, as well as of learning how to learn at university.

In order to establish new mastery, the ways of the past competence must be discerned, and the present possibilities of becoming competent must be explored and the future hopes or fears of mastery or helplessness considered. What is happening, what has happened and what may or will happen, are the three questions, or themes, ever present as background to the counselling transaction. The concrete task of regaining the mastery over present work and study difficulties and personal problems serves as the main operational objective, and, with the returning satisfaction of being able to study effectively, to read selectively, to compose and write essays, dissertations, theses and summaries of facts and figures for examination revisions, the mood of the client turns positive in a relatively short time. True, relapses are frequent as all the therapists know only two well, but these usually tend to recur with the most highly anxious individuals. But even with these, when mastery of the work at hand and catching up with the backlog begins to be more firmly established, the anxiety level tends to subside visibly. The student smokes less, drinks less, eats with pleasure, sleeps better, looks healthier and well groomed, behaves less restlessly, reduces the frequency of self-criticism or attacks on others including a decline in the sharp dislike of objects and activities, becomes more tolerant of himself and others, shows a keener sense of humour and above all relaxes his obsessive compulsive interest in extreme views, ideologies and millenarian visions or, on the opposite scale, forgets his lack of interest in anything at all except himself. When the covert cry of 'revenge – my heart bleeds for humanity' turns into overt humanity, the complete mastery of academic tasks and of personal uncertainties also ceases to be an over-riding compulsion. Enjoyment of life, friends and skills smooths the ruffled feathers of despair. But it all takes time! It all takes effort in the 'working through' which, in physiological terms, could be called a process of 'habituation to the unconditional stimulus of fear' – the fear of functional impotence which is mastered through an active exercise of operational potence.

Reflections and provocations: what to do when everyone is different

Scientia non est individuorum – yet, on the human level, it is pursued in a largely idiosyncratic way by every individual in his scientific game of life when, following the working of the brain, an individual

> not only reacts passively to incoming information, but creates *intentions*, forms *plans* and *programmes* of his action, inspects their performance, and *regulates* his behaviour so that it conforms to these plans and programmes; finally, he *verifies* his conscious activity, comparing the effects of his actions with the original intentions and correcting any mistakes he has made.
>
> (Luria, 1973)

Readers will readily recognize that Luria's description of the main functioning of the brain coincides with Kelly's conception of 'man, the scientist' and 'man the therapist'. Kelly's description of his work in the 1930s, as both tutor and therapist, is so very close to my so-called 'therapeutic procedure' that when I read it, in the sixties, I became highly annoyed with myself for having wasted decades of my life in developing a technique for helping incompetent learners which has, most probably, been used, consciously or intuitively, by teachers of all ages.

> One of my tasks in the 1930's was to direct graduate studies leading to the Master's Degree. A typical afternoon might find me talking to a graduate student at one o'clock, doing all those familiar things that thesis directors

have to do – encouraging the student to pin-point the issues, to observe, to become intimate with the problem, to form hypotheses either inductively or deductively, to make some preliminary test runs, to relate data to his predictions, to control his experiments so that he will know what led to what, to generalize cautiously and to revise his thinking in the light of experience.

At two o'clock I might have an appointment with a client. During this interview I would not be taking the role of the scientist but rather helping the distressed person work out some solutions to his life's problems. So what would I do? Why, I would try to get him to pin-point the issues, to observe, to become intimate with the problem, to form hypotheses, to make test runs, to relate outcomes to anticipations, to control his ventures so that he will know what led to what, to generalize cautiously and to revise his dogma in the light of experience . . .

(Kelly, 1963)

Here we must, at long last, part with the pretence of any strictly scientific methods of behaviour modification and turn to the well tried ways of the ordinary humanity of social transactions – to me, still the most potent, efficacious, and pleasant way of learning and being. (Readers with a rigorous scientific bent and seekers of formally structured therapies should, I think, stop reading here.)

The first principle of the so-called 'educational counselling' therapy is *to put the client socially and emotionally at ease.* So what do we do? We receive the student with all the usual trimmings of a pleasant social introduction: a relaxed, pleasant reception, a not too inquisitive social chat, a cup of tea or coffee, in a reasonably furnished room with a comfortable chair, coffee table and an ash tray provided. Clients usually find me working on research papers or preparing material for teaching and tutorial supervision, or reading theses or dissertations etc. – my academic difficulties and frustrations as well as my satisfactions being there to be shared by my clients, if need be. *I regard this 'academic workshop atmosphere' as a very necessary part of 'mutuality' in the learning and teaching transaction on which the counselling technique is based.*

Preliminary pleasantries over, I enquire, what can I do to help? As an educational psychologist I try to see and to understand what the person expects from me. We talk about the client's immediate concerns and difficulties, switching over to any topic of conversation in order to make the interview into an ordinary social point of contact between two strangers, setting out together on the same journey in search of the lost learning competence, or the lost 'self' or 'soul'. Within this framework of sociability and mutual concern we touch on many points concerning learning difficulties, fears of incompetence or failure, fear of loneliness or misunderstanding by others, fear of everything that might be feared! But we also talk of strengths and competencies, hopes and joys of living and acting – we pick up and illuminate more pointed issues of personal or academic difficulties, formulate trial procedures of work and study, compare notes on how they work, set ourselves tasks for the next meeting.

All we really do is *set out to work together*, over a period of a few sessions when the objective of our mutual concern is quite clear: we both understand that the student has a problem and that he/she understands that I have a problem of him/her having a problem of not being able to be successful in studying, in personal happiness, in interpersonal happiness, in transcendental happiness, in happiness to enjoy life, friends, food, holidays, pastimes, flowers, books and fresh air etc. So what do we do? We simply try to find the ways and means of developing a new style of learning how to learn the things which seem impossible to learn, and how to learn to like the things which are the common joy of mankind when the enjoyment has been soured by the sadness, anger and guilt of missing out on these legitimate joys.

This seems to me just about everything that can be said about the individual educational counselling therapy, except that we do take care to check – as indeed we must – if the new styles of learning match the formal rigours of academic expectations set up by departmental tutors. The 'cure' is not a 'cure' – if the student intends to sustain the course – till he feels that he can proceed successfully under his own steam and has the results of his exams and tests to prove it!

If it comes to describing some less usual 'methods of desensitization' from the state of nervous over-stimulation which usually lies at the roots of apathy, hysterical euphoria, or desperate overacting in extramural activities, as an escape from getting on with the job of learning and facing up to the criticism of tutors or examiners, we do resort to helping the student to teach himself the normal range of relaxation techniques: the 'transcendental meditation' (shifting of attention from obnoxious thoughts to a contemplation of a mild, neutral, largely unresolvable problem such as infinity etc.); we use biofeedback and tapes, and books to train people in such techniques; we practise techniques of 'cognitive self-regulation of consciousness' and 'stress inoculation training' (Borkovec, 1976; Meichenbaum, *et al.*, 1975); and we use books on how to study, including Tony Buzan's very helpful *Use Your Head* and *How to Make the Most of Your Mind* (Buzan, 1975, 1977).

But, again and again, during the many years of 'remedial teaching' and 'counselling' students, I find that an occasional lunch in the staff house (the client pays for himself), when the student can meet my friends over coffee and a chat, or chat over a half-pint of beer in the common room bar, or an occasional coffee in the refectory, shortcuts hours spent in 'desensitization therapies' and makes for a more cheerful outlook, uplift of depression and dispersal of morbid gloom. Readers of parsimonious disposition, touchy on purse or time economies need not be alarmed – it happens rarely, 3–5 times in a session. It does take up my lunch hour, but this is freely given as it saves 3–5 hours of formal 'therapeutic' interviews!

I recall two severe cases of examination panic, both last minute referrals, whom I invited to have lunch on two occasions – each a full examination day – with some of my colleagues in the staff house; right inside the 'den of examiners'! Both managed to control their panic, both passed their exams successfully – a letter of thanks from one included a reciprocal invitation to lunch – a perfect example of a pleasant form of social learning through mutuality; the formula is, as I said before, simple enough: 'To get and to be a giver' (Erikson, 1967). Where it obtains in a learning-cum-teaching situation the learning, which is mostly a social transaction, is efficient. Where it does not, through shyness, coldness, vain academic snobbishness or lack of concern, the formal learning is difficult, inefficient and often a hateful preoccupation. It is, of course, quite possible for a learner to establish mutuality (object relation) with a subject of study, craft or professional skill, but it is invariably a substitute for a human relationship which has arisen from some peculiar bent or disposition to form some addictive obsession. Mutuality is the basis of individuality – in learning and in life. Only in death one learns how to die alone, in life one learns how to live together!

Have I provoked the reader enough to say 'this is not counselling you are talking about'? Well, I agree, it is probably far from it, but to me it is nevertheless an activity of mutual assistance in learning a skill. For a student, it is an opportunity to learn how to learn at university; for me it is an opportunity to learn about a student's difficulties so that I can update my pedagogical skill to help another student. But, it can, of course, be considered as mere sociability, formalized by the working hours and an academic setting. Hard work, nevertheless, I reckon; but worth a try.

An example of study assistance procedure

(i) Educational counselling and learning-through-teaching

Interest in learning how to learn is growing rapidly in education, industry and everyday life. Many people are aware that their difficulties in learning might stem from such causes as inhibitions of intellectual function due to emotional blocks; or obsolete habits of thinking and acting which handicap the enjoyment and efficiency of learning. Most people are not consciously aware how or why they learn, and the art of becoming an autonomous learner is as difficult as the art of competent living. There are, however, many techniques that can help in this process. The learning-through-teaching procedure is only one of them.

The efficacy of this procedure became apparent to me in my work as a remedial teacher. I noticed that even the most retarded, shy, apathetic and nervous children became bolder, more enterprising and perceptive when explaining something that they knew well. The obvious step was to find out if they could master new things by trying to learn about them by themselves and by explaining what they had learnt to a sympathetic listener. The method worked well, and I have since used it extensively in my teaching and counselling work, particularly with students who experience severe study difficulties.

In particular, I found that lecturettes delivered by students in counselling sessions helped them in overcoming their reluctance to study what they had hitherto regarded as a difficult subject. It seems that a student preparing a talk for an interested but non-competitive listener can relax his apprehensions and concentrate on clarifying his concepts without fear of appearing ignorant in the face of an expert. The preparation of the lecturette enables the student to sort out his material, to classify it in order of importance, to formulate clear statements, to explain technical points, and to create simple models of presentation which should help the layman to understand such instructions. In preparing the notes for the lecturette, the student is forced to subdivide the subject matter into smaller units, and to plan the steps of the teaching process with great care, in order not to confuse the layman. This exercise gives the student an opportunity of reorganizing his own knowledge of the subject and thereby induces deeper understanding.

Further, the delivery of the lecturette provides the student with an opportunity for an active recapitulation and consolidation of his study material in a relaxed atmosphere of mutual concern. The student can afford to reflect on what he thinks and says without apprehension. It is often in such moments of relaxed reflection that the difficult points of the problems he is trying to understand become clearer. Moreover, in observing the reactions of the listener, the student is provided with instantaneous feedback on the extent to which he is making himself understood, and with a challenge of small 'learning dilemmas' when the listener asks questions and needs further explanations. The student adapts instantaneously his ways of presentation by using simpler language or diagrams, or by giving clearer definitions.

(ii) Theoretical assumptions: mutuality, k.r.s, and 'hot' and 'cold' knowledge

A formal psychological analysis of the learning-through-teaching procedure is likely to reveal principles and assertions drawn from a number of psychotherapies (see Wankowski, 1973a). But for the present purpose it may suffice to remind the reader of some of the most important features of the learning process. The first amongst these is that, since teaching involves at least two people, it must be regarded as a social transaction, and that the most satisfactory social transaction is one of mutuality.

Mutuality may of course exist not only between two people, but also between the individual and an object of his physical or mental operation. The psychoanalytical concept of 'object relation', in which objects or imagery are often substitutes for interpersonal relationships, is a rich and useful area for studying the deeper layers of the learning process. For the present, however, I will focus on interpersonal mutuality.

'To get and to be a giver' is not merely a description of our constant relationship with the world, but also a prescription for healthy, useful and happy living. For in this statement we discern a harmony of needs and fulfilment, both intimately personal and intimately social. The teacher helps the pupil to get the skill or the knowledge; the pupil rewards the teacher by understanding what is being taught, and often improves the teacher's mastery of his own skill or knowledge by questioning, doubting and misunderstanding. The currency of the transaction of mutuality consists primarily of feelings, and these constitute one of the most important factors in learning.

Studies of feelings accompanying learning in general, and unsuccessful learning in particular, have indeed become my chosen path for learning about learning, and I have pursued them through the last three decades. It was from these studies that I conjectured that the social aspect was probably the most important catalyst of the learning process. It was there that, to me, the magic of learning lay. But this magic proved most elusive to analyse and to evaluate; it certainly did not lend itself easily to formal scrutiny even with the aid of an entire library of psychometric tests and procedures, however versatile, however rigorous. Yet I sensed all along that the magic of feeling was the key. I am now convinced of it. You can catch the joy of it in a fleeting glance of the learner's and the teacher's eye, in an almost imperceptible movement of some muscle in the corner of their mouths, the move of a hand, a slight lean towards one another when things go well in teaching and learning, or the sadness of it in the signs of disappointment and detachment when things do not seem to go well.

There can be little doubt that, as teachers and students, we get 'hooked' on the positive feelings exchanged in the process of mutuality in learning, no less than in any other satisfactory social transaction. When we say 'we like learning and teaching', we like just that; and when we say 'we hate it', we hate the breakdown in the transaction of mutuality. The magic then becomes a 'black magic' of aversion, apathy and depression – the negative side of all that is good, humane, compassionate, cheerful and full of hope; it also becomes the 'black magic' of despair, which swamps the minds of many students – from whom, alas, it is so tempting and so easy for tutors to avert the eye and to say, 'if they can't do it, they surely should not be here'. The satisfactions of mutuality in teaching another person are the same as those in learning together, when two people desire to pursue the same skill or knowledge; a fraternity of interest invested in the object of the study.

Yet another vital factor in learning-through-teaching is the availability of the palpable consequences of learning (Peel, 1956). The knowledge of results (the k.r.s) are read by the 'teacher' in the copious array of signals radiated by the 'learner'. This intuitive, almost subliminal, level of communicating understanding or puzzlement is vital to efficient learning. Both the teacher and pupil sense the breakdown of communication as readily and as acutely as they pick up the lines of common understanding. And when the involvement in the learning-through-teaching session is genuine, it is impossible to mislead, or to be misled. I tried it, as an experiment, only to be told by the clients, 'I see you don't seem to have grasped the point . . . let me put it to you in another way'.

Furthermore, the mutuality of learning-through-teaching and of learning together forge the elements of 'cold' knowledge into the new brand of 'hot' knowledge (Kozielecki, 1977). This distinction between the superficial, intellectual perception of the elements of information and the intimately felt inference is very useful in thinking about learning and teaching transactions. The learning theorist refers to it in terms of the relative strength of 'ego-involvement'

(Allport, 1955). My experience of discussing problems of learning with my clients suggests that the terms 'hot' and 'cold' knowledge are more easily understood and acceptable by laymen.

A deep-level assimilation of knowledge is an important concomitant of the learning-through-teaching procedure. An assembly of factual information gleaned from books and lecture notes often presents an incoherent picture. It appears as loosely-knit, superficial, superfluous, or simply boring. The necessity of explaining it to another person helps integration and remembering, if only by virtue of having to make oneself clear. The information must be presented as a coherent package and delivered in the simplest terms. The commitment to an exploration of any topic for the benefit of another person becomes, moreover, a social commitment. The acuity of attention given to the topic at the time of preparation derives from an undertaking to fulfil a social contract which, though friendly and hopefully a mutually shared experience of learning, is nevertheless an obligation. Thence, I think, its edge, which, cuts a deep and not an easily erasable trace in the memory.

It goes, I hope, without saying that the atmosphere needed for reaching the deeper levels of understanding must, with a hitherto unsuccessful learner-turned-teacher, be created by a genuinely interested, non-competitive, non-authoritarian teacher, or a friend-turned-student. It should also be obvious that the role of the learner should be played by a person who is less knowledgeable, or genuinely ignorant of the subject taught by the person who acts as a teacher. An unsuccessful, frustrated and incompetent learner is usually in such a state of stress, due to an imaginary intellectual impotence, that anything or anybody presenting a perfect model of success, confidence and mastery is likely to increase the level of his anxiety (Bandura, 1969; Morris *et al.*, 1977). A frustrated learner, fearful and hateful of his own incompetence, can only begin to relax his apprehensions when put at ease in a genuine atmosphere of non-competitiveness. It is his own deep ('hot' knowledge) feeling of being competent when he explains the intricacies of his chosen subject, that helps to break up the vicious circle of his 'learning neurosis'. Anything less genuine than curiosity mixed with ignorance on the part of the counsellor acting as learner tends to delay the client's recovery of his learning prowess.

(iii)   Selection of clients, procedures, and atmosphere

Successful learning is the outcome of a highly idiosyncratic procedure, and learning-through-teaching cannot be expected to suit every student who has difficulties in academic work. Most students coming for help do not need and do not wish to try it, since most can evolve their own ways of coping with pressures of work, backlogs of essays etc., through more stereotyped study assistance procedures. Learning-through-teaching requires an agreement to prepare and to deliver two, three or more lecturettes, and economy of time and effort – both the students' and mine – dictates that not too many clients are encouraged to try it, though almost all are told about it and are free to take it up.

Generally, it is the depressed and the disenchanted who are particularly encouraged to try it, especially those whose history of school learning suggests that they were greatly dependent on a supply of feedback (the k.r.s), and approval from parents and teachers or important peers. Depressive states, whatever their nature and aetiology, usually have strong components of social anxieties, and even if the need for social contacts and acceptance is not the main problem, the social context of active learning seems to be beneficial in combating apathy and despair. Sharing the problems of tuition and learning is perhaps the most important factor in reducing anxiety and stress, provided the milieu of the learning-through-teaching session is not too competitive. Care must be taken not to create an atmosphere of undue criticism and of too frequent questioning.

Fostering a genuinely encouraging atmosphere in learning and teaching is a difficult art, particularly with the apathetic and the disenchanted students, and tutors-turned-learners should probably be carefully trained in suitable pedagogic methods. Immaturity in coping with human problems, impatience, and a wish to be a masterful guru or to 'cure' the student of his weakness, must not intrude into the learning-through-teaching sessions. A Freudian warning against the therapist's own complex of 'furor analysandi' is a most apt summary of a faulty approach (Glover, 1955). The counsellor, or a tutor who uses this procedure, should preferably be an amateur in the field of study in which the student has prepared the lecturette. All forms of academic snobbery – the most monstrous annihilator of the joy of learning – as well as authoritarian attitudes and anxiety to restore the student's competence slide naturally into the background when the 'counsellor' or a tutor is ignorant in matters which the student is trying to explain in the simplest terms. Humility, laced with genuine curiosity and gentle questioning when matters are not quite understood, will then win the day in the learning-through-teaching sessions. Only a complete mastery of the teaching session – including mastery of materials and the context of the lecturette – delivered in an atmosphere of mutual concern can help a student to regain the confidence and calm required to straighten his own crooked thinking.

Only a few sessions, usually one to three, are needed for the feeling of confidence to be securely restored, and the 'counsellor' is advised to do a little 'homework' before each session in order to deepen his interest and to show genuine concern. Mutuality of interest and concern must also provide the prevailing theme for linking these sessions together. In my own case I try to preserve these links by setting myself a task for the next meeting: e.g. the student undertakes to prepare a further talk on quantum mechanics, and I undertake to read a chapter on it in Asimov's Guide to Science; or the student prepares a translation in Russian, and I go over the BBC tape of Svidaniye v. Moskvye to brush up my Russian; or a student agrees to prepare a talk on thermodynamics, and I agree to read it up in an elementary physics textbook. Sometimes I participate as a learner in no less than three or four different areas of studies in a day! This is where most of the time and energy go in applying learning-through-teaching.

The method can have many variants. It can take place between pairs of students, or in very small groups of willing participants. The delivery of lecturettes can be shared between two or more students, each one illuminating different aspects of the common problem which tends to present particular difficulty. Students' self-help in organizing such talks and lecturettes, particularly in areas poorly taught by teachers, is another obvious development which could be tried.

A further criterion for selecting students for the learning-through-teaching procedure is their ease or difficulty in communicating with other people. Some students seem to excel in discussions, and to gain insights and understanding through verbal communication. It is in conversation that their thinking is clearest, sharpest and confidently expansive as well as cautiously critical. Others, frequently those in pure sciences, are at their best when reasoning and communicating through numbers, formulae, graphs and tabulations. The verbally fluent ones often suffer from fear of committing themselves to writing, note-making and summarizing; whilst the verbally shy suffer pangs of emotional blockage when they have to explain their work, or to discuss their learning problems. Students who excel in verbal communication often tend to be easily bored and frustrated while learning from reading; they get easily confused and cannot gather up their scraps of knowledge into a meaningful passage of notes or reflections. The word-shy may learn readily from reading, can summarize and make pertinent notes, but may be reluctant to write a plain language essay or a comprehensive laboratory report.

The learning-through-teaching procedure can be very helpful to both these extreme types of disenchanted learners. The euphoric verbalizers must knuckle down to reading relevant literature and notes whilst preparing the lecturette. The main benefit here comes from planning their talk. It seems that by sharpening the outlines of the topic at hand they obtain a clearer picture of what they could not grasp, or where they had gaps in understanding. The word-shy, having meticulously prepared their material, can expand on the topic freely in delivering the lecturette. They visibly enjoy the opportunity of talking about the intricacies of their subject, delight in making themselves explicit, and often readily agree with the truth of the old adage: 'When matters we foreknow, the words easily flow'. Thus the same procedure of helping the distressed and disheartened students to learn how to learn may serve to alleviate a variety of intellectual difficulties and emotional afflictions.

(iv) *Tape-recording as an aid in learning-through-teaching*

Although the learning-through-teaching sessions provide the student-turned-teacher with immediate feedback (k.r.s), it does not provide him with the assurance that what he says is right. The ignorance of the layman, though helpful in creating a genuinely non-competitive atmosphere, creates also an obstacle, by not providing expert confirmation or criticism of the student's understanding. These important features of the learning process can, however, be built into the session by tape-recording the lecturette. The student, playing back the recorded talk in the privacy of his room, can check it with the sources of his information and assess to what extent he is satisfied with his treatment of the topic. Most find that listening to their own talk helps them in discerning their weak points as well as in confirming the strong ones.

Tape recording can also be used to help students suffering from a 'writing block' who are unable to write essays, or lab reports, in spite of working hard in preparing material and data. This is a very common and crippling disability, but like most study difficulties it is 'curable', provided the client is encouraged to get down to practical means of combating procrastination rituals which prolong apathy and fear of commitment to writing. The student is encouraged to talk freely and without too much reflection about the essay or the report he has to do. He can just ramble on about what he has read or had thought about his reading on the subject, what he has not read or thinks he ought to, etc. The taped discussion around the subject of the intended written work is used by the student as a background for the essay. Here again the easing of the tensions of the blocked, petrified mind may be attributed to the catalytic function of mutuality, so essential to creative production. A trace of it can be met in Joseph Conrad's admission to Ford Madox Hueffer: 'It is a fact I work better in your home, in touch with your sympathy' (Meyer, 1967).

(v) Conclusions

All knowledge and all skills are meaningful only as part of the mastery of living. They take root and grow, as it were, in three phases, distinct to a discerning eye and yet occurring almost simultaneously: perception through the senses, internalization through neurological activity, and assimilation through externalization in action. If these phases do not for some reason occur, the knowledge may be eschewed and the skill atrophied. Ineffective, unimaginative and passive attempts at learning – particularly academic learning which appears, for the most part, alien to everything that is overtly useful, applicable and actively enjoyed – must lead to boredom and frustration. All teaching of a similarly ineffective and boring nature must contribute to further alienation from studies. Learning-through-teaching ensures that all these essential phases occur, and that they occur twice over for every lecturette. They are all present in the active preparation for teaching the topic to a layman, when the model of the intended exposition must be clear and well exercised in the student's mind. They occur again with all the accompanying satisfactions, in a masterful exposition delivered for the benefit of the listener.

But the secret of restored competence lies largely in the feeling of mutuality in the social transaction of learning. Its efficacy may also be regarded as being due to the operation of the principle of 'reciprocal inhibition' that:

> if a response incompatible with anxiety can be made to occur in the presence of anxiety evoking stimuli, it will weaken the bond between these stimuli and the anxiety responses.
>
> (Ban, 1966)

The tutor-turned-student is of course the main factor in producing this 'incompatibility'. Formal psychological theories and principles are often confirmation of common sense (Wankowski, 1979a).

Note

1. Eysenck, H. J. and Wilson, G. (1975). *Know your own personality*. London, Temple Smith.

   A convenient model of these traits, which I had in mind, may be found in a brief and accessible form in Eysenck's and Wilson's book, where the more inclusive trait (type) of Extraversion involves the more specific ones of Activity, Sociability, Risk-taking, Impulsiveness, Expressiveness, Lack of reflection and Lack of responsibility; whilst the more inclusive type of Emotionality involves specific traits of Low Self-esteem, Unhappiness, Anxiety, Obsessiveness, lack of Autonomy, Hypochondriasis and Guilt.

10

Reflections and Operational Prescriptions

Janek Wankowski

Teaching and learning is not a process

I have tried to induce in the reader an impression that in spite of any organized educational treatment or provision, involving groups of people, large or small, there will be found those whose idiosyncratic, negative interpretation of the learning and the teaching situations will suddenly, or gradually, deprive them of the *spark of awareness of inner strength* and induce feelings of disenchantment, boredom, futility, helplessness and an unexpressed anger turned into depression. However skilled, benign and considerate the ways and means of helping people to learn in an assembly or in a group, some individuals, at some time, will not be able to proceed competently. And yet, it does not at all mean that most of them are, have been, or will be incompetent. But when in a formal educational enterprise, such as a university, the pedagogical skill and the considerations are sometimes absent, the attrition amongst many able but disenchanted individuals will increase in an exponential manner.

There is nothing new about this disenchantment. As H. G. Wells, writing about his sojourn at the Normal School of Science at London University from 1884 to 1887, has said:

> No one bothered to find out why I had got loose in my setting, much less did anyone attempt to readjust me in any way. I was not the only struggler from the steady pursuit of the ordained course. The schools, I repeat, ignored pedagogics and had no shadow of a general directive control . . .
>
> (Wells, 1966)

For neither learning nor teaching is a process, nor can they ever be fully controlled. They are, if they can ever be defined, a continuous social interaction between individuals, who are themselves a product of interactions with the world around them. Even a relationship with an object, a problem, or a subject of study has a strong element of interaction. The objects, the problems or the subjects of study act on the learner, or an observer, no less than the living beings. *Whatever we do, the doing does something to us!* This is an inescapable, instantaneous relationship. Sentient beings are affected by this reciprocity always – even plants are known to respond to animals and people.

It is not even an interaction; that would be far too simple to even attempt to describe learning and teaching as such. It is an inter-reaction. For apart from interacting with the outside world, the individual interacts within himself as to how he interacted in the past, interacts now and hopes or fears to interact in the future. Hence, to think of students learning and teachers teaching as a process is to simplify the nature of learning to an analogy of a factory, or a means of transport, or communication, in terms of input and output within the circum-scribed frameworks of man-made devices.

Neither can the nature of learning and teaching be regarded as an acquisition or a dissemination of intellectual competence. This obsolete way of understand-ing learning and teaching must also be regarded as largely superficial. As Oleron (1978) writing on the development of cognitive skills pertinently remarks, it is impossible to separate intellectual competence from psychological or social competence, which he defines as relations concerning other indi-viduals. He also argues that 'psychological competence is not limited only to relations with others. It also includes reference to oneself (self-consciousness, behaviour adapted to this consciousness, and self-management)'. Oleron's common sense remarks that 'a large part of the life of the child (and of the adult) is made up of contact with other people in the framework of social organisations, institutions, and habits', and that 'life is determined by motivation, reactions, attitudes, emotions, enthusiasms and rejections, all of which are linked to the origins of actions and reactions and are not easily understood via the theories of either physics or logic', should warn academic teachers that with such a plethora of influences no single way, or provision, including even the training or hiring of the most skilled person to cope with learning difficulties, will ever solve the problems of a great number of students. Individual students must be consciously prepared to help themselves when they stumble in their studies or, at least, to know where to go for help.

Learning and tuition, inter-reaction and 'stress innoculation training' through challenge and protection

An acquisition of knowledge or skill, or of competence to cope generally, or specifically, is not an input-output process either; even if it tends conveniently to be so regarded by scores of teachers in schools, by a far greater number of teachers in academies, and by the swelling cadres of educational administrators.

Effective and competent coping in life is the perennial goal of learning and teaching or, as I like to regard it, of teaching oneself to cope through inter-reaction with others. And the most important part of teaching oneself, or others, how to cope is to experience what it feels like when one seems unable to cope and to teach oneself, so to speak, *how to cope with failure to cope.*

And that is where the skill of the person who helps others to teach themselves this very lesson comes in. For skilled teaching and self-teaching is but a careful 'regulation of the learning dilemmas', which must provide conditions for the encouragement of challenge and for the assurance of security. The signs of success and the knowledge of results must be copiously provided, and so must the experiences of non-success, as well as an occasional experience of the lack of knowledge of results. As Sandven (1979) summarizing his important work on self-realization, says:

> the environmental world should be shaped not only to give the necessary protection to foster the feeling of security, but at the same time also provide the necessary amount of challenge in order to allow the developing individual an opportunity to reach forward, to make efforts to do or manage something which goes beyond what has already been mastered . . . When talking about conditions for self-realization . . . the concept of protection and the concept of challenge may be regarded as of fundamental importance.

Recent trends in therapeutic procedures in neurosis and depression have at last tumbled to it and regard it as the so-called 'cognitive regulation of conscious-ness' (Schwartz and Shapiro, 1976) and 'stress inoculation training' (Meichen-baum, Turk and Burstein, 1975). This is again a rediscovery of a very powerful means of self-control through experiences of the bearable discomforts of stresses. The principle is, of course, as old as the hills. The poets, sensitive to the numberless extensions of the struggling human spirit, captured it centuries ago. Shakespeare's line, 'Sweet are the uses of adversity', in *As You Like It* can be regarded as an apt summary of whole volumes of the most up-to-date counselling and 'self-management' training therapies (Waitley, 1987; Davies, 1986).

And how can training to endure the hardships of bouts of incompetence be best arranged if not in experiencing these stresses in the company of others who can, such is the nature of sociability, help to shock-absorb doubts, loss of hope and helplessness? Since from the beginning of life coping is learnt in a social context, coping in schools and at universities is an essential part of the pedagogical interaction. Its nature cannot, of course, be a replica of the earliest coping lessons in the family, but the elements of mutual support must be there, if only as contractual arrangements in order to create a matrix for the fulfilment of the principles of security and challenge.

The supreme importance of the two conditions of *security* and *challenge* which make for effective learning cannot be overestimated. All success in learning to live fully and courageously depends on these two being in a state of 'relative equilibrium' (I say relative, since switching from one to another is, I think, the spring of its creative dynamic; the most important feature seldom appreciated by teachers at all levels of education). New learners must experience a secure base of protection from which to venture forth to seek and to master new things and new opportunities. Universities themselves should be the embodiments of these principles being, as institutions, set aside and funded for exploration and expansion of the frontiers of knowledge. Whether the senior members (the tutors) can provide this, or are fulfilling this function by providing conceptual and pedagogical frameworks of security and by encouraging exploration, is another matter. Many, to my mind, make use of these vital elements of 'knowledge making' (Wankowski, 1980) primarily for the advancement of their own careers as experts in their fields of research. The junior members (the students) do not consciously set out to create for themselves a secure base of exploration, though most who are successful stumble on it intuitively, by trial and error.

Certainly all remedial, rehabilitative and corrective training schemes depend for their success on these two conditions being present and a glance at the most popular schemes for improving students' study skills might be an appropriate illustration of this fact.

Let us then have a brief look at the collection of writings about ways of assisting students in learning how to learn.

Study methods, techniques, and sociability

I propose briefly to review the main points of the useful publication of the Society for Research into Higher Education (Hills, ed., 1979) and of the Symposium of Practical Approaches in Higher Education published in the British Journal of Guidance and Counselling (1979).

All I am concerned with in reviewing these publications is to point out that, in both these compilations, the methods, or the ways of helping the student to cope with his studies are clearly based on the principle of mutuality and as such depend entirely on the provision of social interaction in learning/teaching transactions which creates a climate of security and challenge.

Thus, in the first monograph there are, apart from valuable chapters discussing a variety of important topics about study courses and counselling, eight separate descriptions of methods in study assistance. Seven of them state very clearly that the mainsprings of building up coping skills in study are those of mutuality of social transactions. And so Hills and Potter ('Group Counselling and Study Skills', 1979) explicitly state that help in adjusting to new circumstances implies an attitude change which comes about mainly through increasing elements of participation and mutual group support. Da Costa ('Profile of a Study Skill Workshop', 1979) says that the main transaction in the workshop is learning from one another and picking up skills from the experiences of academic staff participating in the workshop. The object of the workshop is to bring about a change of attitude to the problems of study through the use of social encounter; as if proclaiming: *we are all in the same boat now, or were when we learnt how to teach our subjects, let us now help each other.* Chibnall ('The Sussex Experience', 1979) states that the main vehicle of help is the fact that students became involved in what is being discussed about study methods amongst themselves. He describes the so-called 'snowball' effect of interacting first with a neighbour, then with the small group, then with a tutor. The method, to me, relies mainly on graded experience of familiarity with the problem examined and discussed in a social situation which serves as a source of security and thus of encouragement towards independent learning how to learn. It is again essentially a social learning situation. Elton's *et al.* ('Study Counselling at the University of Surrey', 1979) method depends on a one-to-one help which, they say, produces benefit from the interaction with an experienced learner/teacher. It is, of course, an example par excellence of the old craft apprenticeship; the most effective, though often maligned method of inducing learning competence, mainly through imitation of a skilled model. Here mutuality and contractual effects are both highly operative. Goldman ('A Contract for Academic Improvement', 1979) gives another variant of the one-to-one transaction of working through the problem. James ('Counselling the Mature Student', 1979) describes the way the counsellor and the student work together through the problem, where both teacher and student have to grow into new roles.

As for my own contribution in the same book, it obviously fits the general pattern of the theme of mutuality which, I hope, showed through my discussion in previous chapters. Nelson-Jones ('Counselling Approaches to Increasing Students' Learning Competence', 1979) summarizes his reviews of counselling by saying that he views the role of counsellor as facilitating learning competence in his institution through co-operation with his academic colleagues. This is, of course, the core of any attempt to develop a study assistance service at any university by creating an atmosphere of trust and mutuality in the interpersonal transaction between subject teachers and study assistance advisers.

The symposium on study skills published in the British Journal of Guidance and Counselling (1979) is also quite explicit about approaches to the problems of study assistance work based on the principle of social inter-reactions. Thorne (1979), introducing the individual contributions, concludes the review by saying:

> It is perhaps not over-fanciful to predict that as institutions become increasingly concerned to offer opportunities for acquiring learning skills, they will inevitably become characterised by a growing recognition that learning is more likely to take place where individuals listen to each other and value each other's co-operation in the *shared pursuit of knowledge*.

Goldman ('When "Knowing How" is Not Enough', 1979) presents two case studies where the co-operation in a 'working through' of students is the key. Both the counsellor and the student work out a solution for which neither of them have, to begin with, an obvious prescription. Hari-Augstein's *et al.* ('Learning Conversations: A Person-Centred Approach to Self-Organized Learning', 1979) technique is clearly a re-application of the old Socratic method of dialogue, with the aid of the technology of a recording as feedback to the learner. It is essentially learning, through a tutorial conversation, how to organize self-tuition. They are again exercises in gaining experience of interacting with the individual's chosen world. Gibbs's and Northedge's 'Helping Students to Understand Their Own Study Methods', 1979 is again essentially a social interaction technique where 'students can easily question the purpose of their own studying and compare their ways of tackling tasks with their colleagues'. Gibbs and Northedge, both shrewd and perceptive young educationalists, see their design of study skill interventions as fitting within the obvious fact 'that learning to learn is a continuous life-long process'. And how right they are, for helping people to teach themselves how to learn one thing must always evoke the 'spin-off' effect of a transfer of training: 'If I can teach myself to learn one thing, surely I can teach myself another'. A well performed task always provides a powerful stimulus of joy and self-satisfaction. Since all, or most, stimuli must obey the law of stimulus generalization (the natural endowment of the working brain), the pleasure of coping with one task is very likely to contribute to the pleasure of being able to cope with another and thus to learn even more.

Most study assistance techniques, because they are rooted in the sociability of co-operative interaction, fulfil the principle of mutuality which satisfies both the learner and the teacher, not only as two individuals meeting for the purpose of solving a common problem, but also as facilitators of their own and their partner's mastery of learning new and often difficult skills. That is where the addiction of Chaucer's Clerk comes in – poetry again: 'Gladly wolde he lerne, and gladly teche'.

It is my seriously considered opinion that both the excellence of the Oxford and Cambridge tutorial system and their smallest student wastage rate amongst British universities is due mainly to the pedagogical advantages of the social transaction of 'apprenticeship' to the personal tutor, which fulfils the conditions of security and exploration. Neither their special selection procedure, nor the collegiate system, nor even the weight of their tradition of academic 'crack battalions', would contribute as much to the successful graduation of their students should the close tutorial system be abandoned.

The magic of learning competence acquired in these universities is not difficult to discover. All students have to produce essays once a week, or once a fortnight in some colleges, and to read and discuss their efforts with their tutors. The essays are usually well pointed towards examination requirements. The principles of security and challenge, the give and take of mutuality, the knowledge of results (feedback) and the contractual nature of the tutorial relationship all contribute to the effectiveness of tuition and learning. Students in other universities in Britain have to write comparatively fewer essays as their course proceeds: in some courses as few as two or three a year, or at most three a term. The essays are seldom marked or returned quickly, or discussed at length with the tutors. The writing of the essays is not, in the main, considered as directly helping students to learn how to write quickly, cogently and reflectively during the major, sessional examinations. They are not, as at Oxford and Cambridge, the means of training the mind in summarizing and in reflecting on reading and thinking about the subjects of study, neither are they considered as directly relevant exercises towards the mastery of examination techniques. Thus the main principles of effective learning which I have mentioned above are seldom, if ever, fulfilled. These systems of university traditions in teaching create less disenchantment in the former and more disenchantment in the latter institutions. Pertinent research into educational procedures of these two systems would, I am quite convinced, result in a similar inference. The contractual relationship in tuition and learning at Oxbridge cannot fail to result in more competent learning by their students, at least as far as the formal requirements of satisfying these universities' examination systems are concerned. This is because the contract of working for and with a tutor provides security of awareness and hope that things in the end will work. The fact that the learner is able to attribute, at frequent intervals, some measure of certainty about the outcome of his learning endeavours creates positive feelings of safety which, reducing the tension of helplessness and fear, contributes to a more relaxed intellectual functioning. And the palpability of the attained objective, such as, say, the completion of an essay, a laboratory report or a seminar paper, automatically evokes *the feeling of approval and recognition from another human being*, the teacher or the co-learner. It is this latter element of the contractual fulfilment that is, to my mind, most important. It is also, alas, the most elusive and seldom overtly acknowledged value in the social relationship of teaching and learning. Any attempt at assisting students to learn how to learn must be built on this value. It is also here where Raaheim's scheme of helping students links most pertinently with what these writers and I have to say. The contractual transaction of the teaching/learning inter-relationship is the basis of competent learning together; not only as teachers of learners but as learning from those who come to be taught. The mutuality of trust, that fruitful efforts and clear signs of guidance will be worked out in the course of tuition, is the key to this interpersonal transaction. All that is necessary is just a dose of mutual trust, so that the novice can rely on the older partner to see him through the greatest difficulties, and the senior partner will himself benefit by the competence of his junior co-learner. For many students it is just this that makes the difference between success or failure to complete the course: a strong dose of mutual trust which engenders the feeling of a worthwhile inter-relationship.

Here I might just as well mention that throughout writing my contributions to this book I have been very keenly aware that the elements of sociability in co-operative contractual learning and tuition are not yet at all well understood and appreciated by teachers at all levels of education, though pertinent and promising research in this line is already in progress (Sandven, 1979a). There are, to me, many obvious reasons for the reluctance to ponder on the benefits of the transactional nature of pedagogic activity, but to describe them in detail would require too much space. It is, however, often from the perceptive people, who are outside the formal educational setting, that the most valuable insights about the practical, common sense nature of education come. An example of such a gem of insight, put most succinctly, came from a journalist, Polly Toynbee (*Guardian*, 1979) who, writing about the Canterbury Cathedral choirboys' school, had this to say:

> But I sensed in those children an astonishing adult pleasure in their work, a kind of fulfilment. What most children's education lacks is the idea that children are of *any use to anyone*. They are, implicitly, expected to accept the

charity handed out to them day after day with gratitude. Teachers and parents are always giving, teaching, ordering with absolute authority. But these children are givers as well as receivers. They have rights, they are valued employees and have a correspondingly adult self-confidence.

Now, if the reader substitutes the word 'students' for the word 'children', Polly Toynbee's insight into the principles of competent learning becomes also a prescription for an effective tuition transaction at any university. All the reader has to do is to ask himself, if he is a university teacher – albeit this is a great deal – if his manner of tuition helps his students to feel that they are also contributing to this transaction.

Conclusion, recommendations and operational prescriptions; when wishful thinking leads to wishful doing

It is quite possible that the variety of themes and schemes touched upon in this collection of chapters will not 'jell', in the reader's mind, into a distinct point of view about matters of teaching and learning in higher education in general, or about matters of helping students how to learn in particular. It is therefore necessary to gather up my views into a more connected unity of thoughts, contentions and operational prescriptions.

I contend, in the first place, that individual differences of children, students and adults are so marked that any unitary scheme of education, or even a variety of schemes, will never provide satisfactory conditions for all students to become competent learners. Flexibility and extensive allowances for individual differences must be built into any educative milieu. This flexibility can be most economically provided by helping students themselves to develop their own individual patterns of effective study. This help should, of course, be a part and a parcel of skilled teaching, both at the level of personal one-to-one tuition transaction and at the level of group or even mass teaching, as in Raaheim's scheme. I define skilled teaching as a facility for organizing people's learning in such ways that they can become competent self-teachers for life.

Unfortunately, I do not hold much hope that universities or institutions of higher education will, for a long time yet, pay more than lip service to the necessity for professional pedagogical training for 'the faculty' which would enhance learning competence of students. Only a widespread fear of some major disaster, such as dire scarcity of energy for maintaining basic technology could make an impact on the traditionally and bureaucratically entrenched attitudes of the great majority of academics and administrators. Monetary rewards for professional training qualifications, awarded for the duration of academic tenure, would of course soon bring about the softening up of the tightly held inference that teacher training is unnecessary for university dons. But this, I am told by many of my colleagues, is a thoroughly unrealistic approach and one which is also not exactly 'academic cricket': in a sense, that, in Britain, financial remuneration for acquiring a professional teaching qualification is, for some reason, considered as beneath the dignity of a university academic. Another administrative variant for loosening up the grip of aversion to training for teaching in the academies would be to make the governmental allocation of finance to faculties and departments, on the bases of the last three years' trends in the *number of graduating students* rather than, as now, according to the *numbers recruited*. But this again, I am told, is a far too drastic prescription.

However, if it is true that universities are now becoming somewhat more sensitive about the training of teachers, as they indeed appear to be in Britain, we can gauge this upsurge of interest in palpable terms of finance spent by them to support professional training. The figures, recently available from the report of the Co-ordinating Committee for the Training of University Teachers (Committee of Vice Chancellors and Principals, 1986), indicate that 'universities spent less than *one twentieth of one per cent* of their grant on staff training'. And if we reflect that teaching is supposed to be a half of the universities' official function and objective – the other half being research – this minuscule provision does not seem to indicate any serious change of heart in matters of professional training of the staff.[1]

So the student must be quite frankly told that he has to find ways to teach himself how to be an effective and competent learner and, since just telling him that would not solve the problem, he must be provided with information where to seek help in these matters.

And it must, of course, be obvious that an effective study assistance service cannot just be a period in the department's timetable, when the student can see some voluntary member of staff to help him. It must be a permanent establishment, manned by a group of pedagogically trained and skilled workers, who would make the problems of study methodology their own professional interest. It might not, in the present climate of academic attitudes and finance, be feasible for such a service to be established in every faculty and the fact must also be recognized that a major advantage of such services derives from their position of neutrality in matters of formal academic assessment.

I do not see any reason why, in Britain, with every university endowed with either a faculty, an institute, or a department of education, a firmly established unit for *the study of the problems of higher education*, and including an efficient study assistance and educational counselling unit and permanent courses for diplomas in teaching in higher education, should not be regarded as a logical possibility. University departments and institutes of education in Britain were established to meet the need for training of teachers for secondary education which was rapidly expanding in the first half of this century. Higher education is expanding now and it is, I think, high time to spend some more money on professional training of teachers for this advanced educational sector.

In the second place, the reader might have conjectured that I have paid much attention to the problems of anxiety and stress as an inhibitor of effective learning. And if, in some places, I suggested that high emotionality, transformed into an obsession with an intellectual activity as a defence mechanism against greater anxiety, might be helpful to some people, I consider this a marginal phenomenon. Generally and with most people, high anxiety is detrimental to balanced and rational thinking. Fear and high nervous tension make us react muscularly rather than intellectually. Speed and a quick 'yes-no' and 'black-white' solutions are most satisfactory when the mind is in an emergency state. Many people may remain in that state for a very long time, for weeks, months and years. With some, it becomes a chronic way of adjustment to the contingencies of life. It is basically immaterial, for the purpose of helping a student to regain learning competence, whether anxiety states come about in response to specific situations, or arise from some genetic proneness, or if they evolve from both (Rozycka, 1979). The fact is that almost any person, in a prolonged state of anxiety, will develop 'reactive depression', when it is absolutely useless to keep telling him or her overtly what he or she should do. People in this state have passed the point of ordinary reasoning and a barrage of reassurance from well-meaning helpers will be of no avail. They must be helped actively to teach themselves and, also in an active way, to loosen up their tight neurotic inferences about themselves, their work, their failure and their helplessness.

It does not matter how a prolonged anxiety or stress is defined, whether as 'incubated anxiety' (Eysenck, 1975), or as 'a state of exhaustion' in Nixon's (1976) scheme of describing human functioning in terms of relationship between arousal and performance. What matters is to recognize what stress does to people who experience prolonged states of helplessness. Nixon's description of the states of functioning is relevant to the point I am making here. Healthy functioning exists 'when arousal enhances performance and the individual feels well' and 'his qualities required for success, namely rapid and flexible thought, originality, vigour, expansion and capacity for sustained effort are abundant'. But then the person reaches a state of exhaustion.

> Increasing the arousal worsens the performance and sets up a vicious circle, because widening the gap between the actual and the intended performance increases the arousal by generating anxiety and insecurity, unrealistic views of the gap are adopted, errors increase and personal relationships deteriorate. Others can see the growth of unhealthy tensions and the symptoms of strain: bad temper, continual grumbling, longer hours worked but less achieved, repeated minor sickness and preoccupations, together with insecurity about health and the future, procrastinations, losing sight of long-term aims in pre-occupations with minor matters, feelings of frustration and persecution by colleagues with complaints of lack of co-operation, technical jargon and catch-phrases replacing original thought.

(Nixon, 1976)

Students in such states of exhaustion often need a specially trained person to help them. And such help is better obtained away from the faculty or department. As Chandler (1978) aptly remarks in her valuable book on counselling: 'the concerned and sympathetic professor can be seen as hypercritical and threatening by students whose guilt about their failure distorts their perception.

Equally, those in authority can often fail to perceive that their advice is inappropriate'.

I would, therefore, like to contend that psychological services are also needed within the scheme of study assistance services at university. Educational Psychologists taking up this work should have a sound training in clinical psychology. Such a provision cannot be done 'on the cheap', but the cost is not all that great, and the service could pay for itself out of tuition fees saved by 'rescuing' the disorientated students.[2]

Virtue is practice: research-cum-study assistance and university teachers' training service

In my third point I should like to say a few words about the nature and the function of a new service within the institutions of higher education which would create and combine those conditions of educational innovations which are now, for a variety of reasons, impossible to include in the formal structures of faculties and departments.

Let us, first of all, look at the objectives, the nature and the function of such an extra-disciplinary service. Though let us remember that, as I said before, it fits only too well into the already existing and well developed field of educational studies, with almost every university in Britain having an established faculty, institute or a department of education. So what I am proposing here is nothing more than just another branch of this field of academic discipline which grew out of the sheer necessity, early in this century, of training school teachers, mainly for the secondary education sector. Now, with the continuing expansion of higher education, it is time, I think, to extend pedagogical studies of this important tertiary stage in a similar manner. There are, of course, already some centres of study of higher education in Britain, Lancaster, Bradford and London being the foremost examples. There are also the well known projects of such studies in many countries in Europe. The invaluable work of the European Association for Research and Development in Higher Education, as reflected in the publications of their Congress proceedings of 1974, 1976 and 1980, gives the most clear indication of the widespread need to examine the problems relating to higher education.

What I now plead for is really the creation of a standard provision for research-cum-study and teaching assistance services in every university, polytechnic and other establishments of higher education. I have in mind a service, which would attract committed and experienced educationalists from a variety of academic disciplines who would be interested, not only in the study of the nature of teaching and learning in their own academic disciplines, but in an extension of these interests into a more comprehensive conception of pedagogics in higher education. Briefly, such services would be engaged actively in four areas of educational provision which are now sadly lacking in most establishments of higher education.

The four areas of operations are as follows:

(a) systematic research into problems of attrition and wastage of students;
(b) study assistance and educational counselling service for students;
(c) assistance in problems of tuition and an advisory service on students' problems for teachers;
(d) permanent institution of courses leading to advanced diplomas for teachers in higher education.

I have reflected at length in the first edition of this book, and will not repeat it here, on the need for all these four aspects of the study assistance services to be co-ordinated into one integrated unit.

All I should like to say is that such a service would become a natural resource and a base for long-range, ongoing pedagogical research, where the individual and the group phenomena of teaching and learning could be observed and evaluated through the discipline of rigorous and systematic enquiries.

The most wasteful feature of the contemporary trends in the research and practice of education is the gap between learning theories and experimental findings and their application at the level of tuition and learning. This gap is widest at the level of higher education as pertinently argued by Elton and Laurillard (1979) and Lambourn (1979). Lambourn contends that teachers in higher education eschew any effort to imagine how the findings of educational research may be utilized for the improvement of their tuition skills or for improving their students' competence in learning. There are, of course, many reasons for this resistance but the point made by Lambourn is, I think, valid when he says that teachers tend to disregard the research because it is not their own and therefore not immediately relevant and not arising from their daily work of struggling with (or of enjoying) their teaching. My contention is that this understandable syndrome of professional alienation cannot be prevented except by encouraging teachers to research into their methods of tuition and learning as they teach and to evaluate them. The service I am proposing would be well placed to encourage this kind of development. It would provide a permanent point of reference and activity whereby the experimental research in the higher education pedagogics would thus become an integral part of applied tuition and learning methodologies. It should grow healthily and pertinently from the demands for pragmatic solutions and lead to theories and models of thinking about the nature and function of higher education itself. The components of challenge met squarely every day and throughout every university session would enhance a greater integration of knowledge of why and how people learn or cannot learn.

The results of research, *particularly if the research can be carried out jointly with tutors in departments*, would provide a basis of security of the professional know-how for further exploration of what happens when certain procedures of skilled teaching are applied or modified in a given course, with a given group of students or with certain individuals. *By encouraging teachers in the departments to take part, or to conduct their own experiments in tuition and learning methods and procedures, we can expect greater involvement in the pedagogical side of their work.* It might even be that a larger number of tutors in the university will, for example, realize early in their teaching career that one of the very simple but effective ways of encouraging students to enhance their competence in learning is to mark their essays constructively and to discuss them as soon as possible after submission, rather than after one month, when the student, who has by then written another three essays, has forgotten what his first essay was all about.

It is surprising how an act of asking yourself a very simple question about your own tuition procedure and following it up with a simple research exercise can, on analyzing the results, bring about a sobering inference that what one has assumed to be an effective method proves to be no better than any other or perhaps even worse. It is from such experiences that improvements in ped-agogical skill are evolved. And the advisory service for teachers, combined with rigorous and enterprising research in tuition and learning methodology, should become a centre for conducting and encouraging such research.

The proposals I have made above are only an extension of my continued work in all those four areas over the years of my service in education. But mine was only a microcosm of experience growing slowly, from a need to cope with daily challenges, into a spark of positive awareness and thus into a conviction that it is possible to teach oneself what can be done to enhance other people's competence in learning. This conviction can, I think, be expanded into a more enterprising and more effective help for students.

Notes

1. The case for serious efforts in pedagogical training of university teachers has not been much advanced in the late eighties, and probably, to my knowledge, not even now. The most important recommendations in this document produced by the Committee of Vice Chancellors and Principals, issued after nearly twenty years of deliberation, ends with an invocation to the Senior Officers and Senior Staff of departments to demonstrate their interest in these matters.

    The recommended period of time over a three-year cycle which is regarded as sufficient for professional training of the university teacher is as follows:
    '15 days for a newly appointed lecturer,
    9 days for experienced staff,
    7 days for the heads of departments'.
    One cannot help but wonder which other trade or profession would consider these few days of training as sufficient for 40 years of professional practice?
    Source: Committee of Vice Chancellors and Principals (1986). *Academic Staff Training: Code of Practice for Consideration and Comments by the Universities*. CVCP, 29 Tavistock Square, London WC1H 9EZ. April 1986.

2. This point has been developed in Chapter IX of the first edition of this book: Raaheim, K. and Wankowski, J. A. (1981) and in the first evaluation report on my work as a study assistance tutor: Wankowski, J. A. (1983). A replication of this study has been carried out in 1988 and reported in: Wankowski, J. A. (1990).

11

Increasing Students' Power for Self-teaching

Janek Wankowski

The five models of thinking about teaching and learning

The aim of this book is to show teachers in Higher Education some ways and means of enhancing student learning, based both on research and on practical experiences. The operative words are quite explicitly on demonstration and exposition. Since, however, the aim of the book emphasizes research as part of the basis of pedagogical procedures it might be worthwhile to mention that the material for the ideas presented here has been culled from my and my colleagues' formal researches and investigations comprising analyses of data from over 13,000 individual students and from personal one-to-one study assistance work with over 1,700 students who came to me for help.[1]

I must now acquaint the reader with the scope of my assumptions about human learning and teaching and with the consequences of these assumptions when applied in my pedagogical practice. Here I must say frankly that in formulating and accepting these assumptions I have adopted both the points of view and the consequences of two models of thinking. The first, as I said before, is the model of the 'Man the Scientist' of Kelly (e.g. 1955), and the second the model of deductive thinking held by Popper (e.g. 1986).

The key to Popper's view, to put it at its simplest, is that confronted by a percept, or a problem, the mind proceeds to examine it by at first making an assumption of what it may be (a dogma, if you like), and then by a critical examination of it. He goes on to say that even this activity of examination and checking is guided 'by the context of expectation. The scientific method of seeking an answer to a problem proceeds by way of *(dogmatic) trial and (critical) error eliminations*, which was the mode of discovery of all organisms from the amoeba to Einstein'. And consequently, to quote Popper more fully:

> We try to impose (our theories) on the world, and we can always stick to them dogmatically . . . even if they are false . . . But although at first we have to stick to our theories – without theories we cannot even begin – we

can, in the course of time, adopt more critical attitudes towards them. We can try to replace them by something better if we have learnt, with their help, where they let us down. Thus there might arise a scientific or critical phase of thinking which is necessarily preceded by an uncritical phase.

(Popper, 1986)

I have made use of this longer quotation for several reasons, the first one that it is, to me, a link with my thoughts about Kelly's work – an individual as self-teacher ('Man the scientist') and the psychology of personal constructs, and also a link with the view of Kjell Raaheim (1974) on intelligence – a propensity of the mind for 'dealing with the partly unfamiliar in terms of the better known past'.

The second reason is that the views of Kelly, Popper and Raaheim have, to my mind, clear links with the contemporary state of the art of thinking about the biological bases of learning and teaching as represented, if only for the purpose described in this book, by Luria and Hart; Luria's (1973) view that the brain/mind always works towards an intention, and Hart's (1983) that it conducts its way of processing its contents by relatively distinct programmes sets (prosters) – an

> organizational device that enables humans to rapidly categorize down the patterns as they are detected, so they can be identified quickly.

Hart's conceptions of 'biasing' that affects choices from prosters (below conscious level) are also of great help in remedial teaching and learning which must facilitate a shift of the 'biases', or the development of some new ones, which might enable a person to change from the unadaptive 'biases' to the adaptive ones in decision-making and problem-solving.

I can select a few loosely knit working models from my equally loosely knit repertoire of assumptions and procedures which I found useful in my work as a teacher and a study assistance tutor. Here I have selected a group of five with the following headings:

(a) Individual as self-teacher;
(b) the master-apprentice model of learning and teaching;
(c) the brain-compatible theory of learning;
(d) two standpoints for approaching learning and teaching: the didactic stance and the co-operative-exploratory stance;
(e) a model for 'remedial action' when things go wrong with learning and teaching.

On closer examination it can, I think, be quite easy to reflect that each of these models compels one to an instant inference, and that all of them are closely interdependent when reflected upon in the light of a theory from which they arise and of a practice to which they point; practice, of course, being more important than theory for the purpose of this exposition.

(a) Individual as self-teacher

Thus, firstly, an assumption and the model of an individual as self-teacher puts the teacher squarely into the role of *a proposer and organizer of his student's self-teaching* in the first place, and as the necessary model of a skilled master of academic, or of any other craftsmanship, in the second.

(b) The master-apprentice model

Secondly, assumptions about the master-apprentice model of learning and teaching, which is most obviously linked with the reflection about the previous model, begs an immediate question of how often they work together to the same purpose of creating more palpable products or results of their craftsmanship; (In our case we must, I suppose, think of an 'academic craftsmanship'). And how often, or how readily, can the apprentice see his master (teacher) actually working in his craft, in order to fulfil his role as a good model of 'academic craftsmanship'? If the answer is very seldom, or never, as it is most often the case in schools and in the universities, then the model is, of course, useless. Well, not quite. There are many ways to go around it, which leads us to some reflections on the third model: the brain-compatible theory of learning and teaching.

(c) The brain-compatible theory of learning model

Again, as in the case of models one and two, this third model is also linked intimately with the first two. For, as far as we know anything about the brain, it actually works according to these models or, at least, according to some principles which are like them. The brain is, no doubt, a self-teaching machine, for it has, for millions of years, taught itself how to survive and to master the world around itself, and even how to employ teachers to help it to teach itself. In this sense, and to that extent, it is both the *master* i.e. the proposer and the model of learning something and the *apprentice* of itself and to itself, both of them wanting to learn, or having to learn something out of sheer necessity – which is often both the case and the predicament of human learning; necessity being the most effective mother of invention.

(d) The didactic and the co-operative-exploratory model

Touching upon the aspect of willingness or unwillingness to learn (and often to teach) we come to the fourth of my assumptions and models of learning and teaching; the two basic standpoints of approach:

(i)   The 'Didactic stance', subsumed by the statement: 'This is what you have to learn!' and

(ii) the 'co-operative-exploratory stance': 'Let's see what we can learn from this'.

Here we are beginning to run into some problems, for both the master and the apprentice – irrespective of whether they are seen as two separate persons, or as two aspects of the working brain – begin to have their habitual, or their 'wishful', or their 'wilful' tendencies; the brain, just as much as individuals, being susceptible almost permanently to ambiguities which are only sometimes resolved into a harmonious co-existence. But, in spite of its difficulties, it is, I think, a useful and workable model, well worth reflecting upon.

There can be no doubt whatever that the 'Didactic' approach to teaching subsumed by the statement: 'This is what you have to learn', is most effective for the purpose of passing on information or knowledge, since learning by imitation is most economical, as far as the expenditure of energy is concerned; acquisition of language being the most perfect and powerful example. Willing learners, or even unwilling ones in some circumstances, are only too ready to be told what they have to do in order to get something they want, or to achieve, in their life. Teachers, as retailers of ready-made knowledge, can be very effective in using this approach, and students of such teachers become themselves, only too easily, the uncritical, willing buyers of that knowledge. With certain types of person who are 'educationally tractable', it is very effective, acceptable and even welcome. The knack of helping such people to teach themselves whatever they want, or must do, is very easy to acquire. All you have to do is to help them to turn themselves into 'didactic teachers' for as long as it may suit their purpose. There are many ways of doing this, particularly via the 'learning through teaching' mode of study which I have already described and to which I will return later.

With other types of people who may not have developed their skills of advantageous adaptation by the knack of 'stooping to conquer',[2] but who don't seem to be unduly threatened by some impositions, the didactic approach and procedures are also effective. It is with the reluctant learners, or with people who happen to have become blocked in learning, or who have, as it often happens, developed a 'conditional response of aversion' to learning in general, or to some specific studies, or their components, in particular (as well as in aversions to teachers and some significant figures), the 'co-operative-exploratory' mode of pedagogic procedures is, in my opinion, the most effective and powerful means for self-teaching and knowledge making.

The methods of self-teaching, following the natural consequences of the need for exploration and integration of the field of knowledge, must be effective because they usually generate a sense of the self-developed self-esteem, as well as the esteem of the partners – the co-operating learners, or teachers. It is particularly effective with all kinds of reluctant learners, at all stages of formal and informal education, because it enables such people to switch over from the fearful and defensive 'fight or flight' state of their nervous system towards the more relaxed and hopeful functioning of 'rest-digest' which enhances deliberative processes of dealing with problems. It is through this facility for deliberate coping with learning difficulties that they become competent self-teachers.

Having used this approach in most of my work with reluctant learners and with students who had difficulties in studies, as well as with my students of psychology, I am well satisfied that it works – for me, at least.

(e) The 'remedial action' model

Finally, I would say that any teacher or student, and indeed any scholar, who wishes to help others or themselves *to cope with not coping in learning and self-teaching*, would be well advised to have some ready-made, or at least partly thought-out, ways or procedures to overcome their specific learning difficulties; a system of remedying or correcting their shortcomings in self-teaching and knowledge making. In a moment I will describe one of the ways and means of doing this, but a brief caveat may not be out of place to set the stage.

Any way, or any method, of coping with not coping must, of necessity, include, or involve reduction of strong emotions arising from the defensive-aggressive state of fear, anger, guilt and, very often, of hate. Aversive feelings, in however small doses and however deeply repressed from conscious thoughts, inevitably accompany any kind of failure to solve any kinds of problems at hand, or in the future; and alas, for most people, even those of the past. The most effective way of reducing all such negative feelings is basically by means of an increased dose of 'approbation', before, during and after some learning (self-teaching) task or operation, be it mental or practical. Now, 'approbation' is best translated into the elements which will make the learning of anything pleasant, acceptable and rewarding, both instantly and in the long run. These elements are: Attention, Praise, Encouragement, Correction and Blame which, in turn, evoke the *Positive Primary Affects (feelings)* of Excitement, Enjoyment, Surprise, Competence and Trust, all of them making for success and competence in learning how to deal with the world. Conversely, the prolonged absence of the signs of Approbation will evoke the *Negative Primary Affects* in the form of Anger, Fear, Boredom, Shame and Contempt, which make learning difficult and induce feelings of incompetence and guilt (Tomkins, 1966).

Basically, so it seems to me, the thing is very simple and it can easily be described 'commonsensibly' and 'quantitatively'. Recently I found it most succinctly put by Polgar (1989) whose approach to teaching and learning is that '*The pleasure of the accomplishment must be several times as much as the experience of failure*'. I used this principle, long before reading about Polgar, in one of my ways of helping some pupils and students to teach themselves to observe their most successful ways of self-teaching (studying) and the most unsuccessful ones, by using saucers and a bag of peanuts, and by rewarding them for every pleasant thought about their success, as they proceeded in analysing how they went about their studies. Inevitably, in all such exercises, the saucers of the subjects of study in which they were most successful contained far more peanuts than the unsuccessful ones. Later I found it was easier to use signs of pluses and minuses for this purpose. This training in awareness of what is going on in one's mind when one tries to solve problems paid quick and handsome dividends in the rapid advance in building up students' self-confidence. It was also a good way of training them to spot areas of specific errors and of specific difficulties which were soon regarded not as factors contributing to a sense of failure, but as useful guides to speeding up success. It has never ceased to amaze me how deeply the fear of error – the *'error-terror'* – has been implanted in our civilization and how much havoc this 'terror' has caused in the education of millions upon millions of individuals. Acceptance of errors as positive guides to learning and teaching must be one of the useful attitudes in any method of study, but it becomes most useful and an integral part of the process of self-teaching as knowledge making, or re-making.

The Master-apprentice model of Academic Craftsmanship: a workshop motivation

I will now turn to the problem of self-teaching as knowledge making by developing further my reflections on the use of the 'Master-apprentice' model which, to my mind, subsumes all other models (a)–(e) mentioned in this chapter. It involves most of the major self-teaching operations of the working brain.

In order to explain what I mean I will, however, resort to an analogy and I will invite readers to create in their minds some imaginary pictures arising from it, and to make them as clear as their own familiarity with such an analogy may allow them, if only, again, in their imagination.

Let us, for a moment, drop our traditional academic habit of regarding intellectual activity as something extra special, and let us assume that academic craftsmanship may be just like any other craftsmanship practised in the world. Let us then substitute for the image of a Master of Academic Craftsmanship and his student apprentices an image of a Master Carpenter and his apprentices. Let us now think what would be the essential ingredients of their activity if they wanted to manufacture a table, either for the purpose of their business concern, or even for the purpose of training the apprentices.

Now I think that what would be needed first is the *intention* of making the table which would naturally and automatically involve a clear image of the finished product as the main *objective* of the whole manufacturing operation. Let us, for example, think of some quite specific table: let's say, a coffee table.

The next logical thing would be to prepare *plans and programmes of action* needed for the making of the coffee table: the sketches, or the drawings, the choice of materials, the tools and the space and the time needed. The work would then need frequent *inspection* and *verification*, in order to see if it proceeds in accordance with the plans and programmes which would involve *comparing the effects of the work* with the originally intended objectives of the completed table, as well as the *correction* of any mistakes that have been made.

Even if, as is the case with most apprentices, some of them would not, perhaps, be interested all the time in some aspects of the table-making process, or preferred one kind of work contributing to the manufacture of it, we can be quite certain that, with a *prudent and perceptive master* in the workshop, the majority of the apprentices would derive some satisfaction from their contribution to the making of the table by seeing and sensing its growth towards completion. The most essential ingredients of the work of making the table would be the provision of *frequent knowledge of results* of how well the components for the table are being formed by checking their shapes and dimensions with the plans of the intended, final product, or with another, already completed table used as a model.

The technical hints from the master and observation of his methods of making the table would also be very useful, if not absolutely essential. So, of course, would be the example of his enthusiasm, steady hand and skill and his patience in overcoming unforeseen difficulties and in correcting mistakes.

If, at this stage, we agreed that we have done some justice to the briefest possible description of the main ingredients of activities needed to make an *object of craft* (a coffee table), let us now see how it compares with this most ingenuous, one-sentence description of the working of the human brain as proposed by Luria, which I have already mentioned in Chapter 9:

> An individual not only reacts passively to incoming information, but *creates intentions, forms plans and programmes* of his action, *inspects* their *performance*, and *regulates his behaviour* so that it conforms to these plans and programmes; finally, he *verifies* his conscious activity, *comparing the effects* of his actions with the original intentions and *correcting any mistakes* he has made.
>
> (Luria, 1973)

Now, when it comes to turning this ingenuous summary of Luria's into a working tool for a teacher, or for a student, it is necessary to reflect what would be the consequences of adopting this model in their academic activities as 'knowledge makers' or 're-makers' or, in the case of teachers, as 'knowledge retailers' which is, after all, a half of their prescribed duties in the academe! All that such readers have to do, or need to, is to go over the words in italics in Luria's statement and see if what they do, as teachers or students, conforms to these statements:

 (i) 'Do I, as a teacher (or a student), have a clear picture of my *intention* – the objective of my course? Do my students share this objective, or are they at least aware of them?'
 (ii) 'Have I formed *plans and programmes* of my actions leading to the fulfilment of my objectives, and, since I share it with my students, our objectives? Do my students know what my plans are, and are they sharing them and/or making them their own? Am I being helpful in these tasks since my students are new to this kind of work?'
(iii) 'What do I do, or how do I proceed in order to enhance my own or my students' opportunities for frequent *inspection* and *verification* of how my teaching and their learning (self-teaching) is progressing, and if it is

progressing towards the fulfilment of my/our plans and programmes?' Otherwise, in pedagogical jargon: 'How frequently and how adequately are we, as master and apprentices, able to have a clear knowledge of the results (the k.r.s) of our progress with our academic craftsmanship of knowledge making, as outlined by our objectives and our plans of getting there, which is, of course, the problem of assessment of our own, and of our students', progress and success?'

(iv) 'How often can I and my students *compare the effects of our work* with the original objectives of the course? How far have we fulfilled our programmes and what picture emerges from our efforts? Is it as good as we intended it to be and, if not,

(v) what about *correcting* the mistakes we have made in creating, or re-creating, what we thought an adequate, or good, chunk of knowledge in the subject of our study?'

It is impossible, within the scope of this book, to proceed to further details and elaborations of practical means and ways of proceeding along the paths of the 'brain compatible' theory of learning. But before leaving this way of contemplating its bearings on pedagogical procedures let us remember at least three major components of the work of the self-teaching brain, namely the *intention (objective)* of learning, the *knowledge of results* and the *pleasure derived from successful achievements* of *the desired outcomes*. Incidentally, let me, as an aside, just mention that when I attempted to assess, very crudely, the effect of the intention (goal orientation) of students in the random sample on their success and failure in obtaining their degrees, the results were as follows: for those with very clear objectives the complete failure rate was 1:41, for those with moderately clear ones it was 1:16 and for those with very poorly defined objectives it was 1:6. I leave it to the imagination of the readers which of these three sub-groups would be easiest to teach what they have undertaken to learn, or even to leave alone to their own devices of 'sinking or swimming' without feeling any pangs of professional responsibility as teachers to enhance their students' interest in their subject of study. Obviously, it seems, the 'clear goals' group would be the most amenable to any kind of teaching, skilled or unskilled, but this group, in my studies, includes only 18 per cent of the random sample. The largest group – the 'less clear' – includes 58 per cent, and those with the poorly defined goals 24 per cent. Let me also tell you that when the goal orientation of the random sample was classified into two categories 'clear' and 'less clear' goals, 52 per cent of those with 'clear' goals had highest 'index of stress', as measured by the frequency of illness (visits to the doctors in the University Health Centre). Perhaps it might also be worth noting that 41 per cent of students who had extreme difficulties in studies (those who sought help in the Study Assistance Unit) were also those whose future goal orientation was classified as 'clear', i.e. nearly one in every two were 'well motivated'. Obviously, and as might be expected, clear intentions can help achievement, but they can also magnify fear of not getting there which kills initiative in many a person, particularly the most intelligent ones who often learn too quickly that they cannot learn!

So now we come to the point of addressing 'motivation' and its relation to teaching and learning. Here, before I go on with saying something about how I found it could be done within the framework of the models I chose to mention in this chapter, I should like to recommend to the readers a book which is, to me, one of the most clearly, comprehensively and systematically written treatment of this subject: Raymond Wlodkowski's (1985) *Enhancing Adult Motivation to Learn*. His 68 motivational strategies is a treasure of the most important practical tips for successful learning and teaching. From the first one: 'Share something of value with your adult learners', to the last one, 'Encourage and provide reinforcing events for positive closure at the end of a significant unit of learning', the list exhausts nearly every aspect of his basic mid-chapter on 'Integrating Emotion with Learning'. To me, a student of the problems of how feelings affect learning, the book would become prescribed reading, should I ever again be asked to take part in professional training for teachers in Higher Education.

But a readiness among such teachers, and also among students, to commit themselves to an exhaustive study of such a valuable aid, is not yet here, and I doubt that it will be for a very long time yet. So I had to think of a short-cut and I found it in a quite simple technique, described in Chapter 9 and on which I shall reflect again as a rounding off of my comments on the five models of approach to learning and teaching; the 'method' of 'Learning through Teaching'. To me this way of proceeding in *self-teaching as knowledge making* can become a truly self-motivating activity for life. It answers Wlodkowski's statement that 'continuing motivation is potentially as much an educational outcome as the attainment of any objective of learning'. It is also, in my experience, one of the most successful ways of helping students to study more effectively (Wankowski, 1989a).

There is no need to tell the reader that, since I found that Luria's definition is a most useful checklist of my pedagogic procedures when I work as an academic teacher, I try also to encourage its use amongst the students who come to me for assistance, when I function as an educational counsellor. I gently help them to assume the role of being their own teachers by creating their objectives of learning and, if necessary, by treating me as their student in order to try their self-teaching craftsmanship on a kindly-disposed person.

You might, at this point, object that it is all very well to help a student how to teach himself when a teacher is a specialist in the same subject, but what about if a study assistance tutor or a 'counsellor' is *not* a specialist and does not know anything about the subject which the student finds difficult to learn? 'All the better, in some cases', would be my reply, since, as I have already mentioned in Chapter 9, amongst the methods of helping students to become self-teachers, the reversal of the role, whereby the student becomes a teacher, is most efficacious. Here we can again reflect on what advantages such a method may bring to the 'poorly motivated', 'disenchanted', or simply 'depressed' students, who feel desperate because they cannot prove themselves to be competent in pursuing their studies. Moreover, we can also reflect how the prescription, derived from Luria's model, might help us again to appreciate the advantages of the method 'learning through teaching'.

First of all we must remember that University students, even those who may appear weak or are unsuccessful, know a great deal about their subject of study, either by virtue of their preliminary studies at school, or because, by the time they come to us for help, they have some idea of what their curriculum is about. So when the 'tables are turned' and they agree to teach you, or me – laymen in their subject of study – they are bound to sense that, possessing already at least some degree of mastery, *they can explain even the most intricate elements of their subject with far less fear in their hearts, of proving themselves in our eyes incompetent*, than they would have felt if they were confronted with the problem of 'teaching' their own tutors. There can be little doubt that the expertise of the highly specialized teachers tends to make them over-critical and impatient and, even if this is not so, they invariably appear as if they were like that to their students. So we can say that *the most important aspect of the 'learning through teaching' procedure is reduction, or abolition of the fear of incompetence* which we know diminishes intellectual functioning. The next most important aspect is one of bringing into operation the system of 'Luria's definition', by encouraging the student, now a teacher, to arrange his teaching in such a way that all the major ingredients of the learning activity of the brain are brought into action. In order to teach you or me anything, the student/teacher must, invariably define in terms of *objectives* what it is he is going to introduce to us in his teaching: he must construct *plans* and *programmes* of the components of his task (lecturette, etc.); he must *regulate* his teaching behaviour, so that it includes the items he has planned to teach us and verify that we are satisfied that his activities conform to his plans and his original intentions, correcting any mistakes he or we have made in our understanding of the problem.

It must also be quite obvious that, in taking up the task of teaching himself through teaching us (the laymen), the student must become more deeply involved, hence more interested in the subject of study he is going to teach us. He might even, as I have observed on many occasions, become very absorbed in it, almost against his original wish to treat it superficially, since *confirmed competence in dealing successfully with problems which hitherto appeared difficult or tedious to tackle has its own compulsive motivations*. The human brain seems to function best by building up systems of procedures in order to *adapt advantageously* to the demands and pressures of life, and the human mind takes delight in finding ways of overcoming immediate obstructions.

The 'learning through teaching' scheme of enhancing self-teaching is effective because it works towards the building up of mental structures (systems) which enable us to construct not only sandcastles on the sea shore and castles in the air, but also coffee tables and theses and all manner of technological and artistic creations, including those for survival, and now, unfortunately, even for possible destruction of life on earth. But the keystone of all these systems is, no doubt, *the imaginings of the objectives of all our operations* – the intentions of our striving which include intentions to learn (to teach ourselves) something we have decided to master.

Thus, returning to the problem posed by the title of this section, I would be tempted to contend that the most effective way of maintaining motivation in study is, in the first place, *the intentions*: the act of placing the objective of our self-teaching endeavours clearly before us, and in the second place, by having access to, or the possibility of providing for ourselves a *constant flow of the knowledge of results of our self-tuition*. I am also quite certain that the best effects these approbations have on the progress and economy of learning (self-teaching) are achieved when they are supplied by another person in co-operative learning – learning together, as Masters and Apprentices, how to proceed towards the mutually agreed and mutually pursued objectives of craftsmanship.

Effectiveness of the Study Assistance Tutorship: a personal audit

I am often asked how effective are the methods of helping students to become self-teachers, some of which I have mentioned in this chapter. My reply to this very important question is that, in my estimate, they are very effective, and I will proceed to describe my assessments. Indeed, I could hardly say that I have no idea, since having pursued my pedagogic work along the paths of many models of procedure, the few I mentioned in this book have probably been the most useful ones. And, as the reader might conjecture, all of them, as subsumed by the Master-Apprentice model, implied, nay, demanded that whichever role I have taken up in helping students to become self-teachers, the constant, ongoing necessity of comparing outcomes with the objectives of all such work was the most important part of it – the unavoidable part and parcel of the professional pursuit of my craftsmanship. My judgements of students' reactions were, as to this day they remain, a constant concomitant of my daily work – the tools of my trade. They were the instant estimates of my own procedures of helping each individual student and of the student's procedures of beginning to help himself. They were derived from the close, moment-to-moment observations of the signs of satisfaction that things were getting better, or dissatisfaction when no such positive feelings were engendered. Perhaps here I should also mention that my observations have, I think, been sharpened by the way I have always approached the puzzle of human learning, by formulating a question concerning the motives and the feelings accompanying learning. The question I always had in mind was this: '*What does the particular action, thought, word, or performance in learning or not learning do to the learner?*' I am quite convinced that this way of looking at learning has helped me enormously in understanding a little more about what was going on in learning and teaching transactions, and how this understanding helped me in my estimations of their outcomes. The reading of a large variety of 'signals' of satisfaction, or of displeasure with the way of learning was also most helpful to the students who could quickly invent or adjust their own techniques of self-teaching. The increased sensitivity to a moment-to-moment judgement of the student's own feelings about the outcome of his learning constitute the main vehicle of assessing his own progress – an active basis of the growth of his competence in his own knowledge making. Furthermore, my ongoing assessment of the study assistance work has been continuously enhanced by students' gratitude expressed in numerous letters and personal visits to say thank you and to tell me how they fared, also by letters from parents and from the members of staff who have referred their students to seek help in the Unit.

Thus, I am able to say that throughout my years of working as a Study Assistance Tutor I have formed a strong impression that a considerable majority of students who came for help were satisfied with it and were academically successful. But this is not a wholly satisfactory answer. The answer must be quantified and here I will try to do this.

I have made four formal attempts at estimating the outcomes of the work of the Study Assistance Unit, as carried out by myself for most of the time, and with the help of my colleague as half-time tutor for 3 years in the eighties. Two of these assessments were by a questionnaire sent to students who came for help and two by statistical estimate of the formally registered outcomes of graduation. Three of these exercises have been reported in various publications and papers and the fourth one is in the process of being written up, but I am able to quote some of the overall results. I will give the figures first and then offer some reflections.

My first attempt to assess *how students view the help given to them by the Study Assistance Unit* (Educational Counselling Unit) was made in 1980 by sending out a postal questionnaire to 273 students who came to the Unit during the sessions 1975/76, 1976/77 and 1977/78. Of these 273 questionnaires 150 have been completed and returned. The information from the returned questionnaires, comprising 55 per cent of the 273 sent, has been analysed and a full report of this evaluation exercise has been published as a research monograph by the Unit in 1983.

The main objectives of this exercise were to obtain information from the individuals concerned on how they valued the study assistance service, and to get their comments and suggestions about possible improvements in student facilities for learning how to learn at University, as well as to provide a record of the first-hand statements from each individual student which might be of use to a number of staff who sometimes try to understand the mishaps and difficulties of their students.

Other, subsidiary, issues which I hoped to illuminate by this enquiry were concerned with reasons why students came to seek help from the Unit, their use of other welfare facilities on the campus, and their prospects of employment, or of career when they happened to leave the University without a degree.

An opportunity of replicating this evaluation exercise, involving a shorter period of time, came my way after my retirement, when I was asked to help the Unit for two terms during the 1987/88 academic session.

Thirty-nine students comprising 21 women and 18 men, from 31 courses of study, came to see me. All these students had been sent a questionnaire to their home or lodgings addresses in July 1988, and this communication had been sent again to the ten who had not yet responded at the beginning of the 1988/89 academic session. Altogether 34 students (87 per cent) responded by returning completed questionnaires. The quantitative report on these two evaluation exercises will be confined to three topics only: (a) Students' reasons for seeking help in the Study Assistance Unit; (b) Students' evaluation of help; and (c) The 'recovery or survival rate' amongst students who came for help (Wankowski, 1989a).

(a) *Students' reasons for seeking help* as given by the responders of the 1980 and 1989 evaluations were classified under several headings which, on further analysis, were grouped into two categories of 'study difficulties' and 'personal or other' difficulties or reasons. In the 1980 exercise 123 (82 per cent) came for help because of 'study difficulties' and 27 (18 per cent) because of 'personal and other' reasons. Similar proportions obtained in the 1989 replication: 26 (76 per cent) 'study difficulties' and 8 (24 per cent) 'personal and other' reasons. The similarity of these trends suggest that although the nature of the help offered in the Unit seems to be quite clearly delineated as educational, the elements of mixed effects of personal and academic upsets and difficulties are still clearly there, as they always will be (Blight, 1981). The problem of the students' use of a variety of helping agencies on the campus may be instructive here, as analyses of both these exercises show that the students' first port of call for help is, in the majority of cases (80–90 per cent) their tutor's room, the next is the University Health Centre where they can obtain medical or psychological help (40–50 per cent), with much smaller numbers calling on other welfare agencies. Student difficulties have a multiplicity of factors, reasons and/or excuses contributing to their loss of coping competence, and a benign educational environment must provide widespread safety nets. Co-operation with all helping agencies is, of course, the most important factor in all such assistance. All students seeking help from the Study Assistance Unit were strongly encouraged to seek closer contact with their tutors, even in cases of initial reluctance to do so. They were encouraged to learn to co-operate with their departmental arrangements and demands, and to be clearly aware what those are and how to respond to them advantageously. Conversely, the majority of students (80 per cent) were advised by their tutors to seek help in the Study Assistance Unit.

(b) *Students' assessment of the help received* from the Unit has been classified under three headings in response to the question: 'Were you helped? And if so, in which way were you helped?' The figures for these assessments for the 1980 and 1989 evaluation exercises were, respectively, as follows:

'Yes, helped': 121 (81 per cent) and 27 (79 per cent);
'To some extent': 23 (15 per cent) and 4 (12 per cent);
'No': 6 (4 per cent) and 3 (9 per cent).

If figures for the positive evaluations are run together, the percentages of students satisfied with the help received became 96 per cent and 91 per cent respectively. If this straightforward question is considered as crucial to the problem of evaluating students' satisfaction with the help received from the Study Assistance Service the answers are self-evident and, to me, quite encouraging. Analysis of the students' answers to the question 'In what way were you helped?' was carried out, originally, by classifying their replies arbitrarily (by an external reader) into seven categories, and compacted, for the purpose of this report, into four subheadings for the two evaluation exercises in 1980 and 1989 respectively.

(1) Help with positive, practical attitude to work, realistic outlook on study, study methods and examination techniques: 93 (62 per cent) and 18 (56 per cent);

(2) practical advice, talking things over, sympathy and reassurance: 40 (27 per cent) and 12 (38 per cent);

(3) help with decision to change courses or to leave University: 5 (3 per cent) and 2 (3 per cent); and

(4) no reply or 'not helped' 12 (8 per cent) and 2 (3 per cent).

Both these evaluation exercises suggest that what students seem to value most is some practical help in how to cope with their problems, an opportunity of talking things over in a 'neutral' context, as well as sympathy and reassurance. Finding practical help directly related to their academic work seems to be a predominant feature of their needs. The picture has not changed even after a ten-year gap between these two self-audits.

(c) Moving on to the figures emerging from my attempts to assess the *'recovery'* or *the 'survival'* rates amongst students who come for help I have this to report:

My first attempt to evaluate the effectiveness of the Study Assistance Service in Birmingham, *with main reference to the criterion of academic achievement of students*, was reported in the British Journal of Guidance and Counselling in 1977 and reprinted in *Helping Students to Learn at University* (Raaheim and Wankowski, 1981). The data comprises information about the first batch of all men and women students who came for help between 1964 and 1975. The second evaluation exercise was reported in 1983 in the monograph 'How students view the help given to them by the Study Assistance Unit'. The data comprised information about academic achievement of all 277 men and women students who came for help between 1975 and 1978. The third evaluation exercise is included in this chapter. The data comprises information about academic achievement of all 708 men and women students who came for help between 1978 and 1985, the total of these three groups comprising all 1,588 students who came for help between 1964 and 1985. The information about yet another group of over 100 students who came for help in the 1985/86 session – the last year before my retirement in September 1986 – is not included, as it was not possible to collect and analyse the formal details of their academic achievement. It is in a sense a pity as a rounder figure of some 1,700 students would have been easier to handle in the following analyses. As it is, the *total of the 1,588 students represents about 93 per cent of all students I met in my work as a study assistance counsellor in the twenty-two years of my service in the University*. I believe that this data is in a way quite unique in the counselling world in the universities, and that it might be of some interest to educational practitioners and administrators in higher education.

The total group of the 1,588 students comprising 957 men and 631 women from all six faculties in the University represent respectively, 60 and 40 per cent of the total group. These proportions are almost identical to the total registration of all full-time students in the University. Moreover, the percentages of men and women students in each faculty are also almost equivalent in both these groups, suggesting that in the group of the 1,588 students who used the Study Assistance Service there was no marked bias in referral or self-referral from any major area of studies in the University. It is, however, quite possible that a further breakdown of this data by all departments might have shown some differences in this respect, for I was often aware that the frequency of referrals from departments seems to have been related to the number of academic colleagues I knew personally in each department. I am still under a strong impression that my personal contact with tutors in departments contributed substantially not only to the frequency of referral, but also to the whole process of helping students to regain their lost learning competence. I have no doubt whatever that a friendly co-operation between tutors and students and amongst other tutors concerned with the teaching of a particular student is one of the most effective ways of alleviating students' study difficulties.

The proportion of students who qualified has risen from 56 per cent in the 1964/75 sample, through 71 per cent in the 1975/78 sample, to 76 per cent in the 1978/85 sample, giving an overall average of 68 per cent for the whole group of 1,588 students, when this average was adjusted by an estimate of progress of the 'current' students. The proportion of students who left the University without qualifying decreased from 42 per cent in the 1964/75 sample, through 29 per cent in the 1975/78 sample, giving an overall average of 31 per cent for the whole group of 1,588 students. When the three student samples (1964/75, 1975/78 and 1978/85) are broken down by faculties, the proportions of qualified to not-

Table 11.1   Academic achievement of 1,588 students in six faculties at the University of Birmingham in 1964–85

	Qualifying (%)	Left without Qualifying (%)
Science and Engineering	63	35
Arts	67	33
Law	76	23
Commerce and Social Sciences	67	31
Medicine:	76	24
Dentistry: (single faculty)	58	42
Education	82	17*

*Percentages short of 100 are due to small numbers of occasional students, deceased, or with no information from faculty registries.

qualified students vary somewhat within and between these faculty groups. This trend is illustrated by Table 11.1. The analysis of data of all 1,588 students in separate groups of men and women suggests that women tend to produce a higher proportion of qualified students (75 per cent) than men (65 per cent).

Yet another way of analysing academic progress of students who came for help to the Study Assistance Unit is to look at the class of degrees awarded to the 876 undergraduates of the total group of the 1,588. This group does not include 117 'current' students at the time of final analyses in 1986. Overall, 37 per cent gained an above average degree and the same proportion (37 per cent) gained an average class of degree; 26 per cent gained below average class of degrees. These proportions are comparable within the average class of degrees gained by all undergraduates in the University in 1983 – 38 per cent. The differences occur in the 'above average' class for the whole university and in the 'below average', 51 per cent and 11 per cent respectively. One of the reasons for the larger percentages of the below average class of degree is among students who came for help. A large number of students, particularly in the Science and Engineering Faculty, are traditionally categorized as 'weak' after their first year of studies and placed into the 'ordinary degree' courses. No amount of psychological and pedagogical skill applied in counselling with a distraught student can be expected to succeed to such a marked and spectacular degree that his tutors would actively intervene in order to change the regulations which have formally sealed his 'academic fate' at the beginning of his course of study.

Reflecting on the negative feature of the foregoing evaluations a few words must be said about the considerable proportion of students (484 i.e. 31 per cent of the total group of 1,588) who failed to obtain a degree for which they were registered. It is a formidable figure of wastage as viewed in strict terms of academic success or failure. No apologies need to be made for this in conscience, or in effort, though obviously some responsibility could be accepted with reference to the time-skill component of the Study Assistance Service. With reference to time, it is not so much the availability of time which could be given by the half-time appointment of a study assistance tutor (the other half being my duties of teaching psychology), as the considerable length of time which had elapsed before the students came to ask for help in coping with their studies, and the chronically short length of time in which they had to teach themselves new ways towards becoming competent in their academic craftsmanship. Generally, this, so-called, 'time-loss, time-press' factor constitutes the greatest obstacle to the effective application of pedagogical skill by the study assistance tutor; in fact by any teacher who tries to restore the lost learning competence of his student. Enhancement of learning on the part of a relatively happy individual is, or should be, relatively easy for a skilled teacher to achieve. It is the handicap of the bruised self-image of a failing student which requires extra time to alleviate. And by extra time I mean the passage of time which is needed by the student for gradually building up personal and academic competence through practising the new schemes of better management of their studies. This is the time they often lack, and the awareness of it constitutes the 'psychological press'.

Some indication of the operation of the 'time-loss, time-press' factor can be observed in the course of an analysis of the time of first referral of students who came for help to the Study Assistance Unit. An earlier referral, particularly one prior to the summer term when most students have to face sessional examinations, should result in a greater rate of 'recovery and survival rate' in academic studies. Indeed, analyses of the dates of first referral in two total samples of students (the 1975–78 and the 1978–85) corroborate each other quite closely. Students who came for help in the autumn and spring terms were successful in graduating at the rate of 4 in every 5 (i.e. 80 per cent), whilst those with the first referral in the summer term succeeded at the rate of 3 in every 5 (i.e. 60 per cent) in the 1975–78 sample, and 1 in 3 (i.e. 33 per cent) in the 1978–85 samples. The percentages of students in these two samples who came for help in the summer term are similar, i.e. 29 per cent and 27 per cent respectively: nearly 1 in every 3. If this statistic is applied to an estimate of the numbers of students referred for the first time in the summer term in the total sample of 1,588 students, this average (of 28 per cent) constitutes 445 students; only one third of this group (147 students) would have succeeded. Still further analysis of the summer term first referral shows that 35 per cent of these students came in July, i.e. *after* their sessional examinations in May and June. They came invariably with a tale of woe, having been asked either to leave University or, in a better case, to re-sit their examination in September. In the first case they were usually referred by their tutors who hoped that the Study Assistance Unit might, after talking to a student, write a letter of support for appeal against faculty decision to terminate their studies, and in the second case that the students might be furnished with some 'quick advice' on how to study for their re-sits in September, before they left the campus.

It might be worth noting that in both evaluation exercises 75–77 per cent of students who left without a degree were in further training when replying to the postal questionnaires. In both these exercises there were students who made statements that consulting the Unit had helped them in their decisions to withdraw from their courses of study, or to re-think their career plans. Thus the success in graduation is not the only criterion of the students' evaluation of help received.

Needless to say, although all of these 'past-failure' referrals presented me with an almost hopeless task in doing anything worthwhile in order to help the student, my extra careful and detailed examination of these students' ways of study has been a rich mine of information about the nature of tuition and student care in each particular course, or department. This intimate knowledge of what was happening at the hub of tuition has been invaluable in all my work with individual students. My understanding of how departments manage, or mismanage, their tuition enabled me to help other students to become competent self-teachers, often in spite of the obvious pedagogical shortcomings at the seat of learning. Much of this intimate knowledge and reflections about the manner of tuition in each department has been shared, in general terms, with many departmental tutors who were interested in problems of tuition and its impact on students' learning.

Conclusions and recommendations

My general inference from these evaluative exercises of study assistance work at university is briefly this: students come for help to the Study Assistance Unit, in most cases, as the last resort. The 'buck stops there', in welfare terms, in the university. 'It is rather a last resort in many students' eyes' – as put most aptly by one of the customers. It has always been like that (Wankowski, 1985). Yet in spite of it, the tutorial game of helping such students seems effective and economical; admittedly not a 100 per cent success, though the 70-80 per cent 'recovery rate', in various groups, is not too bad a result. The game, evolved and improved by me over the years of professional work, has been mainly played out via the way of 'self-help in self-teaching', which has in turn been evolved and improved by the students who came for help. They did this by assuming gradually, but persistently, with my help, a role of self-management in study; teaching themselves what they intended to learn for their degrees.

I should also like to reiterate that I found this method of encouraging the students to *assume a role of self-teacher* – quite often by putting myself into a role of a student, to initiate and to test their craftsmanship – both comforting and economical; we both saved ourselves many hours of work. My average number of 'counselling' (study assistance) hours per student fell from an average of six in the early seventies to an average of two hours for the rest of my service; whilst for a student the two, one-hourly sessions (nowadays, usually one) of 'learning through teaching' was often enough to compensate for, as I estimated, an average of 200 hours of wasted time and effort in coming to terms with his or her course.

Most teachers, I think, can train themselves to play this game of helping students to become their own teachers, quite quickly and without much effort. With a hundred students on their course, only about ten may have difficulty in adapting themselves advantageously to the academic requirements put upon them. A total of 10–20 hours spent helping such students is all that may be required in each academic year. The game, because it has to be played in a one-to-one contact in slow motion, provides a rich source of highly pertinent information on how to improve one's professional craftsmanship of teaching.

The lessons learnt from helping a few individual students in each academic session must, in the light of my experience, lead to better understanding of the problems contributing to student attitudes. They should not only serve as a most useful tool for alleviating this largely unnecessary waste of people's time, effort, discomfiture and money, but, more importantly they should, one hopes, be used for the improvement of the effectiveness of teaching and learning in higher education in general. There can be little doubt that, in relation to what is already known about ways of making tuition and learning more effective, many of the standard practices in higher education are still very amateurish. A recent study of 'Staff Perceptions of Student Learning Difficulties and Implications for Staff Development' by Davies, sums up this inference:

It would appear that teachers are overwhelmingly concerned with their own teaching and barely consider student learning problems. Furthermore, they do not appear to possess the *vocabulary* to describe these problems; *many members of staff were unable to articulate* student learning problems. If teachers could suitably identify and clarify problems, effective measures could be devised, providing solutions to many of the problems cited. As it is, most antidotes that are offered by the teachers are haphazard, unsystematic and not potentially matched for the purpose.

(Davies, 1988)

Or, as one student taking part in my recent self-audit said, in answer to the question 'In what way were you helped?': 'It gave me a chance to talk things out with someone who didn't just say, "I don't know what to do either"'. But all this is hardly surprising, if the chances of academic advancement and the promotion of university lecturers are regarded in a cool, level-headed and pragmatic manner. The fact, if faced honestly and squarely, is simply one of the economy of effort which militates against any desire, or indeed any need, to learn how to help students to teach themselves how to learn what the lecturers profess to teach.

This brings me to the point of advocating that what is needed in higher education is *a scheme whereby the numbers of pragmatically inclined teachers should be greatly increased.* This should be done by a large-scale operation of practical pedagogical training in using the 'active research' approaches in order to learn what goes on in their practice of teaching and learning, and what kinds of schemes and procedures they should themselves try with their students in order to enhance their self-teaching. The idea of 'action research as you teach and learn' is of course nothing else than normal professional procedure in any highly valued skill or craftsmanship. A professional craftsman must be permanently involved in studying his art, if only to keep up with the skill of his colleagues and competition in his sphere of craftsmanship. *This kind of activity of studying their own craftsmanship does not exist amongst the majority of university teachers,* who have no 'felt-need' to study their own methods of 'knowledge retailing'. Neither do many university teachers ever concern themselves with *how* to teach their students effectively in what they, as specialists, excel – i.e. in their own art of 'knowledge making'. In fact a very large number of students whom I specifically asked about it do not even know that they ought to become their own 'knowledge makers'. The main objectives and the philosophy of higher education are seldom, if ever, brought to their attention by their teachers. The demand for 'retailed knowledge' is often embarrassingly staggering, if one enquires closely, or watches it as I did in my own teaching work. Yet, promising examples of successful 'Action research' in teaching and learning in higher education are well underway and the work carried out in Norway by Kjell and Arild Raaheim is definitely one of them (Raaheim, A., 1984).

Many simple, common sense pedagogical procedures already known to us can be used to help students who come to a standstill in learning. So if I were asked what kind of action I would envisage which would be most helpful to the alleviation of student attrition, my reply would be that efforts should be directed towards substantial provision of ways and means which would result in a very considerable improvement in tuition at its most crucial points of contact and co-operative communications between individual teachers and their students. I have no doubt whatsoever that, if these contacts and communications – the working inter-relationships of the Master Craftsmen and their Apprentices in the Art of Academic Craftsmanship – were accompanied by and linked to 'Action Research', the growth of improvement in both the volume and the level of acquisition of the 'retailed knowledge' and in the skills of 'knowledge making' amongst students would become, quite naturally, inevitable. 'Action Research' should be carried out by each individual teacher and in such a way that both the Master of the Craft and his Apprentices become progressively aware of what goes on in their minds when they teach and learn from one another. There can also be no doubt that this kind of serious, professional preoccupation with what I call, 'perceptive teaching and learning' would also contribute to a more rapid expansion in 'knowledge making' in general.

Students, young or old, can very often be extraordinarily perceptive, enterprising explorers of any field of knowledge. The freshness of their curiosity and their boldness due to sheer ignorance, both uncluttered by the awe of the tight structures of the existing state of knowledge, even their recklessness of reflections and spontaneously clinched 'adventitious inferences', can act as necessary stimulants and catalysts for forging new paths in the Art and the Craft of 'knowledge making' in any subject of study.

Consciously designed programmes for co-operative teaching and learning, aiming at the simultaneous functioning of teachers and students as 'knowledge makers' and 'knowledge retailers', are likely to create powerful and challenging bonds in the conceptual framework of human consciousness and enable countless more craftsmen to be 'creators of new knowledge'. I remain constantly surprised by the attitudes of so many of my academic colleagues who seem, as it were, to believe in some kind of a power to which they refer as 'intellectual inspiration', and which they regard as a prime incentive for pursuing knowledge as 'art for art's sake' and as a source of their supreme satisfactions. They somehow do not seem to want to reflect that their zeal may derive from the satisfaction of the total integration of the 'knowledge making' and 'knowledge retailing' via their academic papers and communications which, bonded together, result in the formation of a mental structure known in psychological jargon as the 'Functional Autonomy of Motive'; the sheer habit of experiencing frequent satisfactions with their own craftsmanship which needs no further incentives from the outside world. Teaching and learning can definitely bring their own satisfactions and many more young people could legitimately enjoy them when they commit themselves to university studies (Allport, 1955).

So we now come to the Tolstoyan question of 'What should be done?' And it is here that the greatest obstacle looms immediately on the educational horizon – the icebergs, or indeed the ice-caps of centuries old academic traditions, including the most stubborn resistance to change (Betcher *et al.*, 1976).

Putting it all in the most simple words, what I think is really needed is that *large numbers of teachers in higher education should be formally trained* to teach themselves how to teach effectively, competently and with true professional pride and satisfaction, by studying their pedagogical craftsmanship as they teach their students, whatever they are appointed to teach and to research. This state of affairs cannot possibly be attained by continuing, as hitherto, to indulge in pious wishful thinking and idealistic exhortations by people who have the financial and organizational means of influencing the organization of higher education, nor by the few itinerant, pedagogical enthusiasts like myself. It can only come about by formally setting up courses for professional training for a Diploma in Teaching in Higher Education, the possession of which must be rewarded by an additional salary.

When I referred to the Tolstoyan question of 'What should be done?' the next, far more important one was foremost in my mind: 'Can it be done?' Having written my conclusions and recommendations I must admit that I found it difficult to disregard the note of pessimism intruding into my thinking. The need for improving teaching and self-teaching at all levels of education including its formal apex, the university, is great, urgent and, to me, a common-sense recognition. But can I really expect that it may appear as such to others? After all, I happen to be fully aware of the fact that the roots of my attitude stem from decades of dabbling daily in this field, as the means of earning my living. I am also aware that I am only one of a legion of people who happened to have had the opportunity of being in close touch with the varieties of human zest for learning and of human aversion to it, but this legion is, as yet, relatively very small. So it is, obviously, unfair to expect too much from those who were not so preoccupied.

Yet, the whole problem is so very old, so humanly simple, and has been expressed so clearly and concisely by the genius of some outstanding masters of the pedagogical craftsmanship, that a vignette of it might serve as the neat rounding off of this chapter. Here I wish to refer to Polya, the great Hungarian teacher of mathematics who, in 1948, at the beginning of his small book wrote:

> One of the most important tasks of the teacher is to help his students. This task is not quite easy; it demands time, practice, devotion, and sound principles.
>
> The student should acquire as much experience of independent work as possible. But if he is left alone with his problem without any help or with insufficient help, he may make no progress at all. If the teacher helps too much, nothing is left to the student. The teacher should help, but not too much and not too little, so that the student shall have a *reasonable share of the work*.
>
> If the student is not able to do much, the teacher should leave him at least some illusion of independent work. In order to do so, the teacher should help the student discreetly, *unobtrusively*.
>
> The best is, however, to help the student naturally. The teacher should put himself in the student's place, he should see the student's case, he

should try to understand what is going on in the student's mind, and ask a question or indicate a step that *could have occurred to the student himself.*

(Polya, 1948)

But again, I am aware that this simple summing up of the gist of sound pedagogical advice may not easily be followed. For in order to develop professional sensitivity to the vagaries of human learning and not learning, far more *time and effort* is necessary than the few days, spread over the years, of sporadic attendance at the academic 'workshops' and 'discussions' which constitute the main features of the present-day attempts at pedagogic training of the university teachers. One cannot help but wonder which other professions, from plasterers to high court judges, would consider these few days of training as sufficient preparation for the forty years of their professional practice?

An optimistic counterpoint of this note of pessimism has, however, always been presented in my mind. My assumption that every individual is his own teacher has been so frequently confirmed by observing human learning that I have come to the conclusion that most people, however young, manage to teach themselves in spite of their teachers. Faced with a learning environment most will proceed to master most of what may be proposed by their Masters. And if teachers – the Masters of their subjects – can also train themselves to be organizers of their students' self-teaching, things may become rosier in education without too much effort.

After all, the art of pedagogy is, as I see it, the craft of helping other people to teach themselves even those things which they, at some time and for any reason, may not be inclined to learn, in spite of their desire to do so.

Notes

1. See References: Wankowski (1969–90) also O'Sullivan (1970), Kwiatkowski (1973), Cox (1971), Bevan-Jones (1974) and Willis-Lee (1982).
2. Holder, R. and Wankowski, J. A. (1980). 'It may be this capacity for accommodating which constitutes one of the basic points of inequality in making use of educational opportunities'. As, for example, in the personality profile of a successful mathematician who 'is likely to be a relatively versatile person capable of mastering the skill of his subject through a knack of advantageous adaptation, a cheerful and unresentful conformer to things as they are, with a strong streak of independence ... and readiness to break the rules if necessary – a clear sign of self-confidence and adaptability'.

12

The Teachers and the Taught

John Radford

Departmental experience

Much of the research briefly reviewed in Chapter 1, and the work which both Kjell Raaheim and Janek Wankowski describe in Chapters 2 through 11, show the importance of motivational as well as cognitive factors, within a total educational setting. If this needs further evidence, Ramsden and Entwistle (1981), in a large sample of over 2,000 students at British universities and polytechnics, found clear links between students' perceptions of their main academic department and their reported approaches to studying. Departments perceived as having good teaching and allowing freedom in learning tended to have students with an orientation towards personal meaning in their studies; in those perceived as having a heavy workload and lack of freedom, students aimed more at reproducing. Pascarella (1985) summarizes evidence that a college environment particularly effective at fostering learning:

> . . . is one with the following characteristics: frequent student interaction, with faculty perceived as being interested in teaching and treating students as individuals; a relatively flexible curriculum in which students have freedom in choosing courses and can experiment before selecting a major; an intellectually challenging programme with a stress on intellectual rather than social matters; and strong cultural facilities (plays, concerts, lectures etc.).

He points out nevertheless that when student input characteristics are held constant, institutional structural or environmental factors account for a relatively small amount of variance in post-college learning. But this may be for several reasons: for example in these American studies the usual measure of achievement, the Graduate Record Examination, may mask differences between disciplines; the quantitative institutional characteristics taken, such as staff-student ratio, library, staff qualifications, may be less important than agents of socialization; effects may not be at institutional level, within which students experience subcultures. Premfors (in Kogan, 1989) considers what are the smallest component elements of Higher Education to have a life of their own; for example, departments.

Other units might, of course, be faculties (in the British sense), courses and so on. However, I was for some years Head of a polytechnic department which achieved a degree of success, and which perhaps offers a commentary on some of what has already been said in this book. At what was originally West Ham College of Technology, subsequently (from 1970) North East London Polytechnic (NELP), and from 1989 the Polytechnic of East London, I was fortunate to be able to build up what became the largest Department of Psychology in the UK. It began, however, with two or three students in 1963 taking a psychology option, approximately one third, in an external degree of the University of London. In common with other polytechnics, for a long period nearly all our students had failed to gain university places. The growth of the Department was not an experiment, and no one thought to preserve full data for later analysis; but one can offer one or two evidences of success, before giving an anecdotal account of how this came about. For a number of years the noncompletion rate was below five per cent, which compares well with the best university rates (Chapter 1). Until the adoption of the CNAA system, our students took London external examinations which, in psychology, were the same as were taken by internal students, set by internal examiners who were of course also the internal teachers. Our results, however, were statistically indistinguishable from theirs. Lastly, although the academic field is entered by only a very small minority of students, it offers a direct indicator of academic success. At the time of writing two of our graduates hold university chairs in psychology and a third has an equivalent rank as permanent head of department. A fourth holds a polytechnic chair, while at least one other has done as well overseas. It is doubtful if any polytechnic can match this in any subject.

We had some advantages and some disadvantages, many stemming from our newness. It was possible to appoint new staff, and my general preference was for those with wider than academic experience: business or industry or perhaps especially successful secondary school teaching. Many concomitantly had qualifications besides psychology (I recall at least English, history, geography, economics, German, French, music, Hebrew, zoology, geology, physics, mathematics, drama; they were what my own old Professor, C. A. Mace, a keen gardener, said psychologists should be: 'choice selected hybrids' – Mace, 1948). Students, I think, shared the excitement, even uncertainty, of development, of new problems each day; and for them it was in most cases a second chance, of which they were determined to make the most. We were able to select students, at first from a small, then a larger population as we became known. Nearly all departments select on the basis of grades at GCE 'A' level. We rejected this (although to be eligible for grants students had to have two bare passes or equivalent). We assessed previous record of studying and extracurricular activities; we used a standard intelligence test (at first Raven's Matrices, then Watson-Glaser); and we gave every applicant two independent interviews. These things were given numerical values for ease of comparison, but the final judgment was subjective, balancing one factor against another. A later analysis found that the interviews were the best predictor of success, though only when given by experienced interviewers. This process was very time-consuming, but it probably resulted in picking up students who for whatever reason had missed their way on the conventional route to Higher Education. This was, therefore, an advantage which could not be equally shared by every institution.

'Stone walls do not a prison make', nor an educational setting. Thelin and Yankovich (1987) summarize a sparse literature on architecture in Higher Education. Most institutions, however, have paid as much attention to it as they can afford. Our home at first was two prefabricated huts, apart from the main College building and reputedly due each year for demolition; and then the top two floors of a typical three-decker London primary school even further away. Such isolation itself had advantages: we became a rather tightly knit community (partly because, like the House of Commons, the space was always insufficient for the numbers entitled to use it), with our own library and eating place – indescribable but unavoidably social. These schools were built with classrooms round an open hall, with the Head perched in a mezzanine room commanding a view of the whole. Casual and frequent interaction of staff and students was the result. As Baird (1988) puts it in a review of the evidence: 'the "environment" is where the individual mind, the social group and the organizational structure meet and interact'.

Classes were fairly small, maximum 28 rising eventually to 100, but we made the still rather expensive decision that all students should have a weekly tutorial group not exceeding five, whose functions were both academic and, though less overtly, pastoral. We had little choice as to what was taught, until we introduced our own CNAA degrees, but even this had a silver lining: there was a feeling of a common enemy, the examiners, against whom both staff and students matched themselves. One means to this end was systematic practice: in accordance with what is known of transfer of training, practice on tasks closely simulating the real one, namely the examination. In appropriate terms, each week students wrote an examination answer under more or less exam conditions, and each week I or a colleague gave back the answers of the previous week, with comments and discussion, to the whole group. (I am happy to acknowledge that I copied this plan direct from one of my own teachers, Professor Brian Foss.) There is an obvious comparison with the method described above by Kjell Raaheim.

The enterprise was very much a joint effort, in which non-teaching staff – technicians, secretaries and especially librarian – were all more or less involved. Moses (1985) has described the role of Head of Department in the pursuit of excellence. I was certainly only one factor, though some ex-students have been kind enough to speak favourably of what I tried to do. A comment I particularly appreciate came from a former staff member, who said: 'What I admired was the way you never seemed to do anything. You just used to sit there drinking coffee, and everything happened'. Coffee drinking, and talk, was itself an essential ingredient, partly because (in my experience) notices and announcements are never as effective as face to face interaction, even though the latter entails saying the same thing over and over to different individuals. It was my practice for about fifteen years to visit a local pub almost every Thursday evening, when the beer ran to a bit more than the half-pint prescribed by Janek Wankowski. I did this because I liked it; but there were always at least some students who seemed to enjoy it too, some regularly and some occasionally; and (I think) a larger number who appreciated the possibility, even if they never got around to taking part.

But I might also claim, in the apparent idleness, a touch of *ars celare artem*. If I am pleased with one particular aspect of what I did, it is that I think I hardly ever ceased from a constant search for improvement. This meant both arduous administrative campaigns, largely behind the scenes, and a host of larger and smaller initiatives – such things as watching for and drawing attention to interesting items in the media, encouraging the student psychological society and student magazine (*Psyclops*), facilitating visiting speakers. The effect on students who have been considered, and consider themselves, as failures, of an eminent visitor *who clearly regards the Department and its staff as equals*, has to be seen. The danger with all this, I think, is that of becoming too paternal and 'irreplaceable', and my aim, at least, was always to get things started rather than run them. A Head of Department, or indeed head of anything, I have thought, should work towards his own redundancy, even if he never gets there.

This particular Departmental experience, which has been only sketched here, was not planned deliberately but evolved from the beliefs and resources of a group of staff who were well qualified psychologists but far from being only academics. It also came about in conditions of peculiar restraints, and some opportunities, which would seldom be replicated exactly. But it does seem to me to correspond quite well both with reported research and with what my co-authors have had to say. We did exert some control over quite a number of the variables in Entwistle's 'heuristic model' (Chapter 1). What we sought to do, and undoubtedly did do in many cases, was to raise the level of performance through improved skills and above all enhancement of self-esteem. There are numerous examples of how individuals and groups can excel themselves when they experience both a demand and a possibility (see Radford, 1990); and in some ways the aim of an academic department might be said to be a state of permanent revolution. One strives for an atmosphere in which everyone believes that what she or he is doing is not only well worth doing, but actually can be done. I don't know any way to achieve this that is not extremely demanding in time and effort. To bring about a system in which these can be permanently maximized, however, would demand a reform of Higher Education so drastic as to be outside our present scope.

What makes a good student?

Nelson-Jones and Toner (1978) give the following, perhaps somewhat haphazard, lists of factors involved in student competence: planning, organizing and effective use of study time; effective reading and memorizing; interpersonal relationships and the ability to obtain study help; writing and note-taking;

meeting academic requirements; examination skills; critical thinking, creativity and contributing; handling worries and personal concerns; coping with numerical and statistical data; educational decision making. Thomas (1988) describes a hypothetical model of an 'ideal student', high on these characteristics: focusing on the criterion (e.g. successful completion); spontaneous engagement in (a) knowledge acquisition activities, (b) activities that transform knowledge for some purpose; (c) self-management activities; and a strong sense of personal efficacy.

In such lists we have the familiar mix of the cognitive and the orectic, and the question arises first as to whether we can and should select for such factors. Take first the cognitive. Kjell Raaheim is dismissive of the value of tests; and although we used one at NELP it was only one item in a total picture. It now seems, as mentioned in Chapter 1, that (in the UK) 'A' level grades are a good predictor, though they may well be an index of factors other than intellectual, such as study skills or determination. But it is possible to argue that since entry to Higher Education is already highly selective, any individual who obtains entry ought to be expected to complete, with rare exceptions. But then further, perhaps we should not be satisfied with that, but should seek to raise the general level of achievement. The task of Higher Education, in a sense, may be to make the best of the material it is given by national policy.

It is even more problematic to select on orectic criteria. We could certainly choose fairly reliably using, for example, the characteristics of the good student given by Janek Wankowski in Chapter 6, or even the study strategies described by Entwistle; or traits of self-concept and self-esteem (there is evidence, from Marsh *et al.*, 1988, that distinct mathematical and verbal self-concepts can be identified). The problem is partly that no selection system is one hundred per cent reliable – we may still have admissions who fail and unjustified rejections, what are termed Type I and Type II errors.

However, this is really not a technical question but one of policy as to the purpose of Higher Education. There is no doubt that selection can be made more efficient in the sense of increasing the output of a certain product; but in moderately democratic societies we must put the greatest weight on improving what we do with students once we have them. Most of this book has been about this and, as Janek Wankowski stresses, however autonomous the student the greater burden of responsibility falls on the teacher. The starting point clearly must be the transition from school (or other experience, and there is much to be said in favour of other experience) to university, polytechnic or college. Both Kjell Raaheim and Janek Wankowski have considered this in detail. An important feature here is the need to be explicit about the nature of the education on which the student is to embark. Thomas (1988) puts this at the head of the characteristics of an 'ideal course', the counterpart of his ideal student. One might mention here the practice of the CNAA in demanding very explicit specifications of every course in aims, objectives, methods and content, information which must be available to all students; at least in many cases this has actually resulted in students having much clearer ideas than is sometimes the case in universities. Perhaps not many students consult the full documents, but many courses begin with an outline of the aims and programme. Similarly some teachers at least do not suppose that students on arrival will intuitively know what constitutes a good essay, practical report or project, or how to use library resources. Experience and research suggest, however, that such things are most effectively taught when there is a direct need for them and when they are related to the subject of study. Two or three days of concentrated information at the start of a course, inevitably mixed with much extraneous (though desirable) news about student societies and the next disco, at a time when many students are simultaneously trying to sort out lodging problems and orient themselves in a strange city, is not a good plan.

Similarly many UK public sector institutions have offered study skills courses or packages, as has the Open University. Vermunt and Van Rijswijk (1988) describe a Study Advisory Packet for students of the Dutch Open University. They report two studies showing that: students' learning conceptions and orientations are closely linked to the study activities they employ; students' learning styles are related to their educational experience and to their study results, but only in a small degree to their age; and the Study Advisory Packet raised students' awareness of different ways of studying and contained practically useful suggestions for studying. This is but one instance from a large literature, and Martin and Ramsden (1987), for example, show that it is not necessarily a simple matter. They compared two voluntary study skills programmes, one concentrating on specific skills of note-taking, discussion, essay writing etc., the other on learning to learn through structured group discussions, concentrating on the nature of historical argument (history was the subject of study), and the relationship between students' approaches and lecturers' expectations. The first method was initially seen as more useful but later less so, and it had no influence on student grades. The other was at first seen as too vague, but it did improve grades and came to be considered more useful. Martin and Ramsden suggest that in the second programme the content was tightly linked to teaching and curriculum, and to students' existing knowledge; and that it was embedded in a more supportive department, with less formal teaching, a lighter workload, more student choice, and less stand-offish staff. This is very consistent with what has been said in this volume.

We have also seen the need for organization and for practice on the part of the student. Some students come to Higher Education already equipped in this regard, or able to adapt quickly, but experience shows that most do not. Similarly it has been stressed that techniques are of limited use without motivation, and that this depends on many factors, only some of which reside in the student. It is clear that it is a total learning environment that should ideally be created, within which there is scope for a wide variety of students and approaches to study, though it is reasonable to hope that all will make some progress towards self-directed, autonomous learning. Boud (1988) points out that such a goal is a relative, not an absolute matter, and that not all students can be expected to be at the same stage, although he believes that all students are capable of autonomous learning. One rather extreme example of difficulty arising from variety is described by McKenzie (1987), as a 'surge of religious dogmatism' among a growing number of college students (in the USA) who believe in the absolute authority of the Bible and deem rational discourse to be a waste of time, even satanic. Other texts could also be mentioned. McKenzie believes a commonsense classroom approach is needed to such a challenge: teachers should become familiar with the attitudes and arguments of dogmatic students and cultivate friendly rather than adversarial relationships with them. No doubt that is wise, though it may do little to change things; I have had students sorely puzzled, and even dropping out, due to an irreconcilable contradiction between the science they are offered and what they know to be true from their holy books.

With this, perhaps, we approach that end of the student spectrum where actual remedial action is required, and the need for such services, and how they may work, has already been discussed in detail by Janek Wankowski.

What makes a good teacher?

It was the custom of Ludwig Wittgenstein, when Professor of Philosophy at Cambridge, to give his twice weekly 'lecture' sitting on a small chair in the centre of his austere college lodgings, where for two hours he would think aloud, or engage in question and answer, with every evidence of intense effort; not lecturing but doing original research. Wittgenstein 'was a frightening person at these classes. He was very impatient and easily angered . . . (he) was always exhausted by his lectures. He was also revolted by them. He felt disgusted with what he had said and with himself'. He believed that his teaching was largely harmful, and that as a teacher he was a failure (Malcolm, 1958). Yet what philosopher would not wish to have been there?

We are not all philosophers, and still fewer of us are Wittgensteins, and Sheffield (1974) found that the nominations of 1,000 Canadian students of excellent teachers suggested there was no one best way of teaching. In general, students liked teachers who were masters of their subject matter, prepared lectures well, related material to practical issues, encouraged questions, and were enthusiastic about their subject matter. Waters *et al.* (1988) found that high-rated faculty were described by students in terms of positive personal/ motivational and interpersonal characteristics, whereas the low-rated were described in terms of classroom behaviour. Jones (1989) found a close relationship between student ratings of teaching competence and of teachers' personalities, but argues that this does not invalidate student assessment since there is, in reality, a connection between the two aspects. Marsh (1987), reviewing the evidence, concludes that student evaluations of university teaching are reliable and stable and valid against a variety of other measures. He also stresses that effective teaching, and student evaluations of it, are multidimensional. There is no single criterion of effective teaching. A similar point is made by Kurz *et al.* (1989), in respect of the more general issue of faculty evaluation. They conclude from a review of evidence that different definitions of performance must be included, and that these may even be conflicting. Student evaluations have been less used outside the USA but perhaps should be more widespread.

They do seem to agree fairly well with other research. Sherman *et al.* (1987) for example, find much research to support these characteristics of excellence in university teaching: enthusiasm, clarity, preparation and organization, stimulation, and love of knowledge. Experience is also important, but is insufficient by itself. They argue that excellence should be regarded as a stage in professional growth, which can be planned for and developed through such techniques as guided reflection, guided integration, support and challenge. This development involves a series of stages, in which teaching and learning are successively conceptualized as follows:

Teaching	*Learning*
telling –	reproduction
leading –	comprehension
transmitting knowledge –	processing, integrating and understanding
complex interaction –	a complex process involving intellectual, motivational, personal, emotional and developmental variables indicated by analytic synthetic and evaluative thinking.

More simply perhaps, Common (1989) defines the four primary responsibilities of the teacher as to create, maintain, lead and close teaching settings. Based on research, five generalizations define an effective teaching setting: all the participants are actively engaged; the setting is governed through decentralized management; there is orderly instructional practice; the setting evolves in educationally worthwhile ways; and the setting is closed through the summative evaluation of the worth of its processes and products.

No doubt these are what we all wish to achieve but seldom do. There is no shortage of soundly based advice. Brown and Bakhtar (1983) describe five main styles of lecturing: the visual information giver, the oral presenter, the exemplary (a blend of the two), the eclectic (a less successful blend, self-doubting but with a strong commitment to the subject), and the amorphous – vague and arrogant. They offer straightforward advice to the young lecturer, such as speak loudly and clearly, not too fast, with variation and pauses; plan, prepare and structure the lecture; make it understandable; watch for reactions and feedback; involve the audience; be satisfied with making four or five main points; and so on. Book-length treatments of the practical skills of college-level teaching are to be found in, for example, Beard and Hartley (1984); Brown and Atkins (1988); Lowman (1984); and Newble and Cannon (1989). To my mind Lowman is particularly convincing and practical. Obviously a whole book cannot be summarized, but his premise is that:

> . . . superior college teaching involves two distinct sets of skills. The first is speaking ability. This includes skill not only in giving clear, intellectually exciting lectures but also in leading discussions. The second is interpersonal skills. Such skills allow one to create the sort of warm, close

relationships with one's students that motivate them to work independently. To become an excellent instructor, one must be outstanding in one of these sets of skills and at least competent in the other.

By putting the emphasis on skills, Lowman is able to show that these abilities can be learned; though not necessarily equally well by all. There is perhaps a tendency to think that relationships in particular are matters best left to spontaneity. For teachers, such an attitude is unprofessional. At the same time, Gilbert Highet (1976) may have been right when he argued that new teachers need to learn basic techniques, but more than this they need to recognize that active energetic teaching is good for self-esteem; and this, he thought, could not be learned in short courses on teaching but came best from watching excellent teachers and by constant monitoring of one's own progress. One might add that something can be learned from watching the less good; as a demonstrator I determined, if I became a lecturer, never to brush off a student's enquiry with the remark 'You don't need to know that!', as the man out front did. Kjell Raaheim urges the use of an 'apprenticeship' model of learning which certainly has advantages. I suggested it in a polytechnic setting, but it would have entailed appointments at junior level which were ruled out of court by the trade unions. Yet it is not only a good way to learn, but valuable also both to the senior partner and to the students; I have seen it work very successfully.

Becher and Kogan (1980) among many others, point out that in general teaching has not been a valued part of university activity. They cite the two obvious reasons for this, one that it is research that gains prestige and promotion, and two that student-staff relationships have traditionally been regarded as private and personal; teaching problems are not commonly discussed and teaching has not been thought to require planning or preparation. This is probably changing to some extent, partly from the impetus (in the UK) of the CNAA and the polytechnics. Even in that sphere, my superior at NELP maintained consistently that one should not reward, e.g. promote, individuals for doing well what they were paid to do anyway, that is teach. Promotion must be linked to structure, which in effect meant administration. It is clear to me, however, and to the other writers of this volume, that effective teaching necessitates commitment. It is very difficult to fake enthusiasm, and very difficult to maintain it if what one is doing is not valued by others, both personally and financially.

We may well agree with Janek Wankowski that skilled teaching may be considered a facility for organizing the learning of others in such a way that they can become competent self-teachers for life. McCombs and Whistler (1989) consider that to enhance such autonomous learning, the teacher must, among other aims: understand and demonstrate real interest, caring and concern for each student and his or her needs, interests and goals; challenge students to invest effort in taking personal responsibility and being actively involved in learning activities; relate content and activities to personal needs, interests and goals; structure learning so that each student can accomplish personal goals and experience success. In practice, these rather general sounding aims are often a matter of an attitude which finds expression in numerous very small ways, such as making an effort to learn all one's students' names (as Lowman, 1984, advises), or taking a note of an article that might relate to a student's still vague idea for a project. The restaurateur Marco Pierre White is quoted as saying: 'To be a good chef all you have to do is a lot of little things well', and this can be applied to teaching.

The importance of effective teaching for student achievement, if it needs further demonstration, is convincingly analysed by Brophy (1986) on the basis of research findings. Although he is writing of American schools, his conclusions could be transferred with only changes of wording to European Higher Education:

> Even trained and experienced teachers vary widely in how well they organize the classroom, articulate achievement expectations and objectives, select and design academic tasks, and instruct their students. Those who do these things successfully produce significantly more achievement than those who do not, but doing them successfully demands a blend of energy, motivation, subject matter knowledge, and pedagogical skills that many teachers, let alone ordinary adults, do not possess. Thus, if we as a nation are serious about wanting good teaching in our schools, we will need not only to improve pay and working conditions so as to recruit and retain talented people but also to arm them with the knowledge and skills they need to do their job effectively. Contemporary research on teaching is contributing by identifying the knowledge and skills that are needed.

Taking Higher Education seriously

C. Northcote Parkinson (1957) described to brilliant comic effect the results of the British adoption, in the nineteenth century, of the venerable Chinese system of selection by competitive examination.

> It was assumed that classical learning and literary ability would fit any candidate for any administrative post. It was assumed (no doubt rightly) that a scientific education would fit a candidate for nothing – except, possibly, science . . . Men thus selected on their classical performance were then sent forth to govern India. Those with lower marks were retained to govern England. Those with still lower marks were rejected altogether or sent to the colonies. While it would be totally wrong to describe this system as a failure, no one could claim for it the success that had attended the systems hitherto in use. There was no guarantee, to begin with, that the man with the highest marks might not turn out to be off his head; as was sometimes found to be the case. Then again the writing of Greek verse might prove to be the sole accomplishment that some candidates had or ever would have. On occasion, a successful applicant may even have been impersonated at the examination by someone else, subsequently proving

unable to write Greek verse when the occasion arose. Selection by competitive examination was never therefore more than a moderate success.

It is, we must admit, so with Higher Education. Lecturers agree, as Entwistle has shown, that they seek to produce 'critical thinking' (rather than Greek verse); but it is by no means clear how the present systems of instruction and assessment are supposed to achieve this result (Marton *et al.*, 1984). More encouragingly, McMillan (1987), reviewing 27 studies, found evidence that students' critical thinking does improve while they are at college, but it is uncertain what features of the experience, if any, bring this about. In practice, students are assessed largely on subject knowledge which, as we have seen in Chapter 1, may be only loosely related to their subsequent lives.

Ideally, if we are to help students to learn, we must start by asking, learn what? and why? There is, in fact, no shortage of such questions and attempted answers, and no systematic review will be offered here. But it does seem to this writer that much is at a rather general level, and little appears to have had much impact over the last half century or century. As several writers have pointed out, for example Fulton (1988), Trow (1989), British Higher Education retains assumptions that have been superseded in most other 'developed' countries: it is restricted to some 14 per cent of the population (1988; planned rise to 18.5 per cent – Fulton), and it is seen as typically consisting in a three-year full-time single honours course, of equal high standard wherever it is taken. Of course much of this is fiction. Standards are manifestly not equivalent; even if final examinations can be approximately equated, the educational experiences in different institutions certainly cannot. Very large numbers of students do not follow the standard pattern; but they are massively discriminated against in terms of resources and prestige. This may or may not be the wisest national policy. Of course other countries have their own problems, as Kjell Raaheim has mentioned in respect of Norway. As to aims, in contrast to the view of lecturers, British official policy, as presented to Parliament by the Secretary of State for Education and Science (*Higher Education: Meeting the Challenge*, 1987) is that Higher Education should: serve the economy more effectively; pursue basic scientific research and scholarship in the arts and humanities; and have closer links with industry and commerce and promote enterprise. Quality will be enhanced by: improvements in the design and content of courses and in validation procedures; better teaching through staff training, development and appraisal; and more selectively funded research, targeted with attention to prospects for commercial exploitation. Efficiency will be increased by: improvements in institutional management; changes in the management of the system; and the development and use of performance indicators.

This book is not about educational policy, but as Barnett (1988) remarks, we can speak of two levels of educational aims: the operational, e.g. the aims of a course; and the philosophical, the ends an educational process must serve if it is . to count as education. Our purpose is to suggest ways of enhancing student learning, but by way of stimulating discussion and drawing attention to evidence and experience, rather than by prescribing set methods. Part of this must be the consideration of aims, at both levels. There is, indeed, some recognition that a re-appraisal is overdue (e.g. Becher and Kogan, 1987; Ball and Eggins, 1989). There is some recognition that appraisal of the process is not only possible but desirable; as Elton (1989) puts it: '. . . it is certainly possible to appraise both teachers and teaching in higher education, and . . . the widely held belief that such appraisal presents very great technical difficulties is false'.

An example of how appraisal can be given practical application comes, perhaps not surprisingly, from the USA, although even there it appears to be the first of its kind. In the 1983–5 biennium, the state of Ohio (population approximately 11 million) set an appropriation of $3,000,000 for Programme Excellence in undergraduate education. The purposes were (1) to recognize and reward high quality academic programmes at state-assisted colleges and universities; (2) to increase the quality of instruction through enrichment grants; and (3) to encourage academic excellence in associate and bacca-laureate programmes. These ends were served by defining excellence, by developing a competitive process for selection, based on peer review, and by grants of around $75–$200,000. The report of this initiative (Skinner and Tafel, 1986) cannot of course say anything about the long-term effects. But it is of interest to note the characteristics of excellence that were developed. These include: purposes and objectives of programmes clearly related to needs and interests of students, and curriculum appropriate to the objectives; match between student characteristics and quality and type of resources; faculty rated as outstanding, with particular attention to their role in undergraduate teaching and curriculum development; numerous examples of internal and external recognition of faculty and students; undergraduate involvement in research, publication and scientific and professional associations; careful internal pro-gramme reviews, with feedback used to improve system. It might be said that none of this would be at all unfamiliar to anyone who has served on a CNAA Subject Board; but the $3,000,000 certainly would be.

In the UK, at least, the search for excellence in undergraduate teaching has to be largely self-motivated. The present writers have offered views as to how students may be helped to learn, largely within the system in which they and their teachers happen to find themselves. Essentially, perhaps, our message has two parts. One is that education – at any level, but certainly at ours – is unavoidably and desirably a personal process; that is to say, it is a matter of interaction between individuals, and it is a matter of each assisting the development of the other, though the greater responsibility for this naturally rests with the teacher. It follows that effective teaching is unlikely without commitment and enthusiasm on the part of the teacher; and this implies both conditions that foster these attributes, and mastery of techniques by which they can have practical effect. This brings us to the second point, which is that student learning needs to be planned for. This means not only planning and appraisal of programmes, resources, and the conduct of teaching itself, but also the provision of back-up educational services and, perhaps the greatest of the present *lacunae*, proper training of teachers in Higher Education. On this point we would agree with Elton:

My credo then is that the academic profession needs training in much the same way as academics consider that other professions need it and indeed provide it for them. This means that the training itself must be professional, that it should normally lead to recognized academic qualifications, that it should be closely allied to practice and that – above all – it must be associated with relevant research.

(Elton, 1989)

It might be said that even if it is accepted that Higher Education presents a problem (and not all do so accept), then our solution is merely to throw money at it. Our answer is first, that every society must decide priorities, and we think a good case could be made for the value of more effective education; but second, that it costs little for the individual practitioner to reflect on what is being done, or invest in a book or two, or initiate a Departmental seminar, or experiment with student evaluation; as many do. We hope that this book may have contributed to the thinking of at least some readers – teachers, administrators, policy-makers and others.

Bibliography

Adams, M. J. (1989). 'Thinking skills curricula: Their promise and progress', *Educational Psychologist*, **24**, 25–77.

Alexander, P. A. and Judy, J. E. (1988). 'The interaction of domain-specific and strategic knowledge in academic performance', *Review of Educational Research*, **58**, 375–404.

Allport, G. W. (1955). *Personality: A psychological interpretation*. London, Constable.

Apps, J. W. (1988). *Higher Education in a Learning Society: Meeting new demands for education and training*. San Francisco/London, Jossey-Bass.

Baird, L. L. (1988). 'The college environment re-visited: A review of research and theory'. In Smart, J. C. (ed.), *Higher Education: Handbook of Theory and Practice*, Vol. IV. New York, Agathon Press.

Ball, C. and Eggins, H. (eds), (1989). *Higher Education into the 1990s*. Milton Keynes, Open University Press/SRHE.

Bamford, T. W. (1960). *Thomas Arnold*. London, Cresset Press.

Ban, T. A. (1966). *Conditioning and Psychiatry*. London, Allen & Unwin.

Bandura, A. (1969). *Principles of Behaviour Modification*. New York, Holt, Rinehart & Winston.

Barnett, R. A. (1988). 'Does higher education have aims?' *Journal of Philosophy of Education*, **22**, 239–50.

Batty, W. R. H. and Wankowski, J. A. (1974). *Admission Grades, Temperament and Degrees of Chemistry Students*. Birmingham, University of Birmingham Educational Survey and Counselling Unit. Mimeograph.

Beard, R. and Hartley, J. (1984). *Teaching and Learning in Higher Education*. London, Harper & Row.

Becher, T. and Kogan, M. (1980). *Process and Structure in Higher Education*. London, Heinemann.

Becher, T. and Kogan, M. (1987). *Calling Britain's Universities to Account*. London, Education Reform Group.

Beck, F. A. G. (1964). *Greek Education 450–350 BC*. London, Methuen.

Berg, C. (1957). *Being Lived by my Life*. London, George Allen & Unwin.

Bergendal, G. (1983). *Knowledge and Higher Education*. National Board for Universities and Colleges. Stockholm, Almquist and Wiksell International.

Betcher, T., Hewston, E., Parlett, H., Simon, A. and Squire, G. (1976). *Making the best of it; reconciling ends, means and resources in Higher Education.* London, Nuffield Foundation.

Bevan-Jones, H. (1974). *Degree Achievements, Use of Welfare Services and Reported Experience of Anxiety/Depression.* Birmingham, University of Birmingham Educational Survey and Counselling Unit Monograph.

Bligh, D. (1981). 'Study Counselling: The Exeter Experience'. In Frederick, J., Hancock, L., James, B., Bowden, J. and Macmillan, C. (1981). *Learning Skills: A Review of Needs and Services to University Students.* Parkville, University of Melbourne Centre for the Study of Higher Education.

Block, R. A. (1985). 'Education and thinking skills reconsidered', *American Psychologist,* **40**, 574–5.

Borkovec, T. D. (1976). 'Physiological and Cognitive Process in the Regulation of Anxiety'. In Schwartz, G. E. and Shapiro, D. (eds), *Consciousness and Self-Regulation,* Vol. 1. New York and London, Wiley.

Boud, D. (1987). *Appreciating Adults' Learning: From the learner's perspective.* London, Kogan Page.

Boud, D. (ed.), (1988). *Developing Student Autonomous Learning.* 2nd edn. London, Kogan Page.

Boys, C. J. and Kirkland, J. (1988). *Degrees of Success: Career aspirations and destinations of college, university and polytechnic graduates.* (Higher Education Policy Series No. 3.) London, Jessica Kingsley.

Bransford, J., Sherwood, R., Uye, N. and Rieser, J. (1986). 'Teaching thinking and problem solving: Research foundations', *American Psychologist,* **41**, 1078–89.

Brennan, J. and McGeevor, P. (1988). *Graduates at Work: Degree courses and the labour market.* (Higher Education Policy Series No. 1.) London, Jessica Kingsley.

Brennan, J. L. and Percy, K. A. (1976). *What do students want? An analysis of staff and student perceptions in British higher education.* Paper presented at The 2nd Congress of the European Association for Research and Development in Higher Education, Louvain-la-Neuve.

Breskvar, B. (1987). *Boris Becker's Tennis: The making of a champion.* London, Springfield Books.

British Journal of Guidance and Counselling (1977, January). 'Fieldwork: a Symposium of Practical Approaches in Higher Education', *British Journal of Guidance and Counselling,* **7** No. 1.

Brookfield, S. D. (1986). *Understanding and Facilitating Adult Learning: A comprehensive analysis of principles and effective practice.* Milton Keynes, Open University Press.

Brophy, J. (1986). 'Teacher influences on student achievement', *American Psychologist,* **41**, 969–1077.

Brophy, J. (1987). 'Socializing student motivation to learn'. In M. L. Maehr and D. A. Kleiber (eds), *Advances in Motivation and Achievement,* Vol. V. Greenwich, CT, TAL Press.

Brown, G. A. and Atkins, M. (eds) (1988). *Effective Teaching in Higher Education.* London, Methuen.

Brown, G. A. and Bakhtar, M. (eds) (1983). *Styles of Lecturing.* Loughborough, University of Loughborough, UK ASTD Publications.

Buzan, T. (1975). *Use Your Head.* London, BBC Publications.

Buzan, T. (1977). *How to Make the Most of Your Mind.* London, Colts Books.

Cannon, T. (1986). 'View from industry'. In G. Moodie (ed.), *Standards and Criteria in Higher Education.* Milton Keynes, Open University Press/SRHE.

Chance, M. R. A. (1979). *A Biological Systems Synthesis of Mentality Revealing and Underlying*

Functional Bi-Modality. Birmingham, Hedonic and Agonic Social Systems Institute. (Private communication.)

Chandler, (1978). *Student Counselling, When and Why?* Exeter University Teaching Service, Exeter, Devon.

Chibnall, B. (1979). 'The Sussex Experience'. In Hills, P. J. (ed.), *Study Courses and Counselling: Problems and Possibilities*. Research into Higher Education Monographs. Guildford: University of Surrey, The Society for Research into Higher Education.

Chipman, S. F. and Segal, J. W. (1985). 'Introduction'. In Segal, J. W., Chipman, S. F. and Glaser, R. (eds), *Thinking and Learning Skills*. Hillsdale, NJ, Lawrence Erlbaum Associates.

Choppin, B. H. L. *et al.* (1973). *The Prediction of Academic Success*. Slough, National Foundation for Educational Research Publishing Company Ltd.

Clarke, S. (1988). 'Another look at the degree results of men and women', *Studies in Higher Education*, **13**, 315–31.

Committee of Vice Chancellors and Principals (1986). *Academic Staff Training: Code of Practice for considerations and comments by Universities*. (Available from C.V.C.P., 29 Tavistock Square, London wc1h 9ez.)

Common, D. L. (1989). 'Master teachers in higher education: A matter of settings', *The Review of Higher Education*, **12**, 375–87.

Cox, J. B. (1971). *Six-year trends in undergraduate wastage*. Birmingham, University of Birmingham Education Survey Monograph.

Craik, F. I. M. and Lockhart, R. S. (1972). 'Levels of processing: A framework for memory research', *Journal of Verbal Learning and Verbal Behaviour*, **11**, 671–84.

Da Costa, M. (1979). 'Profile of a Study Skill Workshop'. In Hills, P. J. (ed.), *Study Courses and Counselling: Problems and Possibilities*. Research into Higher Education Monographs, Guildford: University of Surrey, Society for Research into Higher Education.

Dahlgren, L. O. (1984). 'Higher education: Impact on students'. In Huren, T. and Postlethwaite, T. N. (eds), *International Encyclopaedia of Education*, New York, Pergamon.

Danziger, D. (1988). *Eton Voices*. London, Viking Books.

Davies, D. (1986). *Maximizing Examination Performance: A Psychological Approach*. London, Kogan Page.

Davies, J. (1988). *Staff perception of Students' Learning Difficulties and Implications for Staff Development*. Ph.D. Thesis, University of Manchester.

Derry, S. J. and Murphy, D. A. (1986). 'Designing systems that train learning ability: From theory to practice', *Review of Educational Research*, **56**, 1–39.

Dunstan, J. (1978). *Paths to Excellence and the Soviet School*. Windsor, NFER.

Dunstan, J. (1987). 'Equalization and differentiation in the Soviet school 1958–1985: A curriculum approach'. In Dunstan, J. (ed.), *Soviet Education Under Scrutiny*. Glasgow, Jordanhill College Publications.

Dweck, C. S. (1986). 'Motivational processes affecting learning', *American Psychologist*, **41**, 1040–8.

Eccles, J. S. (1985). 'Why doesn't Jane run? Sex differences in educational and occupational patterns'. In Horowitz, F. D. and O'Brien, M. (eds), *The Gifted and the Talented: Developmental perspectives*. Washington, DC, American Psychological Association.

Elton, L. (1989). *Teaching in Higher Education: Appraisal and Training*. London, Kogan Page.

Elton, L. R. B. and Laurillard, D. M. (1979, March). 'Trends in Research on Students Learning'. *Studies in Higher Education*, **4**, No. 1.

Elton, L. R. B., Hodgson, K. and O'Connell, S. (1979). 'Study Counselling at the University of Surrey'. In Hills, P. J. (ed.), *Study Courses and Counselling: Problems and Possibilities*. Research into Higher Education Monographs, Guildford: University of Surrey, The Society for Research into Higher Education.

Entwistle, N. (1987). 'A model of the teaching-learning process.' In Richardson, J. T. E., Eysenck, M. W. and Warren-Piper, D. (eds), *Student Learning: Research in education and cognitive psychology*. Milton Keynes, Open University Press.

Entwistle, N. (1988). 'Motivational factors in students' approaches to learning'. In Schmeck, R. R. (ed.), *Learning Strategies and Learning Styles*. New York, Plenum Press.

Entwistle, N. (1990, January). *How students learn and why they fail*. Paper presented at the Conference of Professors of Engineering, London.

Entwistle, N. and Tait, H. (1989). 'Approaches to learning, evaluations of teaching, and preferences for contrasting academic environments'. *Higher Education*, **18**, 1–24.

Entwistle, N. J. (1981). *Styles of Learning and Teaching*. Chichester, Wiley.

Entwistle, N. J. (in press). 'How students learn, and why they fail'. In Radford, J. (ed.), *Talent, Teaching and Achievement*. London, Sigma Forlag/Jessica Kingsley.

Entwistle, N. J. and Ramsden, P. (1983). *Understanding Students Learning*. London/New York, Croom Helm/Nichols.

Entwistle, N. J. and Wilson, J. D. (1977). *Degrees of Excellence: The Academic Achievement Game*. London, Hodder & Stoughton.

Erikson, E. H. (1959). *Young Man Luther*. London, Faber.

Erikson, E. H. (1967). *Childhood and Society*. Harmondsworth, Penguin.

Erikson, E. H. (1971). *Identity, Youth in Crisis*. London, Faber.

Eysenck, H. J. (1965). *Fact and Fiction in Psychology*. Harmondsworth, Penguin.

Eysenck, H. J. (1970). *The Structure of Human Personality*. London, Methuen University Paperbacks.

Eysenck, H. J. (1975). 'The Learning Theory Model of Neurosis: A New Approach', *Behavioural Research and Therapy*, **14**, London, Pergamon Press.

Eysenck, H. J. (1988). 'Intelligence and personality in school learning', *Educational and Child Psychology*, **5**, 21–38.

Eysenck, H. J. and Wilson, G. (1975). *Know Your Own Personality*. London, Temple Smith.

Eysenck, H. J. and Wilson, G. D. (1976). *A Textbook of Human Psychology*. Lancaster, M.T.P. Press.

Fazakerly, M. (1972). *Wastage: A Survey of a Sample of Early Leavers from a Polytechnic Department of Education*. An unpublished paper. In Discussion of Papers Presented at Eighth Annual Conference of the Society for Research into Higher Education 1972.

Foster, J. J. (1985). 'Assessing student learning: Psychologists in blinkers?', *Bulletin of the British Psychological Society*, **38**, 370–4.

Fraser, B. J., Walberg, H. J., Welch, W. W. and Hattie, J. A. (1987). 'Syntheses of educational productivity research', *International Journal of Educational Research*, **11**, 145–252.

Freud, S. (1949). *An Outline of Psychoanalysis*. New York, Norton.

Fulton, O. (1988). 'Elite survivals? Entry "standards" and procedures for higher education admissions', *Studies in Higher Education*, **13**, 15–25.

Furneaux, W. D. (1961). *The Chosen Few*. Oxford, Oxford University Press.

Furneaux, W. D. (1962). 'The Psychologist and the University', *Universities Quarterly*, **17**, No. 1. London, Turnstile Press.

Gibbs, G. and Northedge, A. (1979). 'Helping Students to Understand Their Own Study Methods'. *British Journal of Guidance and Counselling*, **7**, No. 1.

Gibson, A. (1986). 'Inspecting education'. In Moodie, G. (ed.), *Standards and Criteria in Higher Education*. Milton Keynes, SHRE/Open University Press.

Glaser, R. (1984). 'Education and thinking: The role of knowledge', *American Psychologist*, **39**, 93–104.

Glover, E. (1955). *The Techniques of Psycho-Analysis*. London, Baillière, Tindall & Cox.

Goldman, G. (1979a). 'When "Knowing How" is Not Enough'. *British Journal of Guidance and Counselling*, **7**, No. 1.

Goldman, G. (1979b). 'A Contract for Academic Improvement'. In Hills, P. J. (ed.), *Study Courses and Counselling: Problems and Possibilities*. Research into Higher Education Monographs, Guildford: University of Surrey, Society for Research into Higher Education.

Grey Walter, W. (1961). *The Living Brain*. Harmondsworth, Penguin.

Gutteridge, R. and Giller, N. (1987). *Mike Tyson: For whom the Bell Tolls*. London, W. H. Allen/Star.

Hajnal, J. (1972). *The Student Trap*. Harmondsworth, Penguin.

Hari-Augstein, E. and Thomas, L. F. (1979). 'Learning Conversations: A Person-Centred Approach to Self-Organized Learning'. *British Journal of Guidance and Counselling*, **7**, No. 1.

Hart, L. A. (1975). *How the Brain Works*. New York, Basie Books.

Hart, L. A. (1983). *Human Brain and Human Learning*. New York and London, Longman.

Hatch, S. (1972). 'Change and Dissent in the Universities'. In Butcher, H. J. and Rudd, E. (eds), *Contemporary Problems in Higher Education*. Maidenhead, McGraw-Hill.

Hawkins, C. A. (1982). *A study of access to higher education and student attrition written in answer to a question 'On which point is the articulation between school and university problematic?' Skimming the milk and whipping the cream*. Utrecht: Rijksuniversitteit, Afdeling Onderzoek en Ontwikkeling van hat Onderwijs. Monograph.

Hemery, D. (1986). *Sporting Excellence. A study of sport's highest achievers*. London, Collins (Willow Books).

Highet, G. (1976). *The Immortal Profession*. New York, Weybright & Talley.

Higher Education: Meeting the Challenge Cmd 114. London, HMSO.

Hills, P. J. (ed.) (1979). *Study Courses and Counselling: Problems and Possibilities*. Guildford: University of Surrey, Society for Research into Higher Education.

Hills, P. J. and Potter, F. W. (1979). 'Group Counselling and Study Skills'. In Hills, P. J. (ed.), *Study Courses and Counselling: Problems and Possibilities*. Research into Higher Education Monographs, Guildford: University of Surrey, Society for Research into Higher Education.

Holder, R. L. and Wankowski, J. A. (1980a). *Personality and Academic Performance of Students at University*. Research into Higher Education Monographs, Guildford: University of Surrey, Society for Research into Higher Education.

Holder, R. and Wankowski, J. A. (1980b). *Personality and Academic Performance*. Research into Higher Education monographs, Guildford: University of Surrey, Society for Research into Higher Education.

Hollin, C. (1989). *Psychology and Crime: An introduction to criminological psychology*. London, Routledge.

Hudson, L. (1970). *Frames of Mind*. Harmondsworth, Penguin.

Huxley, A. (1937). *Ends and Means*. London, Chatto & Windus.

Jacobsen, B. F. (1978). 'Studenter og studievansker'. *Forskning fra Psykologisk Institutt i Bergen*, 1978, 2.

James, D. (1979). 'Counselling the Mature Students'. In Hills, P. J. (ed.), *Study Courses and Counselling: Problems and Possibilities*. Research into Higher Education Monographs, Guildford: University of Surrey, Society for Research into Higher Education.

James, W. (1890). *The Principles of Psychology*. New York, Henry Holt.

Johnes, J. and Taylor, J. (1987). 'Degree quality: An investigation into differences between UK universities'. *Higher Education*, **16**, 581–602.

Johnes, J. and Taylor, J. (1989). 'Undergraduate noncompletion rates: Differences between UK universities'. *Higher Education*, **18**, 209–25.

Jones, J. (1989). 'Students' ratings of teacher personality and teaching competence'. *Higher Education*, **18**, 551–8.

Katkin, E. S. (1975). 'Electrodermal Lability: A psychophysiological Analysis of Individual Differences in Response to Stress'. In Sarason, I. G. and Spielberger, C. D. (eds), *Stress and Anxiety*. New York and London, Wiley.

Keith, T. Z., Pottebaum, S. M. and Eberhardt, S. (1986). 'Effects of self-concept on academic achievement: A large-sample path analysis'. *Journal of Psychoeducational Assessment*, **4**, 61–72.

Kelly, G. A. (1955). *The Psychology of Personal Constructs, Vols. 1 and 2*. New York, Methuen.

Kelly, G. A. (1963). 'The Autobiography of a Theory'. Unpublished Manuscript. Ohio State University. In Bannister, D. and Mair, J. M. M. (1968), *The Evaluation of Personal Construct Theory*. London and New York, Academic Press.

Kiell, N. (1964). *The Universal Experience of Adolescence*. London, University of London Press.

Kipnis, D. (1971). *Character Structure and Impulsiveness*. London, Academic Press.

Kogan, M. (ed.) (1989). *Evaluating Higher Education* (Higher Education Policy Series, No. 6). London, Jessica Kingsley.

Kornbrot, D. E. (1987). 'Degree performance as a function of discipline studied, parental occupation and gender'. *Higher Education*, **16**, 513–34.

Kozielecki, J. (1977). *Koncepje Psychologiczne Czlowieka*. Warszawa, Panstwowy Instytut Wydawniczy.

Kurz, R. S., Mueller, J. J., Gibbons, J. L. and Dicataldo, F. (1989). 'Faculty performance: Suggestions for the refinement of the concept and its measurement'. *Journal of Higher Education*, **60**, 43–58.

Kwiatkowski, J. W. (1973). *A Study of Academic Attitudes and Their Relationship to Personality*. Unpublished thesis. Department of Mathematical Statistics, University of Birmingham.

Lambourne, D. (1979). 'Seeing a Model of Learning'. In *Proceedings of a Joint Conference of the Society for Research into Higher Education and Staff Development and Educational Methods Unit*. Manchester Polytechnic Conference Papers, No. 27.

Leff, G. (1989, September 8). 'Inventions of mediaeval minds'. *The Times Higher Education Supplement*.

Lowman, J. (1984). *Mastering the Techniques of Teaching*. San Francisco, Jossey-Bass.

Luria, A. R. (1973). *The Working Brain*. Harmondsworth, Penguin.

Mace, C. A. (1948). *The idea of a faculty*. Reprinted in Mace, M. (Ed.), *Selected Papers*, 1973. London, Methuen.

MacMurray, J. (1961). *Person in Relation*. London, Faber.

Malcolm, N. (1958). *Ludwig Wittgenstein: A memoir*. Oxford, Oxford University Press.

Malleson, N. (1972). 'Student Wastage in the United Kingdom'. In Butcher, J. H. and Rudd, E. (eds), *Contemporary Problems in Higher Education*. Maidenhead, McGraw-Hill.

Manske, M. E. and Davies, G. A. (1968). 'Effects of simple instructional biases upon performance in the Unusual Uses Test'. *Journal of General Psychology*, **79**, 25–33.

Marsh, H. W. (1987). 'Students' evaluations of university teaching: Research findings, methodological issues, and directions for future research'. *International Journal of Educational Research*, **11**, 253–388.

Marsh, H. W., Byrne, B. M. and Shavelson, R. J. (1988). 'A multi-faceted academic self-concept: Its hierarchical structure and its relation to academic achievement'. *Journal of Educational Psychology*, **80**, 366–80.

Martin, E. and Ramsden, P. (1987). 'Learning skills or skill in learning?' In Richardson, J. T. E., Eysenck, M. W. and Warren-Piper, D. (eds), *Student Learning: Research in Education and Cognitive Psychology*. Milton Keynes, SHRE/Open University Press.

Marton, F., Hounsell, D. and Entwistle, N. (eds), (1984). *Cap the Experience of Learning*. Edinburgh, Scottish Academic Press.

Mathieson, M. and Bernbaum, G. (1988, August 19). 'Preach, don't just teach'. *The Times Higher Education Supplement*.

McCombs, B. L. and Whistler, J. S. (1989). 'The role of affective variables in autonomous learning'. *Educational Psychologist*, **24**, 277–306.

McKenzie, D. (1987). 'Teaching students who already know the truth'. *Cultic Studies Journal*, **4**, 61–72.

McMillan, J. H. (1987). 'Enhancing students' critical thinking: A review of studies'. *Research in Higher Education*, **26**, 3–29.

Medawar, P. B. (1972). *The Hope of Progress*. London, Methuen.

Meichenbaum, D., Turk, D. and Burnstein, S. (1975). 'The Nature of Coping with Stress'. In Sarason, I. G. and Spielberger, C. D. (eds), *Stress and Anxiety, Vol. 2*. New York, Wiley.

Meyer, B. C. (1967). *Joseph Conrad: A Psychoanalytical Biography*. Princeton, NJ, Princeton University Press.

Mill, J. S. (1873). *Autobiography*. Oxford, Oxford University Press, reprinted 1924.

Morris, L. W., Brown, N. R. and Halbert, B. L. (1977). 'Effects of Symbolic Modelling on the Arousal of Cognitive and Affective Components of Anxiety in Pre-School Children'. In Sarason, I. G. and Spielberger, C. D. (eds), *Stress and Anxiety*. New York, Wiley.

Moses, I. (1985). 'The Role of Head of Department in the pursuit of excellence'. *Higher Education*, **14**, 337–54.

Mumford, M. D., Weeks, J. L., Harding, F. D. and Fleishman, E. A. (1988). 'Relations between student characteristics, course content, and training outcomes: an integrative modeling effort'. *Journal of Applied Psychology*, **73**, 443–56.

Musgrove, F. (1971). *Patterns and Authority in English Education*. London, Methuen.

Nelson-Jones, R. and Toner, H. L. (1978). 'Approaches to increasing student learning competence'. *British Journal of Guidance and Counselling*, **6**, 19–34.

Nelson-Jones, R. and Toner, H. L. (1979). 'Counselling Approaches to Increasing Students' Learning Competence'. In Hills, P. J. (ed.), *Study Courses and Counselling: Problems and Possibilities*. Research into Higher Education Monographs, Guildford: University of Surrey, Society for Research into Higher Education.

Newble, D. and Cannon, R. (1989). *A Handbook for Teachers in Universities and Colleges: A guide to improving teaching methods*. London, Kogan Page.

Nielsen, G. (1971). *Prediksjon av problemløsere*. Thesis on file, University of Oslo.

Nixon, P. G. F. (1976). 'The Human Function Curve, with Special Reference to Cardiovascular Disorders'. *The Practitioner* (1976), 217, 765 and 935.

Nucci, L. and Pascarella, E. T. (1987). 'The influence of college on moral development'.

In Smart, J. C. (ed.), *Higher Education: Handbook of Theory and Practice* (Vol. III). New York, Agathon Press.

Oleron, P. (1978). 'Development of Cognitive Skills'. In Lesgold, A. M. (ed.), *Cognitive Psychology and Instruction*. New York, Plenum.

O'Sullivan, D. A. (1970). *A study of the relationship between education attitudes and personality*. Unpublished M. Sc. Dissertation, Department of Mathematical Statistics, University of Birmingham.

Parkinson, C. N. (1979). *The Law: Or still In Pursuit* (revised edn. of *Parkinson's Law: Or The Pursuit of Progress*, 1957). London, John Murray.

Parkyn, G. W. (1967). *Success and Failure at the University*. Wellington, New Zealand Council for Educational Research.

Pascarella, E. T. (1985). 'College environmental influences on learning and cognitive development: A critical review and synthesis'. In Smart, J. C. (ed.), *Higher Education: Handbook of Theory and Practice* (Vol. 1). New York, Agathon Press.

Pask, G. and Scott, B. (1971). *Learning Strategies and Individual Competence*. London, Systems Research Ltd.

Peel, E. A. (1956). *The Psychological Basis of Education*. Edinburgh, Oliver & Boyd.

Perry, W. G. Jr. (1970). *Forms of Intellectual and Ethical Development in the College Years: A scheme*. New York, Holt, Rinehart & Winston.

Pickering, G. (1949). *Creative Malady*. London, Allen & Unwin.

Piechowski, M. and Colangelo, N. (1984). 'Developmental potential of the gifted'. *Gifted Child Quarterly*, **28**, 80–8.

Polgar, L. (1989, November 10). *Guardian*.

Polya, G. (1948). *How to solve it*. Princeton, NJ, Princeton University Press.

Popper, K. (1986). *Unended Quest: An Intellectual Autobiography*. Glasgow, Collins (Flamingo/Fontana Paperbacks).

Powell, J. P. (1985). 'The residues of learning: Autobiographical accounts by graduates of the impact of higher education'. *Higher Education*, **14**, 127–47.

Powell, J. P. and Cracknell, G. (1987). 'The enduring effects of science education: Graduates' views on what they learned'. *Research in Science and Technological Education*, **5**, 107–19.

Prawat, R. S. (1989). 'Promoting access to knowledge, strategy and disposition in students: A research synthesis'. *Review of Educational Research*, **59**, 1–41.

Raaheim, A. (1984). 'Can students be taught to study? An evaluation of a study skill programme directed at first year students at the University of Bergen'. *Scandinavian Journal of Educational Research*, **28**, 9–15.

Raaheim, A. (1987). 'Learning to Learn at University'. *Scandinavian Journal of Educational Research*, **31**, 191–7.

Raaheim, K. (1964). 'Analysis of the missing part in problem situations'. *Scandinavian Journal of Psychology*, **5**, 149–52.

Raaheim, K. (1974). *Problem Solving and Intelligence*, Bergen, Oslo, Tromsø: Universitetsforlaget.

Raaheim, K. (1984). *Why intelligence is not enough*. Bergen, Sigma Forlag.

Raaheim, K. and Manger, T. (1983). 'Hvordan går det til eksamen?' *UNIPED*, No. 1, 1983.

Raaheim, A. and Raaheim, K. (1982). 'Hvem egner seg til å studere?' UNIPED, **3–4**, 36–7.

Raaheim, K. and Wankowski, J. A. (1981). *Helping Students to Learn at University*. Bergen, Sigma Forlag.

Radford, J. (1990). *Child Prodigies and Exceptional Early Achievers*. Hemel Hempstead, Harvester-Wheatsheaf.

Radford, J. and Rose, D. (1989). *A Liberal Science: Psychology education past, present and future*. Milton Keynes, SHRE/Open University Press.

Ramsden, P. and Entwistle, N. (1981). 'Effects of academic department on students' approach to studying'. *British Journal of Educational Psychology*, **51**, 368–83.

Reid, W. A. (1971). *The Universities and The Sixth Form Curriculum Report No. 1*. Birmingham: University of Birmingham and Schools Council Sixth Form and Examination Projects. Mimeograph.

Reid, W. A. (1979). 'Making the Problem Fit the Method: A review of the "Banbury Enquiry"'. *Journal of Curriculum Studies*, **11** (2).

Rest, J. V. (1988). 'Why does college promote development in moral judgment?' *Journal of Moral Development*, **17**, 183–94.

Richardson, J. T. E. (1989). 'Cognitive skills and psychology education'. In Radford, J. and Rose, D. (eds), *A Liberal Science: Psychology education past, present and future*. Milton Keynes, SHRE/Open University Press.

Rogers, J. (1989). *Adults Learning*, 3rd edn. Milton Keynes, Open University Press.

Roizen, J. and Jepson, M. (1985). *Degrees for Jobs: Employers' expectations of higher education*. Guildford, SHRE and NFER/Nelson.

Rozycka, J. (1979). 'Neurotyzm w Aspekcie Psychologicznym na Podstawie Badan Empirycznych (The Psychological Aspect of Neuroticism on the Basis of Empirical Investigations)'. *Acta Universitatis Wraclaviensis No. 483. Prace Psychologiczne XV* Wroclaw, Wydawnictwo Universytetu Wroclawskiego.

Ryle, A. (1972) 'Student Health and Counselling'. In Butcher, H. J. and Rudd, E. (eds), *Contemporary Problems in Higher Education*. Maidenhead, McGraw-Hill.

Saenger-Ceha, M. M. T. (1970). *Psychological and Social Factors in Student Drop Out*. Amsterdam, Swetz & Zeitlinger.

Salomon, G. and Perkins, D. N. (1989). 'Rocky roads to transfer: Rethinking mechanisms of a neglected phenomenon'. *Educational Psychologist*, **24**, 113–42.

Sandven, J. (1979a). 'Conditions for Self-Realisation. A Theoretical Diversion'. *Scandinavian Journal of Educational Research*, **23**.

Sandven, J. (1979b). 'Social Sensitivity as a Factor in the Teaching Process: A Theoretical Discussion'. *Scandinavian Journal of Educational Research*, **23**.

Savell, J. M., Twohig, P. T. and Rachford, D. L. (1986). 'Empirical status of Feuerstein's "Instrumental Enrichment" (FIE) technique as a method of teaching thinking skills'. *Review of Educational Research*, **56**, 381–409.

Schwartz, G. E. and Shapiro, D. (1976). *Consciousness and Self-Regulation Vol. 1*. London and New York, Wiley.

Seligman, M. E. P. (1975). *Helplessness: On Depression, Development and Death*. San Francisco, W. H. Freeman.

Serna, L. A. (1989). Implications of student motivation on study skills instruction. *Academic Therapy*, **24**, 503–14.

Sheffield, E. F. (ed.) (1974). *Teaching in the Universities: No one way*. Montreal, McGill University Press.

Sherman, T. M., Armistead, L. P., Fowler, F., Barksdale, M. A. and Reif, G. (1987). 'The quest for excellence in university teaching'. *Journal of Higher Education*, **48**, 66–84.

Skinner, P. and Tafel, J. (1986). 'Promoting excellence in undergraduate teaching in Ohio'. *Journal of Education*, **57**, 93–105.

Smith, C. U. M. (1970). *The Brain: Towards Understanding*. New York, Putnam.

Smith, P. K. and Cowie, H. (1988). *Understanding Children's Development*. Oxford, Blackwell.

Snow, R. E. (1986). 'Individual differences and the design of educational programs'. *American Psychologist*, **41**, 1029–39.

Stern, G. G. (1970). *People in Context: Measuring Person-Environment Congruence in Education and Industry*. New York, Wiley.

Taylor, P. H., Reid, W. A. and Holley, B. J. (1974). *The English Sixth Form*. London, Routledge & Kegan Paul.

Tennyson, R. D. and Rasch, M. (1988). 'Linking cognitive learning theory to instructional prescriptions'. *Instructional Science*, **17**, 369–85.

Terenzini, P. T. and Wright, T. M. (1987). 'Influences on students' academic growth during four years of college'. *Research in Higher Education*, **26**, 161–79.

Thelin, J. R. and Yankovich, J. (1987). 'Bricks and mortar: Architecture and the study of Higher Education'. In Smart, J. C. (ed.), *Higher Education: Handbook of theory and practice*, Vol. III. New York, Agathon Press.

Thomas, J. W. (1988). 'Proficiency at academic studying'. *Contemporary Education Psychology*, **13**, 265–75.

Thorne, B. (1979). 'Study Skills – A Symposium of Practical Approaches in Higher Education'. In *British Journal of Guidance and Counselling*, **7**, No. 1.

Tobias, S. (1989). 'Another look at research on the adaptation of instruction to student characteristics'. *Educational Psychologist*, **24**, 213–27.

Tomkins, S. S. (1966). 'The Psychology of Commitment. In Tomkins, S. S. and Izard, C. E. (eds), *Affect, Cognition and Personality*. Empirical Studies. London, Tavistock.

Toynbee, P. (1979, December 24). 'Canterbury Cathedral Choir Boys'. *Guardian*.

Trow, M. (1989). 'The Robbins trap: British attitudes and the limits of expansion'. *Higher Education Quarterly*, 45–75.

University Grants Committee (1968). *Enquiry into Student Progress*. London, HMSO.

University of Birmingham (1978). *Where to go for advice*. Birmingham, University of Birmingham Publications.

Vermunt, J. D. H. M. and Van Rijswijk, F. A. W. (1988). 'Analysis and development of students' skill in self-regulated learning'. *Higher Education*, **17**, 647–82.

Waitley, D. E. (1987). *The Psychology of Winning*. Chicago, Illinois, Nightingale-Conaut Corporation.

Wankowski, J. A. (1969a). *Students – why some fail: An interim report on enquiries into failure and withdrawal of students*. Birmingham, University of Birmingham Educational Survey Unit.

Wankowski, J. A. (1969b). *Random Sample Analysis: Motives and Goals in University studies*. Birmingham, University of Birmingham Educational Survey. (Monograph, 1969, and part 2 in 1970).

Wankowski, J. A. (1970). *GCE's and Degrees: Some Notes and Reflections on Studies of the Relationship Between Admission Requirements and Achievement at University*. Birmingham, University of Birmingham Educational Survey. Mimeograph.

Wankowski, J. A. (1970). 'Residence and success at University'. In *Alta* University of Birmingham Magazine.

Wankowski, J. A. (1973a). 'Educational Counselling: A Helping Hand in Restoring Shattered Learning Competence'. In *Proceedings of a Conference of the British Student Health Association*, 25th edn.

Wankowski, J. A. (1973b, October 12). 'Disenchanted elite'. In *The Times Higher Educational Supplement*.

Wankowski, J. A. (1973c, December). 'Academic Degrees and Personality of Students in one British University'. In the *Proceedings of the First Congress of the European Association for Research and Development in Higher Education*. Rotterdam.

Wankowski, J. A. (1974, May). 'Teaching Method and Academic Success in Sixth Forms and University'. *Journal of Curriculum Studies*, **6** (1).

Wankowski, J. A. (1977, January). 'Learning How to Learn at University: The case for an Experimental Centre'. *British Journal of Guidance and Counselling*, **5** (1).

Wankowski, J. A. (1977b, January). 'Educational Counselling and Learning Through Teaching'. *British Journal of Guidance and Counselling*, **7** (1).

Wankowski, J. A. (1979a). *Reluctance Towards Professional Training of University Teachers: Taboo or Prudence?* Unpublished paper written at the request of the editor of Impetus, the Forum of the Co-ordinating Committee for Training University Teachers. CVCP, Tavistock Square, London.

Wankowski, J. A. (1980). 'A search for knowledge: The student's perception of his courses'. In the *Proceedings of a Joint Conference of the Society for Research into Higher Education and Staff Development and Educational Methods Unit, Manchester Polytechnic, Conference Papers No. 27*. Mimeograph.

Wankowski, J. A. (1983). *How students view the help given to them by the Study Assistance Unit*. Birmingham, University of Birmingham Educational Counselling Unit Monograph.

Wankowski, J. A. (1985, July 2–5). 'A brief outline of proposals for improvement of Professional Training of University Teachers: A case for a Diploma in Teaching in Higher Education'. In the *Proceedings of the Eleventh International Conference on Improving University Teaching*, Vol. II. Utrecht, Netherlands.

Wankowski, J. A. (1989a). *Study Assistance Work in a British University: Implications, reflections and recommendations for research and teaching in higher education*. Occasional publication in connection with the 'Action Research' project in the University of Bergen: 'New forms of education at the first stages of study at the University'. University of Bergen Department of Cognitive Psychology, 5007, Bergen, Norway.

Wankowski, J. A. (1989b). *Study Assistance Tutorship: Personal Audit: Second evaluation exercise of how students view the help given to them in the Study Assistance Unit*. Birmingham, University of Birmingham Educational Counselling Unit Monograph.

Wankowski, J. A. (1990). *Study Assistance Tutorship: Personal Audit; second evaluation exercise of how students view the help given to them by the Study Assistance Unit*. Birmingham, University of Birmingham Educational Counselling Unit Monograph.

Wankowski, J. A. and Cox, J. B. (1973a). *Temperament, Motivation and Academic Achievement: Studies of Success and Failure of a Random Sample of Students in One University*. Birmingham, University of Birmingham Educational Survey and Counselling Unit.

Wankowski, J. A. and Cox, J. B. (1973b). *Temperament, Motivation and Academic Achievement*. Full version. Birmingham, University of Birmingham Educational Survey and Counselling Monograph.

Wankowski, J. A. and Reid, W. A. (1982). 'The Psychology of Curriculum Theorizing: A Conversation'. In *The Journal of Curriculum Theorizing*. New York, Plenum.

Wankowski, J. A., Reid, W. A., Raaheim, K. and Jacobsen, B. F. (1984). *Upper Secondary Students in Norway, England and USA: their personalities, study habits and occupational interests*. Department of Curriculum Studies and Educational Counselling Unit, University of Birmingham Monograph.

Waters, M., Kemp, E. and Pucci, A. (1988). 'High and low faculty evaluations: Descriptions by students'. *Teaching of Psychology*, **15**, 203–4.

Weiner, I. B. (1970). *Psychological Disturbance in Adolescence.* New York and London, Wiley.

Wells, H. G. (1966). *Experiment in Autobiography, being the Autobiography of H. G. Wells.* London, Victor Gollancz and the Cresset Press.

Willis-Lee, R. (1982). *Towards a New Model of Order and Change in Counselling Provision at Birmingham University.* Research Fellowship Final Report in Educational Counselling (1979–1982). University of Birmingham Educational Counselling Unit. Unpublished Monograph.

Wlodkowski, R. J. (1985). *Enhancing Adult Motivation to Learn: A Guide to Improving Instruction and Increasing Learner Achievement.* San Francisco, Jossey-Bass.

Name Index

Subject Index

The Society for Research into Higher Education

The Society exists both to encourage and co-ordinate research and development into all aspects of Higher Education; including academic, organizational and policy issues; and also to provide a forum for debate, verbal and printed.

The Society's income derives from subscriptions, book sales, conference fees, and grants. It receives no subsidies and is wholly independent. Its corporate members are institutions of higher education, research institutions and professional, industrial, and governmental bodies. Its individual members include teachers and researchers, administrators and students. Members are found in all parts of the world and the Society regards its international work as amongst its most important activities.

The Society is opposed to discrimination in higher education on grounds of belief, race, etc.

The Society discusses and comments on policy, organizes conferences, and encourages research. It is studying means of preserving archives of higher education. Under the imprint SRHE & OPEN UNIVERSITY PRESS it is a specialist publisher of research, having some 30 titles in print. The Editorial Board of the Society's Imprint seeks authoritative research or study in the field. It offers competitive royalties; a highly recognizable format in both hard- and paper-back; and the world-wide reputation of the Open University Press. The Society also publishes *Studies in Higher Education* (three times a year), which is mainly concerned with academic issues; *Higher Education Quarterly* (formerly *Universities Quarterly*), mainly concerned with policy issues; *Abstracts* (three times a year); an *International Newsletter* (twice a year) and *SRHE NEWS* (four times a year).

The Society's Committees, Study Groups and Branches are run by members (with help from a small secretariat at Guildford). The Groups at present include a Teacher Education Study Group, a Staff Development Group, a Continuing Education Group, a Women in Higher Education Group and an Excellence in Teaching Group. The Groups may have their own organization, subscriptions, or publications; (e.g. the *Staff Development Newsletter*). A further *Questions of Quality* Group has organized a series of Anglo-American seminars in the USA and the UK.

The Society's annual conferences are held jointly; 'Access & Institutional Change' (1989, with the Polytechnic of North London). In 1990, the topic will be 'Industry and Higher Education' (with the University of Surrey). In 1991, the topic will be 'Research and Higher Education', with the University of Leicester: in 1992, it will be 'Learning &

Teaching' (with Nottingham Polytechnic). In 1993, the topic will be 'Governments, Higher Education and Accountability'. Other conferences have considered '*HE After the Election*' (1987) and '*After the Reform Act*' (July 1988).

Members receive free of charge the Society's *Abstracts*, annual conference Proceedings, (or 'Precedings'), *SRHE News* and *International Newsletter*. They may buy *SRHE & Open University Press* books at 35 per cent discount, and *Higher Education Quarterly* on special terms. Corporate members also receive the Society's journal *Studies in Higher Education* free; (individuals on special terms). Members may also obtain certain other journals at a discount, including the NFER *Register of Educational Research*. There is a substantial discount to members, and to staff of corporate members, on annual and some other conference fees. The discounts can exceed the subscription.

Annual Subscriptions
August 1990–July 1991

Individual members		£ 43.00
Students & retired members		£ 12.00
Hardship		£ 20.00
Corporate members		
less than 1000 students		£155.00
1000–3000 students		£195.00
more than 3000 students		£290.00
Non-teaching bodies	up to	£295.00

Further information: SRHE at the University, Guildford GU2 5XH, UK Tel: (0483) 39003 Fax: (0483) 300803
Catalogue: SRHE & Open University Press, Celtic Court, 22 Ballmoor, Buckingham MK18 1XW. Tel: (0280) 823388